DEAD, INSANE, OR IN JAIL

A CEDU Memoir

✝

Zack Bonnie

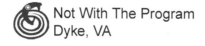

Not With The Program
Dyke, VA

✝

ISBN 978-0-9963378-2-3

✝

Book development, editing, and production – Anne M Carley, of
Chenille Books, who thanks Mollie Bryan, Jane Friedman, and J.W.
Stryder. Thanks go, as well, to C.E. Cameron, Ayla Palermo, and
the other beta readers, for their commentary.

Cover design and illustrations – Jonathan Weiner

For Mom and Dad:
Without you there is nothing.

✝

For the staff at Rocky Mountain Academy:
You showed me both the without and the nothing.

CONTENTS

LIST OF ILLUSTRATIONS

Cover artist Jonathan Weiner created seven lino cut prints to illustrate the book. He editioned the prints on Japanese rice paper and scanned the prints into the digital images used herein.

Print titles and their locations in the book:

EDITOR'S PREFACE

Before I met Zack Bonnie, I knew nothing about the "troubled teen industry" or brainwashing techniques. I had only a limited awareness of trauma injury, or the process of recovery from it.

After reading Zack's manuscript, I was struck by two things. Clearly, he had a story to tell. Second, I noticed I had become hyper-aware of the words I used in my emails and conversations with him. I wondered why.

I had become sensitized to the CEDU vocabulary. So much of the abuse at Rocky Mountain Academy was verbal: Words, enforced with intimidation – immediate, physical, and emotional, as well as institutional, architectural, environmental, and subliminal. RMA gave ordinary words special, ominous meanings.

Take "agreement." During Zack's years at RMA, the "Agreements" were the house rules, yet anyone who called them rules was rebuked for it. I found that so telling: The basic terms under which these teenagers were forced to live were presented in such a coercive and sly way, as though the kids were willing agents of their own betrayals.

Adding to the travesty, some of these agreements were not disclosed until a staff member found it convenient. As Zack writes, "I would have to wait until I was out of agreement to learn what many of the Agreements were. However, one of the first things I learned [at RMA] was that we didn't call the Agreements rules...which they clearly were."

When I began research into CEDU and programs like it, I learned that they didn't just happen for a brief period decades ago. Although they relocate and change their names, the facilities still exist. Advocates and lawmakers are now working to eliminate the gaps in this country's legal framework that have permitted these places to thrive largely unregulated and unmonitored by educational and medical authorities.

Completing this first book of the series has launched Zack into his calling as a public advocate for reform and regulation in the world of treatment, confinement, and care for troubled teens and their troubled families.

I have great respect for the author, particularly his resolve to tell his story for posterity, and "without the violins playing." Writing this memoir required him to re-live severe, repeated trauma, and then transmute those unwanted memories into words. Words that readers new to the CEDU world could comprehend. Words that could elicit empathy and effect change.

I'm grateful that Zack did the work. He opened my eyes. I hope Zack Bonnie's words, in this and future books, reach a wide audience. We all need to know.

Anne M Carley
Chenille Books
Charlottesville, VA
July 2015

PREFACE

I began writing this book series as a kind of personal project, an exploration into a time of purposefully calculated emotional duress that occurred during key developmental periods of my young life.

However, over the years, I became aware that there were very few detailed, accurate accounts from people involved with facilities like Rocky Mountain Academy. Fewer still were told from the perspective of a teenager sequestered there. So, I decided to close the information gap and share my story. These are my memories of the time I was at Rocky Mountain Academy – a CEDU school in Idaho.

In attempting this project I had two goals that sounded easy: To be accurate in describing events and experiences, and to coherently relate my thoughts and mental processes during those experiences. I would tell a true story – stranger than most fiction – and gain some satisfaction from describing my recollections with accuracy.

First, I needed to re-unite my thoughts and feelings. With the invaluable help of Robin Bernhard, that process took years. As a consequence, I re-experienced the CEDU program a second time, and with the memory of an older man.

In theory, I had a choice. I could turn my back on what had happened, and stay in my CEDU-sanctioned trajectory to "move on and get over" any injustices (or gaps in my programming). However, I realized I could stop, and recognize the impotence I felt at that time, in my role as the victim of a systematic withholding of my self-determination and autonomy.

I can say that the emotional curriculum at CEDU was meant to induce significant and irrevocable psychological changes in those who completed the program. It intentionally separated students' intellect from their emotion, using verbal abuse, peer pressure, sleep deprivation, and other recognized tools of thought control.

Beyond that, I cannot possibly understand or explain the intentions of a place like CEDU. I can describe a small bit of what it was like to be a kid there, although any description only hints at the helplessness I felt. All I have are words. In contrast, the staff at RMA had an arsenal of tools and artifices to impel physical, mental, and emotional change.

This series may interest students of persuasive coercion, undue influence, and tactics used by cults or fringe religious groups to induct new members and retain existing ones. It portrays the repeated traumatic process of breaking down natural mental defense mechanisms and personal autonomy in young people, in order to deny them a sense of self-identity. It describes the cortisol dumps that occur between brain and body under ongoing stress. It illustrates how mind control can be achieved without the use of immediate physical violence.

Numerous programs continue to thrive in insular communities that focus on deconstructing their residents' inner emotional lives and their human relationship with nature. Thousands like me have been sent off to live in these mandatory situations with contrived, abusive social dynamics that, to me, defy reason. Keep this in mind, and please do not keep it to yourself. Attention must be paid to programs for minors – in all segments of society – left unregulated and unchecked.

Zack Bonnie
Charlottesville, VA
July 2015

ACKNOWLEGMENTS

There are those in the world that deserve true praise. From the advice of two women I derived the basic principles behind my daily work: Tell what happened, and capture the pathos and catharsis feelings of the ordeal. Do both without exaggerating, they said, and I might have a good story without the violins playing. Thank you, Frauke Regan and Claudine Cowen, mothers to two of my personal friends. Whether in this life or the next, I want to thank you for forming the backbone to my memoir of this turbulent time. You helped a soul brother out! Without those two nuggets in mind, the project would have been hindered with explanations, assumption of other identities, and the opinions of an apologist to insult. Simply being truthful in telling "what happened" turned out to be the tool I needed.

Ample thanks cannot be expressed in these few words for the people who encouraged me to publish this book. First I have to thank Anne M Carley of Chenille Books for her dedication to editing and taking me to task to fill in gaps so that uninitiated readers can keep up. There is no telling how much help she has been in these final steps. Jonathan Weiner is the illustrator for the book, and was a participant in my peer group's Truth propheet. His continued support of the project, and the astounding art he provided, have enhanced the vision and perspective of this book.

I must acknowledge the numerous readers over the years who encouraged me when I had started to lose hope of completing and publishing this book. Through the years I received generous support, help, friendship, and sound advice from those readers and my personal support networks: the Danis family, the Corey families, the Lizsts, Westmans, Regans, Cowens, and Bonnies. Rebecca Danis, my long-time partner, has done more than anyone to keep me, and this project, in motion. Without those close to me, I would not know the importance of pursuing continued beneficial self-actualization. I am remiss not to name dozens more readers and supporters of the project: Know that your notes have sustained me, and I sincerely thank you.

Finally, without friends who have known me, and adversaries too, I'd be a perambulating island. Becoming masterful at explaining the expression of futility in recognition of the mystical, mysterious, ways of God and Man, you have been kept in mind throughout...

-ZB

Author's Statement

Anyone familiar with the program structure at Rocky Mountain Academy will notice that I reduced the number and changed the names of the "families" in the school hierarchy. To convey a sense of the program philosophy's vague attempts to appropriate a Native American theme, I lifted inspiration from true experiences that did not make it into this book. Also, I took some artistic liberty with my descriptions of music and references to songs. The psychological impact of the music that was played at Rocky Mountain Academy is almost impossible to overstate. The constant repetition as background music, day in and day out, of what was literally a handful of songs numbering twenty or so at the most, was mind-numbing. The music played during the so-called "emotional growth" experiences, by contrast, was chosen for the purpose of making already sleep-deprived, psychologically abused children dissolve into tears on cue. Music at the school was generally employed as either a tool, or a weapon. It was almost never something to express one's self creatively with, or simply enjoy.

There were so many kids and staff that mashing together personalities into composite characters was necessary. The intimate level of interaction between kids and staff members is not exaggerated, although I have changed the names and combined the personalities of the people that were part of my experience, to preserve individual anonymity.

Accurately describing my own state of mind, as I experienced the unnatural environment and deliberately constructed trauma that comprised daily life in the CEDU program, was my main goal here. To do this with consistency, I reduced the number of "emotional growth workshops" referred to as "propheets," wilderness expeditions, and other events indicating the passage of time during my stay in Idaho. I also combined and simplified some of the themes and concepts of propheets and workshops to make them easier to understand for readers unfamiliar with the experience of being subjected as children to rigorous behavioral modification techniques.

In this book, I have been as true as possible using the reference details available; the only materials I have from CEDU are those the school provided to my family, for their approval and continued philanthropy.

Other intentional inaccuracies and discrepancies are listed below:

1. A sneeze guard was put on the food bar while I was away on Survival, which makes me wonder if some health inspection occurred while I was in the high desert of Southern Idaho.

2. The names of the families, buildings, and rooms have been changed in some cases. Whether a room or a building is called "Emerson" or "Einstein" or "Energy" makes very little difference. I also condensed the six RMA "families" into four, and changed their names to reflect Native American and pioneer-like influences.

3. I cannot say for certain if the tree that we called Big Ben was a Ponderosa pine (*Pinus ponderosa*).

4. A locked box was available for rap requests. In the book, I have also permitted rap requests to be slipped under the door of "the Bridge" – the room the staff used for their headquarters.

5. In my description of the Truth propheet I took three liberties. First, although costumes were mandatory at later workshops, there was no masked creature in my Truth propheet. I made this change to help illustrate how a kid's perceived "issues" were revealed to the power staff members they would later bond with. Secondly, I adapted the events in the "icebreaker," taking some tools and memories from later stages of the program. I believe that at the beginning of my Truth propheet we had a "battle of the bands" where kids and adults did "air band" renditions – dancing, singing, and lip-syncing – to 80s pop songs. Finally, I took small liberties with my description of the music. I wanted to illustrate the mystical influence and psychological impact of the musical component of the propheet experience. Also, the "shooter marble" was in fact a chrome ball.

6. Frozen tomatoes. Not really. Most of the food at RMA did seem "acceptable." However, it was the case that our diet was restricted, we were allowed to eat only at mealtimes, and the propheet meals were very small.

7. To illustrate the confusion that a new kid would feel during the dancing that takes place after a Summit "gets out," I tweaked the nature of the music playing over the loudspeakers. I did this to lead up to events that occur during later stages of the RMA program, which I will describe in subsequent books in this series. I also added the use of a microphone. I can't recall if a megaphone or microphone was ever used during my time at RMA.

8. Chapter Twenty, and the incident with the character named Herb, did not happen to me. My reasons for insisting that it remain in

the book are twofold. First, I needed a device to portray the shame and self-loathing that I would identify in myself in later parts of the series, while still protecting the privacy of my younger self – as I have done for the rest of the characters in the book. Second, I wanted to tell a small part of the story of some of the kids I know who did experience events similar to those described. Because those experiences happened during their attempts to escape from the program, these kids were simply punished, and it was implied (or in some cases directly stated) that their attempts to escape amounted to invitations to be sexually abused. I stand by my inclusion of the chapter as a plot device for later use in this narrative.

9. I am fairly certain that the dog in a plastic bag that I describe during my account of my experience at SUWS was actually a raccoon. It is probable that over the last 25 years, my memory has combined a conversation between deliriously hungry children with the experience of eating a thawed raccoon.

10. I chose not to include many things that I did witness. During my first few weeks in Idaho there were scandals between students of a homosexual nature. The boys involved were subsequently publicly shamed. Those kids and others were accused of sexual "contracts" with other students. There were also accidents, and cases where suicide was attempted or ideated by RMA kids. Some children did not last long, and were clearly in a fragile mental or emotional state. Some kids arrived and remained in longer, strange periods of shock. Out of respect for them and their stories, I have tried to keep the focus on myself and not the emotional struggles of the people that were around me.

11. Because kids came and went so frequently, I wanted to pay homage to the ones that I simply brushed shoulders with – those who left and never returned. Kids who turned eighteen and chose to leave, and kids who were able to escape – or find some other means of denying themselves a CEDU education – deserve some recognition. My way of doing that is to call them even-numbered peer groups. At RMA, kids who left before graduation were forgotten quickly, unless they died, or were incarcerated, and the school found out. In those cases, the stories of their misfortune were used for expository value, and as proof that all of us kids were as good as dead if we didn't stay the two and a half years necessary to graduate. Graduates earned a kind of respect that even-numbered kids would never attain.

12. Sheriff [Snipes] did carry his gun on our plane ride down to Boise. This was 1988, and I wasn't ever surprised or suspicious about the man's intent. At one time, the Sheriff was one of many supporters of this project! I just want to point it out, in this post-9/11 world.

†

Except as mentioned above, everything I describe happened as I remember it. I have not overstated events, nor have I made allegations for shock value. If anything, I have downplayed or left unmentioned the issues and experiences of other individuals, out of a kind of survivor's loyalty.

Based on facts, written from memory with the aid of my personal journals from that time, archival materials from my family and others, and supported by years of conventional therapy – this is my story.

-ZB

INTRODUCTION

For the reader unfamiliar with CEDU Educational Services, and the schools it has influenced

CEDU's name, pronounced *see-doo*, suggests the educational method that ostensibly guided the for-profit schools. Although the schools explained the acronym as "See yourself as you are and do something about it," history indicates the initials first stood for Charles E. Dederich University, in honor of the founder of Synanon, who strongly influenced CEDU's founder, Mel Wasserman, a California businessman. The CEDU organization was founded in 1967 as CEDU Educational Services, Inc., and was acquired in 1998 by Brown Schools, Inc., under the name CEDU Education – Brown Schools, Inc.

CEDU and Brown Schools closed and declared bankruptcy in 2005, thereby managing to sidestep final financial settlements in a number of lawsuits claiming student mistreatment, employee sexual abuse, and deceptive practices. Universal Health Services subsequently re-opened some of these schools, as "behavioral health centers."

The CEDU schools are generally credited with establishing a new kind of boarding school for troubled teens. Drawing on Synanon's "encounter group" techniques and using interrogation practices, counselors applied what became known as "tough love" to force change on their teenaged charges. The two and a half year program included some academic subjects, and many labor assignments at the school's farm, woodlot, and buildings and grounds. The schools featured extended "raps" – highly confrontational groups derived from Synanon's "The Game" – and "propheets" – overnight sessions of extreme stress, reputedly based on the teachings of Khalil Gibran's The Prophet.

Rocky Mountain Academy ("RMA") opened in 1982 in Bonners Ferry, Idaho, more than ten years after its sister school named CEDU, opened in Running Springs, California. Mel Wasserman founded them both. In later years, more CEDU schools were added, including CEDU Middle School, Boulder Creek Academy, Northwest Academy, Ascent Wilderness Program, and Milestones.

School of Urban and Wilderness Survival ("SUWS") was founded in southern Idaho in 1981 as a therapeutic wilderness program for youth aged fourteen to eighteen. A North Carolina program began in 2000. The SUWS programs became part of Aspen Education Group's portfolio of private teen facilities. Now owned by Bain Capital, Aspen has divested many of their schools and programs, including SUWS Idaho, citing reduced demand.

Synanon was founded in Santa Monica, California in 1958 by Charles E. Dederich, Jr., as a behavior modification facility for addicts. Mel Wasserman was an early member of the organization. After he left Synanon, he founded CEDU. Initially, Synanon was a two-year treatment program, but over time its leaders changed the organization's mission, declaring that members could never leave the program, as addiction could never be completely cured or reversed. Forced to close in the United States 1989 after problems with the IRS, the organization still exists in Germany.

Additional for-profit schools and programs claiming to provide therapeutic interventions continue to draw in families concerned about their teenagers.

For links to more information, consult the Resources page on the deadinsaneorinjail.com website.

Forgiveness means giving up all hope for a better past.
—*Lily Tomlin*

ORIENTATION

ONE

JULY 1988

After my cousin Gail's wedding in Baltimore, Dad let me drink a few beers.

"Zack, I want to take you on a ski trip! I got tickets for a resort this weekend, in, er – Idaho."

"Awesome! But don't I need a jacket from home?"

My weed and Walkman had to be stashed, or Mom would trash them both.

"No, I wanted it to be a surprise. I packed for you. Everything you'll need! Mommy will take the baby home. We're going to the airport by taxi, so say your goodbyes and let's go."

"Sweet! Jeez, thanks, dude!" I was on top of the world.

Maybe the taxi driver wouldn't mind if I had one more beer on the way? I allowed Dad to talk me out of that. Outside the hotel, I was already thinking about burning my dad down the snowy mountain and chatting up girls on the slopes, or ski lifts. Dad looked on me with more patience than he ever had, as I chugged half a beer and slipped the rest into a garbage can.

Our taxi took us away from Maryland's afternoon humidity.

The plane pursued the sun all night.

I chased Dad through a bright, empty little airport. It was pitch dark as we shoved luggage into the trunk of a rental car. None of the interior lights functioned. Dad stabbed at the steering column with a key. The car came alive, wheezing like an old vacuum cleaner. My dad swung the rented white Mercury onto a dark highway.

We must be in Idaho.

Dad said that right after the tour of some boarding school out here, we would go skiing. I knew the Rocky Mountains had a lot of snow, even in July.

The car clock's blue light read 4:00 AM. I closed my eyes.

I would come to regret trusting my father.

The troubled teen industry has grown rapidly, driven by corporations that may be more motivated by profit than by providing quality services. It can be confusing and frightening for parents trying to make the best decision about care for their child, and for professionals trying to advise families about these difficult choices.

—ASTART website http://astartforteens.org/

The white rental car slowed, and the noise of gravel jarred me awake. My ears perked and focused on the clunks of little stones against the undercarriage of the automobile. I blinked. Darkness had been replaced by glowing morning light. The car hadn't stopped moving since leaving the airport, a long time and distance ago. The clock on the dashboard said 7:00 AM.

The sun was up. *Where are we? Was that a ski lodge? What about that boarding school?*

We slowed by an enormous wood bay. There must've been enough wood stacked up to construct a great pyramid, or some other wooden world wonder unknown to me. Enormous mountains and rugged terrain were right in my nose; even the trees were foreign. Big dogs barked as we pulled in next to other parked cars. A chill filled the car as soon as Dad turned the key and the engine halted its hum.

I'd never been out West. I was ecstatic.

With anticipation for the day, I wondered how much snow would be in the higher mountains. The ski lodge must be near the boarding school. Skiing was our priority, so we'd get to the slopes soon. My father despised tardiness.

Kids started to emerge from three similar one-story wooden dwellings. I could see them take note of the shiny rental car as they walked toward the ski lodge. Wait! This must be the school. I had visited other boarding schools before, so it wasn't that strange to be in a new environment looking at a bunch of people close to my age.

I put my straw hat on. It nicely held back my long brown hair. I took a moment to look at my reflection in the flippy car mirror. I put on sunglasses. The hair was nice, I have to say, though it was so thick and wavy that I almost let my mother talk me into cutting it before summer camp, a couple of weeks earlier.

While my father shuffled papers between his pockets, the glove box, and the visor, I peered toward higher elevations. Shrouds of clouds obscured distant peaks. I checked out some of the hotter females pouring out of another area of wooden buildings and instinctively wondered if there could be sexual possibility. I had gone on a school-organized ski outing in seventh grade – last year. I spent the ski trip in the back of the bus with a girl. That was the most fun I'd ever had skiing. I was hoping for a repeat of that experience if I could get away from Dad. I hoped some of the girls I spied forming morning ponytails would be on the slopes later. I was also hopeful that one would have pot. I'd been smoking more and more because I liked it.

We ignored the dogs' dry, bored barks, and got out to stretch our legs by the car. For the first time I noticed the Washington State license plate. Another massive dog had detected our arrival and bounded toward us. Impossible to ignore, so big and black was this beast that even my father exclaimed out loud, as the dog approached with a dark-furred, lumbering, meaty swagger. Hoarsely barking, his girth provided a slobbery, happy momentum as he trotted a primal circle around the rest of the pack, my father, and me.

"Sancho! Cut that out!" A voice commanded in our direction. "Hello. Mr. Bonnie? Yes, hey there, I'm Andrew Oswald, and welcome to Rocky Mountain Academy!"

Andrew Oswald and two burly dudes in collared shirts waved off Sancho and his canine cohort. I readjusted the straw hat on my head. Andrew Oswald shook hands with my father and then me. His grip wrapped all the way around my hand, and his squeeze was impolitely tight. He said these two younger guys would show me the campus.

Campus. I hated that word. Last fall, I was "not invited back to dorm on the campus" for eighth grade at the Hill School. While Andrew Oswald attempted to peer through my sunglasses at my eyeballs, the guys, Paul Renssalaer and Tim Chalmers, observed me. They asked me if I liked my hair long and what state I was from. We walked away together from the two older men – neither of whom could be trusted.

My tour guides were seventeen. Both were from California and hadn't ever been to Virginia. I'd never been west of West Virginia.

"That's near D.C., right?" Paul asked.

"Like three hours away. It took forever to get here, though."

"That was your father?" Tim questioned.

"Yes. So's far as I know." I chortled. They both seemed pretty stiff to me.

Somewhat out of the blue, Tim said he had to leave San Francisco on account of a drug problem. He had a big tattoo on his arm, a cross with skulls at the four points. He seemed pretty cool but clearly was "assisting" Paul, who was sort of bland. Flimsy, like a puppet missing a hand, or a marionette with severed strings. He seemed to be just…a shell. Tim seemed sharper. I don't mean smarter. Or do I? If Paul was like the Blue Ridge back in Virginia, Tim's face and aspect seemed jagged like the Rocky Mountain peaks surrounding the campus.

Paul steered us past other kids. They flashed furtive glances in my direction, but then their necks snapped forward if I made eye contact, and they quickened their pace. I felt shunned, as if I wore something repulsive. I stashed the sunglasses in a pocket. The passing boys didn't wave or nod. The girls avoided us. The only voices around seemed to be our own.

Also, we seemed to be the only people not walking quickly. Paul and Tim were letting me lead this tour, I realized.

"Yup. This is it. Rocky Mountain Academy. I helped make the sign at the entrance. You saw it, I own it. I'm in late Warrior. Or Leadership."

"What grade are you in?" I tried to understand.

"Like I said, I'm in Warrior family...I guess I would be a senior by now," Tim ominously added.

"And I'm in Summit, and I'm next to graduate so Tim's peer group will move up to Summit. The program operates by a family system."

"How old are you?" Paul wanted to know.

"Fifteen," I lied.

Tim's pointy chin bobbed to ask another question: "Did you know that you were going to be coming to RMA today?"

"We're going skiing after this," I replied.

They exchanged a sideways glance.

They must be envious.

Magnificent, stringy barked trees stood to the right, in piles of their own dead brown needles. I would come to know them as tamaracks. These oddly deciduous conifers created a dense curtain that blocked the view into the steeply sloped forest beyond. Everything looked different from my world back East. Larger. As I walked with Tim and Paul, I gazed up at the surrounding mountains. They were jagged and uninviting, a different species than those in my ol' Virginny. My Blue Ridge Mountains were rounding, luscious, and feminine. In Idaho they were masculine, pointy peaks right over us. God didn't lay down foothills here.

I learned their names. Clifty Mountain was on one side of the campus, and Katka Mountain on the other. They rose up out of the clouds like two angry deities, daring and forbidding. Both were much steeper than anything I'd ever hiked at Camp Minnehaha in the West Virginia Appalachians. Clifty's distant rocky face resembled snow, and as the morning fog lifted, I convinced myself the newly eroded scree tumbles were ski runs down the bowl.

Inside a building called La Mancha, the dorm rooms, all carbon copies of each other, had six bunk beds each. I saw little to differentiate the people who slept in each bunk. No music posters. No pictures of girls. No pictures of friends at home. Not even photos of families most of the time. The simple, perfectly made beds were equipped with a big wooden cube for storage at the foot of each bunk.

My guides began telling me the differences between this place and a regular boarding school, although their descriptions were as sparse as the rooms. The confusing undertone made me suspicious. I knew something was amiss. I chalked it up to the fact it was early in the morning and my tour guides were older and better informed. Also, they acted like they thought I was stupid. I felt like they were playing a game with me without telling me all the rules. They tried to placate me but avoided giving me answers. They both looked at me sidelong, making me feel quite queer. I put my sunglasses back on.

Paul and Tim used words I didn't know, and words I did know in a context that I didn't understand or use: RMA, Expeditions, Bands, Programs, Experientials. It reminded me of the several weeks I'd spent in France the previous summer, when I was thirteen. I felt like an anthropologist, studying language barriers between people from the opposite sides of my own country. It occurred to me that they might have different words for things out here in the West!

Whatever. When the tour of this school was over, I was going skiing, and I'd never see these two weird dudes again.

We walked on a dirt road alongside a patch of woods. I spied a giant cargo net and a series of weathered wooden pontoons. About twenty feet away, a big suspended platform, with cables wired at hip level around it, came into focus. Paul pointed at the wood platform and simply said, "That's the Point."

Another massive wooden structure, called Skinner, was still being constructed. We took a quick tour. I should have taken a hint when Paul called it the "academic building." For the first time, "classes" were mentioned. The building, unfinished, reeked of newly cut cedar and pine.

Finally, idiotically, a question sprang to mind. *Why were they here? It's July. There is no SCHOOL in summer? Right?*

There's summer school – I was familiar with that. But a summer boarding school replete with a sauna and a lake?

I asked a direct question trying to kick-start some dialogue. "How long since you were at home?"

"I went on my Five Day last month," Paul replied with a vacant stare.

"Five day *visit*, he means. That was a long one, wasn't it, Paul?" Tim prompted.

"Yes, and it was a good visit. It was good to see my aunt again."

At this moment we came upon two boys. They were heading in the opposite direction and passed close by us. One had a sullen expression on his face and was pushing a wheelbarrow. Inside it, a hard rake and a shovel non-rhythmically banged away. The kid with the wheelbarrow wore a filthy red T-shirt and dark blue jeans caked with mud from the knees down. He had a rather ugly and patchy crew cut, and work gloves on his hands. The clean guy with him wore a collared shirt. A taller, older boy, he carried a big mug of coffee and appeared as if he'd been sprayed with arrogance perfume. His air of having been freshly groomed was a stark contrast to the dirty little dude with the wheelbarrow.

We ambled onward as the clanging wheelbarrow retreated. Tim was looking at me as if sizing me up. I wasn't intimidated, but ready for the tour to end soon. I was thinking it would soon be time to suit up for skiing, *so stop fucking staring at me.* I lit a cigarette. They told me to wait until we were up at the house. They could smoke there.

"If you want to suck a dart with me, why not here?" I asked.

"House porch is the only place at Rocky Mountain Academy where anyone can smoke." Tim flashed a look of irritation.

I took another drag. "Whatever. Well, I'll put it out in a minute then."

I didn't really want any adults to see me smoking, even though my dad already knew I smoked. There had been consequences before. Especially at the boarding school that had already thrown me out. We ambled toward the ski lodge-looking building. I puffed some more, and noticed Paul and Tim were wearing identical work boots. I wanted to say something, but we were already approaching the parking area where my tour had originated.

"This is the house," Paul said, pointing up at the wooden castle that resembled a ski lodge.

I had noticed the kids gravitating toward it, when Dad parked the rental car nearby. Paul and Tim and I stood at the base of the giant building while conversations buzzed, and the din of dozens of boots on wooden floors clunked above us. I looked out toward the rental car, but my dad wasn't there.

"Well, Zack. After the orientation we'll come back and get you and show you the house and the farm," Paul said.

I didn't see the need to continue this tour. I just wanted to make my father happy, not see any more of the campus.

Tim and Paul left me in a big exterior hallway, outside an office-looking room in the basement of the big lodge. They expected me to go inside the open door, but I stood where I was, overlooking the parking lot. I wanted that big wooden office door kept open – wide open. The collar-shirted guys disappeared up the stairs, to the sound of receding clunks.

My father was not by the car, or in the office, and for the first time in years, I urgently wanted to see him.

I stood outside the room, watching the sun heat the campus.

Andrew Oswald's body lifted itself out of a plastic-backed black chair, and he stepped out of the room toward me. I felt his hand on my shoulder.

"Where's my father?" I half gasped.

TWO

Andrew Oswald had been inside, waiting.

Keeping his weighty hand on my shoulder, he veered me past him through the massive doorframe. The darkness inside, and the noise of people upstairs, muffled and distorted my focus, like when I tried on Dad's thick eyeglasses as a child. Then my eyes began to adjust, although the sounds kept fading like the boot clunks upstairs. The room was sparely furnished. I noticed a desk and a stack of black chairs.

Andrew Oswald's head breached the doorway as he reached out to take the metal stirrup door handle. He had to stoop to get back into the tiny room. His balding head was flecked with black and white wisps of hair. These peppered hairs seemed to be sweating, as they clung to his shiny scalp. The head rose back to a human position atop Andrew's neck and my world darkened as his fleshy body stood between me and the thick door that shut behind him. The latch clanked into place.

"Did you have a good tour?"

His voice was nasally and smaller than it should have been, emanating from that big sweaty, hairy body.

"This is an interesting school, hunh? Did Tim and Paul take you to see the sauna?"

"Yeah, that was alright."

I wanted to talk to my father.

"Where is he?" I repeated, in part because of the muffle, "Where is my father?"

There was a woman in the room too, a small, country-looking woman with falsely curled, streaky, stringy blonde hair. Her diminished presence was perfectly invisible to me until after the door closed. She stood meekly in the corner, her hands behind her back.

Creepy.

With her eyeballs directed into the bridge of my nose, the woman whipped her hands forward. She had been hiding something. My eyes were stuck on her serene face.

Wait. Was that...something sharp?

Some sunlight glinted through the window in the heavy door. A magical, slow-motion moment elongated exponentially. I turned into Andrew's body, which blocked my escape. He was still looking at the woman with a sense of mysterious urgency. I'd have bet the moments were flying by rapidly from their perspective.

"This is Kelly Grainger. Kelly."

I looked back at Kelly. *Who is this woman and why do I need to know who she is?*

Kelly's hands hugged the shiny object to her abdomen. She turned and willed me to follow her gaze through the window.

"Where's my dad?" I demanded.

Something was happening and I didn't see it coming. Through that dingy little window in that closed wooden door, I could see the rental car driving away. A wake of wind flicked gravel and dust from the bouncing back wheels of the white Mercury. The car I had been snoozing in an hour before was leaving without any ceremony. Down a long driveway, it left a bumping trail, dry as bones. It was still very early.

The word "Dad" went dry in my mouth. It all snapped together in my mind. I began to turn decisively toward a new threatening sound, but I was too late. I tried to prevent the attack.

Raise your hand! Dammit!

The silvery beast had my wrists. They were immobilized! Long graying mustache hairs reached up and out triumphantly from Andrew Oswald's nostrils above me. Andrew wore circular shaped spectacles. The red frames had little horns on them, and set off his iron gray eyebrows. With bushy eyebrow-hairs peeking out from above the red frames, he appeared like an overgrown and deranged lemur.

What he was wearing in between his scraggly head and furry toes wasn't formal. He didn't even have shoes on. Instead, he wore enormous sandals. His toes were huge. I was mesmerized by Andrew's feet. Those stately dogs – that big toe was as big as my whole foot! I began to get very scared, as the threatening words and sounds came into focus behind my lagging vision.

Andrew Oswald's peculiarly nasal and rounded words floated in my light head. "Program," "processing," "clothes off."

Whoa. Back up. Clothes off?

14

I know I didn't hear that right.

I couldn't move.

I'm trying to, but my wrists are bound to this stranger. I'm trying to back away. Simultaneously, he is demanding that I take off all of my clothes. And there's this woman. From out of the shadows with something sharp!

I wish I had woken up.

I wish I was running, and being chased, and THEN woke up!

But I didn't.

I won't exaggerate. I will be as plain as I can be about my "processing."

About my "orientation" and my admittance into Rocky Mountain Academy on July 11th, 1988.

I was fourteen-and-a-half years old.

Dear Zack,

This is going to be a hard letter for me to write, and, I suspect it might be a hard letter for you to read. During the past two years, I've written you a lot of notes but some of them, you didn't read – or at least you read part and once you got the drift, you didn't finish them.

I asked you on Saturday when we were playing gin, if you doubted that your parents loved you. You thought about it and said, "Well, I doubt it, sure. But I know you do." Zack, that's one thing – one condition of your life that you don't ever have to doubt. Daddy and I love you more than you can ever know.

—Letter from author's mother, 11 July 1988

THREE

[Continued] It's because we love you that it was so
hurtful to see you destroying your life. You'd become
someone unable to take responsibility, unable to
listen and take advice, unable to control some of your
unpleasant impulses. We saw you turn from a very
kind, loving and funny boy, into an angry young man,
resentful of authority and all rules. We couldn't allow
that to happen. We know, those attitudes ALWAYS
lead to failure.

In order to have a happy and successful life a person
must accept authority and must follow rules. You've
shown over the past two years that this was a lesson
you hadn't mastered. In fact, the older you got, the
more disrespectful and irritated you became.

—Letter from author's mother, 11 July 1988

To say the air goes out of your lungs when you're faced with
something terrifying is an understatement. Here's how it goes: first the
heart stops, drops, and rolls, like all of your blood is on fire. I've heard
it called skipping a beat, but it's more like feeling an anchor drop to
the bottom of your stomach. Then your lungs' steady – often pleasant
– uptake of air suffers an incredible shock.

Air escaped.

"Where's my father," I repeated a fourth time, now more a statement than a question.

When you are in shock you forget to breathe. This was the first
thing to happen. Because the brain is fully absorbed in that most exact
and immediate sense – sight – the process to take air in is, unnaturally, not there. I forgot to breathe. This was the first thing to happen.

I was losing freedom. I would be losing control.

Time continued to flip further into slowing motion. This was the
first thing to happen. The rental car bounded down gray gravel like an
unfeeling albino animal. The Mercury on pockmarked, charcoal-col-
ored wheels had fled the scene and left me with the deranged lemur,

his eyes full of nightmares, and his secretive, menacing associate.

I balked. I tried to maneuver out of the way. Who could react? Kelly Grainger bounded out of my periphery. I heard scraping – the sound of metal edges. At the limit of my vision, still processing the sight of the rental car, metal flashed. The scissors made one slick, wavering, metallic, musical note.

The anchor dropping to the pit of my stomach steadied me like a buoy on the open ocean – this weeble wobble almost went down. Andrew Oswald still squished my wrists in his hairy paws. Kelly cut off my hair in an instant. I felt an unpleasant shift in the weight on my head as a slanted line of freshly cut brown curls fell to the floor. Compensating from the shift in weight, or because I was faint, I teetered toward the fingers gripped around my arms.

I wanted to be indignant. I wanted to fight. I wanted to escape. I really, really wanted to wake up. The gray beast's branchlike arms held me firmly and stopped any movement I made. I was out of kicking distance, and unable to summon enough strength to use his weight against him.

Time renormalized as the blood started rushing around inside me again. I became aware of the overwhelming sound of thumping. My burning ears echoed my heart. I obeyed my adrenal glands' primal urging, pulling up the anchor buried in my stomach, and tried flight. No go. I still hadn't taken a breath since my last "father."

When I finally did, I inhaled a beaten, sad, stale, defeated, and utterly foreign northwestern woody flavor. Disgustingly, it had been tainted by the breath of Andrew Oswald, contaminated on its way to me through his shaggy, gray mustache. He was an inch from my face.

"Calm down!" Andrew Oswald squished my wrists until they felt like empty tubes of toothpaste. His spittle sprayed my face, and I had to resist the impulse to vomit on him.

"We're just gonna do a quick search of your clothing so we can get you out of here. You're not leaving the campus with your father. You don't want this fight, and I am not having any of THIS SHIT! YOU GOT THAT?"

His stale air came rushing into my brain and with it a message: brace for impact. Pure oxygen could be pumped into dangling masks in a plummeting airliner – here, that was totally unimportant. I would simply have to acquiesce to imminent doom. Let whatever comes, come.

My mind stretched like a rubber band; it was already searching for a reason for this treatment and surprise attack. It was the blood rushing back up to my face from my feet and that incessant thumping in my head that reminded me of being caught shoplifting. The button had clearly displayed the words: WHITE DOPES ON PUNK! But that had been over a year ago, and my parents hadn't found out. Or had they? I suddenly wondered if that could be the crime that had brought me to this moment. My dizzy mind whipped me between the room I was in, the airplane window seat that I'd been tranquilly gazing out of a few hours ago, and that moment when I was busted in a store for shoplifting the lapel button for my jean jacket. Only dip-shits like my brother and his friends wore pins on ties, suspenders, and snappy letter jackets.

I was unable to do anything but comply. I didn't know how to comply, but class was in session with Mr. Oswald. So, I lost my clothes. What was my crime that I now had to get naked for these strangers? Maybe this related to what happened when I ran away from Camp Minnehaha a month prior? Why was this happening to me? Was one of my teachers to blame? Did my girlfriend's parents do this to me? Fuck, I bet it was the psychiatrist my parents had made me see. The shrink knew I hadn't been taking the Ritalin that my moth-er insisted he prescribe. "To organize the command tower of your thoughts," Dr. D had said.

My mind ceased daydreaming only for a moment.

"Kelly, take his jeans. Zack, take off your watch now. And put it with that stuff. Good. Take off your shoes. Socks. Hand them to Kelly. Check him. OK? Alright, good. Now turn around and take off your underwear. Shake 'em out. I said shake 'em out. OK, I want to make sure you don't have any drugs so bend over. I said bend over, son! Nice."

My face was flushed and the remainder of blood in my veins drooled back toward my ankles as I exposed my asshole to Andrew Oswald. Shame. I was embarrassed, and frightened, and angry all at once, bent over like that. Kelly's face still projected serenity.

Her expression brought memory and distraction together to transport me briefly to the Louvre, the big fancy museum in Paris. I had seen the Mona Lisa's enigmatic smirk, almost one year ago this very day! As Andrew briefly acquainted himself with my bunghole, I took a quick refresher tour of the Louvre, relieved to have my escapist imagination reignited. In this forced daydream, I sensed that I wasn't in my body for a stint.

I certainly wasn't in the long hallway below the piles of construction materials and workers yelling in French. This wasn't the space under the long anticipated, but only half-completed, glass pyramid. A hallway with medieval sculptures adorning long, old, ornate tables; bronze and marble seemed suspended in time. Shields and helms protruded gaudily from overloaded walls. The walls of the halls had texture and volume, as an unencumbered exhibitionist might. All these stimuli started shutting out the shouting from above, and the movement of clunking work boots.

My body winked at Andrew. Outside of my body, I was aloft, viewing his little wooden room from the ceiling, or perhaps peeping into the bizarre scene from the window, like an overly curious butler. A naked man fought a bear – my mind shot to the struggle in sculpted bronze, an enormous piece right at the entrance of one hallway in the crowded museum. My memory flitted to a headless angel atop one of the ornate tables, and numerous Greek archetypes I passed with their noses and sex organs missing.

I began to rematerialize. I noticed some blue jeans on a small table in the corner next to Kelly. They were folded like brown bags from a supermarket. Boxy, stiff, and downright ugly, these jeans were likely already here in this room before I went on my tour with Tim Chalmers and Paul Rensselaer.

That realization never escaped me. Those jeans on the desk became for me the metaphor of imminent doom, like the masks that wait, prepared to drop out during an airplane wreck. Get on the plane: try not to think of the convenient placement of the oxygen mask. Try not to anticipate the need.

Block it all out. I am safe in this moment. Think only of that.

I reached for the pair of plain white underwear briefs, but it wasn't time to dress, yet. Andrew thrust a colorful flannel shirt to my bare chest and held it there.

"Tuck it in."

Kelly finally handed me the underwear and the new pants, not bothering to avert her eyes in the bizarre transaction. I had never seen duds like what they piled in my arms. The jeans were as hard as a cardboard box and as scratchy as mica. As the clothes touched me, I snapped back completely from the memories of the museum, away from my re-imagining of the airplane ride that night, and back into my present self.

My jacket, the clothes I wore, a small pocket knife, my cigarettes, my lighter, a ring, my sunglasses, and my watch all disappeared from the corner of the desk of this ironically named "orientation room," never to be seen again. I'd miss most the silver ring that formed an X, a gift from my girlfriend. I liked that floppy straw hat too.

I dressed quickly, making sure to tuck in my red patterned flannel, and emerged from the office. Andrew Oswald's burly paw steered me upstairs into the hall of clunking boots. The stairwell seemed as contorted and warped in my mind as a painting by Salvador Dali.

A waking dream, a trance that I cannot wake from, haunts my spirit, and always begins with a climb into the entrails of the big wooden building.

†

Our admissions procedure is designed to assist prospective students and their parents in learning as much about the school as possible. The procedure begins upon receipt of a completed application, school transcripts, previous records and evaluations. After these materials are screened, an on-campus interview is scheduled for the applicant and parents which includes a tour of the campus and an orientation to the curricula.

Acceptance into the academy is based upon the application materials and the admissions interview.

—RMA Brochure

FOUR

Everywhere was wood.

Wooden stairs, trim, window ledges. Wooden banisters for wooden steps. The sticky, piney odor of this densely wooded but mostly unpopulated area of the Northwest complemented it all. It smelled of damp sawdust. As we made our way up, I could hear voices from above. The view changed as Andrew and I climbed. Kelly was still back in the little room, probably sweeping or vacuuming up my hair. Into my field of vision came Tim and Paul, waiting for me, to continue the campus "tour."

I fought for clarity. I was too afraid to do anything. The cheery arrival committee consciously downplayed all that had happened to me in the last sixty minutes. I was still blushing from shame; my emotional state a smeared palette of base fury and fear. Andrew departed after depositing me with Tim, Paul, and an arrival group.

A woman with tremendous breasts, wide as over-ripe cantaloupes, stood in front of me. With her hands in her back pockets, she rocked back and forth, smacking on a piece of chewing gum. Her rocking distracted me from my new thoughts. I'd heard that rocking is a habit observed in people in need of constant calming. In her case, the rocking didn't seem to help because Darlayne Hammer was clearly a volatile time bomb. Her intimidating personality did not put me at ease while I met other members of the arrival committee.

The next woman, profoundly skinny and comparatively flat-chested, had dark curly hair. Her name was Tess. "I'm Tess Turnwell. Welcome to RMA."

What? Welcome to Army? Army of what?

Tess continued. "Darlayne and I run Papoose family. We meet in the Papoose room or the tipi. I'm going to be your senior counselor. So starting now, let's see, you're going to be moved into La Mancha. You don't have your ups and downs yet, so, make sure a support or older brother walks you to and from there. Um, I guess that's it. Again, welcome to our home! RMA. This is the right place for you. I know exactly how you feel right now. You are going to do fine, don't worry!"

I would have to walk to La Mancha with big brothers. Hunh?

Who is a papoose – isn't that what Native Americans called babies?

Who is big brother?

What does it mean to go up and down as a privilege?

Where is La Mancha?

Thoughts, smells, lights, and sounds mingled with shamanistic strangeness. My emotions swirled like inlet waters at high tide. These individuals I was now forced to interact with seemed to deny the shameful experience I had just endured downstairs. I had just met these people. Couldn't they see the indignity staining my face?

I didn't know how to express all the anger, intimidation, and contempt that I began to feel. The idea that these people obviously condoned Andrew Oswald's actions was suddenly in the mix, too! Was I safe? Would I always have to strip in front of strangers like I'd done for Kelly and Andrew? Maybe I'd have to strip in front of everybody I met? Would I get to see Darlayne and Tess naked?

Introductions continued informally. I noticed music in the background of the enormous house. Speakers hanging in the corners of the lodge softly pumped out songs by the musicians I would come to know as James Taylor, Kenny G, and Cat Stevens. There was some bustle off and around us as the kitchen and its band of hair-netted workers came into view. I turned and took in the dining room behind me.

Great – everything was wood in there, too. And no books anywhere. *Back home, we have filled bookcases everywhere, pictures on the white-ish walls, and furniture, not picnic tables. Never thought I'd miss that stuff.*

A different hue of wooden browns claimed each corner. The floor was made of big wooden slats. On many Saturday work crews I would become intimate with the thin crevices that separated the floorboards, digging between them with a butter knife, scraping and flicking crumbs of dirt to the surface for removal. There were two rows of identical picnic tables. Wooden booths lined the entire area. None of the tables or booths were covered with tablecloths – shiny and lacquered, they were entirely made of wood.

Light flooded into the dining room from large, clean windows, which further accentuated the light brown booths and tables. A giant, empty food bar reminded me of a bowling alley's glossy wooden paneled lane. I envisioned precisely propelling a fifteen-pound bowling ball right down the middle.

The wooden plates, wooden salad bowls, serving bowls, and tremendous stacks of particularly ugly plaid wood-grained plates bounce and crash. Everything flies into the air, a sustained explosion as my oversized wrecking ball bowls down the colossal lane, spinning maniacally, and sending wooden shrapnel into the air, causing a pleasant ruckus.

FIVE

The first home visit usually happens around the time a student has been in the program for approximately 14 months. It is a very structured visit, five days in length, and involves careful preparation and follow-up with both student and parents.

—RMA letter to parents

I snapped back to attention when Darlayne Hammer clicked a Polaroid and the flash lit up.

"Now we've got your ass documented." The machine whirred and spat out a sandwich of toxic chemicals. Darlayne flapped the magical Polaroid paper in the air and grinned at me.

"It's so the police can recognize you when you split." She stained the border of the photo with a Sharpie. "B-O-N-N-I-E."

"What?"

The smell of developing solution lingered in my nose. Then Darlayne touched me.

She reached out and squeezed my cheek between a chubby finger and thumb that strongly smelled of strawberry bubblelicious gum. Cheap fake jewelry with southwestern-style, plastic blue beads jangled on her plump wrist next to my ear. I stepped back, but instead she squeezed harder, and stared me in the eyes.

"Ooh, you're going to be fun."

She paused, took in my blank expression. Sustaining her dominance, she released me from her grubby grasp. She was off with a smelly smack of her gum and a turn on her heel. Darlayne had the self-assurance and temperament of a wild boar. She wore white tennis shoes and her butt squoze into faded Jordache blue jeans. I informed my younger captors that I needed to use the bathroom. I did.

Paul and Tim walked me back through the lodge-house-thing and waited for me outside the bathroom. I hadn't needed to pee and cry simultaneously since I was four. I looked at the stalls and the woodwork in the bathroom. Besides the mirror, sinks, and toilets themselves, everything was made from wood. There was no back exit. I turned around into my new reflection. I was amazed at several things, simultaneously.

My hair had been horribly chopped. I wanted to punch something or puke with the reminder of all that had transpired in that subterranean chamber of humiliation, with that gorilla and the invisible sociopath woman hiding in the shadows with her shiny scissors. My eyes were bright and alert, but upon seeing my own reflection in the dingy light of the bathroom, I could feel my entire soul shrinking inside as the absolute knowledge of my plight descended around me. Although tears could rush up to my eyes for different reasons, I was able to stifle the crushing feelings. This deep despair might not have a name, but I'd felt it many times after fights with Dad. I'd had a lot of practice at home and I knew how to dam up the liquid behind my eyes.

I stared at myself another moment.

I may have been left here. This is for real. I am scared. Not just at being left here in a mysterious situation, but for my life. Was my father returning or not? He'd have to return eventually, right? This is just his way of scaring me. It just can't be real. Cavity searching is not a proper way to end the tour of any facility.

Later I would learn that most students were searched, though not as thoroughly as I had been. I had just gotten off of an airplane; of course I didn't have any contraband on my person. Especially not IN my person. I was resigned to wait out the day and see what the evening brought. I hauled the bathroom door open by its cold, metal handle to behold Paul and Tim's faces.

"We're supposed to take you to meet Papoose family in the Kootenai Lodge after we show you the farm."

Tim's chiseled chin wobbled on as he explained that the first three families – Papoose, the one I just got initiated into, Brave family, and Warriors – took care of the enormous campus. We passed the spot where I'd just seen kids smoking on the porch of the big lodge. It connected to an outdoor staircase that led us down to a significantly smaller building.

"Those are Brave and Warrior headquarters, their family rooms. They're also in this building. We also call it the Pioneer House or Kootenai Lodge." They started alternating remarks.

"It's where you'll go for Papoose first lights, most every morning."

"These are all rap rooms, too."

25

"Yup. This used to be the only building on campus. Then the pioneers came and, you know, we all helped build most of the rest of the stuff."

"Paul, do you know if pioneers and students also built the dorms?"

"I doubt it. I helped pour the retaining wall around La Mancha, though."

"You're on the greenhouse crew at the farm, aren't you, Bro?"

"Sure am. George says we'll be done building right on time! So fucking awesome."

"OWNING IT! Yeah, Zack, so this Kootenai Lodge was one of the earliest buildings on the campus when the pioneers came and built the school and recreated the family system."

Paul and Tim had totally lost me. Did they really care about a greenhouse that much? I only would if I knew it was filled with leafy, sticky green buds.

"From CEDU."

Paul's straight face insisted on nothing, and broke my visual of the fuzzy plants growing in harmony, like the outdoor marijuana patches a friend had shown back home.

"I'm sorry, I don't know what you guys are talking about. Saw who do what?"

"Yeah. We call them pioneers, because when they came up here from CEDU there was nothing. From California. This is the second CEDU school, OK? They wanted to plant their sword. And they said 'Here Forever'." Tim finished as if reading from a bad script for the first time.

Tim and Paul continued the tour, breaking out in smirks at my horrible guerrilla haircut, and look of total confuzzlement on my face. I was now dressed like them, and my hair wasn't freakishly longer any more. The rest of the kids we passed kept producing the same expression of mimicked empathy.

How could I not have noticed that detail from the onset?

Most kids I could see were hauling wood around the campus, cutting it up by every possible means in their horrid wood corral. I was informed that this would be where I'd spend the next several months! I'd be there the following day, Tim and Paul assured me. They were becoming as familiar as the rough clothes and unexpected new hair-cut. We walked on. Other kids were cutting down trees in the nearby woods and plotting more deaths of more innocent trees for further chopping, chipping, peeling, pushing, pulling, piling, digging, and building uses. The campus reminded me of an early cartoon version of a factory. The two-man saw definitely left that impression, with boys and girls perilously yanking a six-foot blade between them. Why didn't they use a chainsaw?

We walked a lot, and came to a farm, where the tour guides point-ed out the greenhouse they'd been going on about. At the RMA farm was another "family" of kids, the Brave family. Some of them were a year or two older, all dressed in work boots and gloves. Brave family did egg collecting, shit raking, shit hauling, and sheep shearing.

There were outbuildings in various stages of construction around the animal pens. An entire menagerie lived at the smelly farm. All in all, it was a less eventful morning for all of the animals down at the farm than it had been for me. Even the ram my tour guides affec-tionately addressed as "Rambo," notorious for durations of perceived insanity, seemed to be on perfectly good behavior.

We walked down yet another rustic dirt road. Paul pointed out an obstacle course on our left, with chin-up bars, monkey bars, rope swings, stacked tires, and the like. A giant cargo net made from thick, braided strands was almost obscured from view by the forest. They called this big patch of woods with the obstacle course La Mancha Forest. They pointed out the dorm I'd begin living in that night.

We had circled our way back to the house by way of the entrance to the campus, near the place where the smooth state road turned onto the bumpy driveway that woke me earlier. There was much to be apprehensive about, as we approached the main lodge-house-thing again. I missed my hair and my hat and my sunglasses. The dreamy, surreal, in-and-out-of-my-body feeling persisted. Kids were congregat-ing for lunch. They stared at me. I again felt totally insecure. I was the new kid, and it felt as if I was still naked.

The kids were upstairs, smoking, on a tremendous sequence of porches that linked the front to the back of this enormous building. A forty-foot wraparound gangplank called the catwalk separated two porches. One porch was directly over that small dark room where I had just been "oriented." On each section of porch, a gaggle of smok-ers formed miniature factories, spewing obscene amounts of Marlboro smog into the atmosphere. I thought this public smoking by kids very strange. I had been kicked out of the Hill School for getting caught smoking, although I couldn't have lasted there anyway – smoking notwithstanding.

Incidentally, I believe we Virginians are born addicted to nicotine. My father smoked, my mother smoked, and all of my friends and their parents smoked, too. In Virginia, a kid wasn't supposed to smoke until they were sixteen.

I tried to get a view of some of the faces on the porches as we approached. Non-smoking kids sat on the catwalk between the two fuming factories. Everyone looked at me from under the cloud of smoke, scrutinizing me with their universal gaze of curiosity and unbending concentration, summing me up.

I wanted to meet people, usually. I liked social interaction, oftentimes. But, shocked, and extremely confused, how could I be social? I shied from the gazes. This was the longest day of my life.

Would my dad come back?

Tim went and briefed Darlayne about our tour. Paul didn't smoke, though I was thankful that he stayed with me on the smoking porch with the dwindling crowd. I didn't want to be left alone with any of these kids. They wouldn't look me in the eye, now that I was close. Paul didn't say a damn thing, and he didn't do me any damn good, not introducing me to the two girls on the porch with us. One of the girls had brown hair and skin, she was holding work gloves, and, like the boy I had seen with the wheelbarrow, her jeans and work boots were caked with filth. The other, older, girl wore a fuzzy pink sweater. I flipped the butt of the smoke that Tim gave me off the porch when I was done, making sure it wouldn't burn a person or incinerate anything.

Paul had a look of disdain on his face. "You can't do that."

"Hunh? I flipped it like fifteen feet, dude. Let's see you do it better?"

"NO. I mean it's out of agreement not to use the butt can," Paul snarled through his teeth.

His simmering irritation added to the hyper stimulation I was feeling.

"Sorry. What's a butkin?" *What had I done to upset him?*

Before following Paul in to find Tim, I paused to look at the girls on the porch to see if they had witnessed the bizarre exchange with Paul. But as soon as the younger one saw me looking their way, she flinched.

"Bans." The tanned girl lifted her leather work gloves in front of her face to block me from sight.

I caught the door and followed Paul inside. Tim stood near Darlayne Hammer. I hesitated. Still smacking on her gum and rocking to and fro, Darlayne barked at me from across the room.

"Don't know what the fuck is going on, do you? You're a cute one! Well, just follow Tim and Paul. Your big brothers will show you the program. Poor baby – long way from home this time, aren't you?"

She was addressing me from across a wide and not unoccupied space. I had to move my head in agreement with her, as I looked over more students in the enormous living room. I didn't like Darlayne drawing attention to me at this point in my morning. Newly shorn, flannel wearing, and feeling naked, I knew to stay away from her, like I knew it was smart to avoid a rabid Doberman. There was something downright wolfish about the woman, despite her inspiring carriage.

My tour guides pulled me to a couch area in the back of the large room, and schooled me on what a CEDU was. Here's what I heard:

The first CEDU was in California – the founding schools of CEDU each have their own history – and the way Tim and Paul talked about these histories, RMA and CEDU sounded sacred. In this spirit of scripture, the founding figures of CEDU, and current staff members, were talked about as gods might be.

My senior counselor, Tess, was Minerva to the CEDU Zeus – her father, Solomon Turnwell – who originated the entire system back in California some time before. He had a lot of money. Sol had founded both CEDU schools. We were now sitting in his second one.

Paul sounded exuberant when he explained that Sol was building more places for kids like us all over the country. The stories about Sol and his charisma and the sessions he used to run reached mythical proportions.

"You're going to learn a lot about this stuff at Monday Meetings and last lights, so don't worry about this shit too much."

We wandered through a maze of couches and stacked up pillows in the big living room.

"Sol Turnwell lived in California in 1969. He wanted to help kids who were going to be dead, insane, or in jail by the time they were eighteen. So, like, to get them before they got into serious crime, Sol

29

informed a few of these random fuckups from his neighborhood that he had a home they could crash at to get off of the street. To talk about their problems."

"Yeah, Sol's a master...he can hypnotize, and, like, make grown-ups cry." Tim sounded like he was in awe of this dude.

"So, eventually he took those agreements in exchange for free rent in his house, you know – to not do drugs or sex – they could stay."

Before I could ask more about the sex and drugs, Paul droned on. "Then they raised money to buy this place, and that's why we call the ones who came here first, and only had the old Kootenai Lodge, the pioneers. Now your Papoose family's room is in Kootenai."

"Hedwig and Nat Farmer were pioneers, too."

Paul added that, as if it meant something. He opened the door to the smoking porch for me again.

"Hedwig did my haircut at orientation, dude. Zack, the staff who did you is new. Not Andrew. The woman, what was her name, dude?"

"I don't rightly remember right now, Tim."

Forget the woman with the scissors for now, and I'll stash whatever they're saying about hedges and pioneers for later.

I was still stuck on the realization that they didn't mean *my* mother and father and brother and sister when they said my "family's room." It took me several seconds. It was only as Tim droned on about how we'd all be working at the wood corral together that I knew he was talking about a different social group. It would take time to adjust to all these new words and associations.

I had a quick, quiet chuckle as I pictured my real family peeling logs, covered in dirt and pushing a wheelbarrow full of sheepshit.

Six

Referring to family here evidently meant seeing Tess Turnwell again. She was waiting for me next to another giant doorframe, down the flight of outdoor wooden stairs at the entrance to Kootenai Lodge.

Unlike Darlayne Hammer, who could be seen stalking the campus, easily identified by her big breasts, blonde hair, and the direct, predatory manner of her stride, Tess Turnwell walked with a distinct lopsided bounce and reminded me of a brunette mop, with a slinky for a handle. Where Darlayne was big and buxom, Tess was skinny like kite string.

Tess stood in front of the family room waving excitedly.

"This is also called Papoose room, and this will be where you'll come after breakfast every day."

With an unnatural exuberance, her arms akimbo, she took custody from Paul and Tim.

"Come on in, Zack! The rest of your peer group is just itching to meet you!"

Her bouncy demeanor was not infectious and I got the feeling she thought I was nine years old. With her arms outspread, during an uncomfortable little pause, I saw she was expecting a hug before I should enter. I slid by her, but when I stopped for a moment to take in the crowded room, Tess confidently let a hand wipe at the small of my back, urging me into the bustle. The voices paused as I searched for a seat. I found unoccupied floor space by a wall.

Tess's Papoose headquarters was packed tightly with couches and flimsy black plastic chairs filled with about forty kids hanging on one another. The crowd buzzed nervous energy. The girls sat close and fiddled with one another's hair. One of the boys sat in between an older guy's legs. He, in turn, had his arms draped around the kid. This older guy waved at me when I entered the room. His other hand rubbed the boy in front of him on the chest, as you would a dog's belly. The very fucking creepy meter started to rise. Several of the girls were sitting like that, too, leaning back with their heads resting between the breasts of another girl. There were a handful of adults in the room, not just the creepy guy who'd waved at me. While older than the kids, he and Tess were several years junior to a few other adults. I wasn't sure anymore if the waving, boy-rubbing man was a "kid" or not. All my previous rules – when to touch, how to tell who were teachers, what a friendship is – blurred. The new expected normal was very, very fucking creepy.

"Everyone, let's slow it down a level."

Tess closed the door behind me, choking off more distracting thoughts to the control tower in my brain. As she gave instructions, the room hushed.

"Let's do an introduction, so bans are lifted for now while we make the newest member of our community feel welcome! Let's proceed in order from the head of the peer group. Zack, do you want to tell your new family where you're from?"

Is this woman crazy? My new family?

"Virginia, Ma'am."

"Uh, you don't have to call me Ma'am, Mister Bonnie."

One of the kids started to hum the theme from Dueling Banjos.

The young man who had draped himself around a boy snapped across the crowded room. ""Ernesto, knock it off! Ernesto apologizes. Please go on."

The room had gone from a playful and normal teen buzz to silence when the dude barked. I was still inspecting him, and trying to guess his age as Tess prompted me to tell everyone how old I was.

"Fifteen," I lied. Most kids in the room looked older.

"And what's something that makes you happy?" Tess asked.

"Um." I didn't yet have an answer, and I didn't want to be in the spotlight anymore, I was thoroughly overstimulated and needed breakfast or another cigarette. "I dunno. Cigarettes?"

"Hi, I'm Melanie. I'm the head of the peer group, so I'll start the intros. I've been here for five weeks, umm...I'm from Los Angeles and oh yeah! I love warm socks."

"I'm Rob Warner, I'm from Detroit, and I am on bans from you. Oh! Yeah, I like all music."

"Well I guess I'll go. Name's Wally Gold. I'm from L.A. Also. I'm also on bans from you, and I guess I like the farm."

"You guess?" Tess corrected him.

"I like the farm." Wally restated.

"I'm Ernesto Quepa, I'm sixteen, I'm from the Bay Area which is in northern California. I've been here for twenty days."

He raised his thumbs at the northern California reference while all the southern Californians responded with boos and downward turned thumbs. He was the Dueling Banjos offender.

"And I like robots!"

One of the girls had to be prodded. Her name was Ivy. She was beautiful; she liked tattoos, was from San Francisco, and had evidently just arrived the week before.

I'll have to keep an eye on her: Ivy Larrabee. Luscious.

The older guy who had snapped at Ernesto spoke next.

"Zack, I'm Keith Rios. I'm originally from West Virginia, but I've been living out West since I was a teenager. I was in Peer Group One, so I essentially helped build the campus we're now on. I'll be showing you the ropes and, along with Tess, I help run Papoose family. Welcome!"

"Yeah, I'm Jamie. Durant. Dad is in the Force, but I'm most recently from Indianapolis."

Keith drummed both hands against Jamie's chest in a "shave and a haircut" rhythm.

"Right. OK! I like guns – you know – shootin' with my dad."

Jamie had met group muster.

Keith drummed more on the chest of Jamie, the kid who was nestled into his lap. I let my eyes linger on Keith. *Was I looking at a pioneer? This guy worked here? He looked like a kid. Why did he and Tess seem so fucking happy?*

When the twenty or so kids in my "peer group" were introduced, Tess went on to address all forty of the kids crammed into the Papoose family room.

"In this morning's first light, I want to talk about morning chores. It's this family's responsibility to do a good job on daily chores in the house. When I go up there after my family has done chores and I see that one of the wood bays in the pit isn't fully stocked, or that the lights have been left on in the conservatory, it just hurts me so much. I mean it basically says, 'Tess's papooses don't give a fuck.' Right?"

She looked around the room pointedly.

"I take ownership of how we do our chores. I want to take pride in my family. I don't want to have to be policing you and wiping your asses, so let's really love our work today, put yourself IN LOVE with doing the windows, or the dusting. Down at the wood corral, you guys, safety is paramount. It is our responsibility to be safe. Also safety creates love...the love to do our work. OK? Your work now is to love the campus, to respect where we live, and it is visible to all the other families in this special place when we make our love visible. Let's remember that when we do our daily chores today. Keith, do you have something you want to add?"

"Put yourself in love with doing the windows"? Whoa.

Keith set one hand on the Jamie's shoulder, and the other on Ivy's knee. For the fifth time in four minutes, she visibly recoiled. He slithered out from behind Jamie, stood up, and smoothed his shirt. Checking that it was tucked in, Keith continued to stick his hands in and out of his pants while he acknowledged Tess.

"Yeah, Tess, thanks. I want to add to what you said about safety down at the wood corral. It's really important, guys. The Agreements aren't in place for you to shit on them. OK? Don't. Fuck. Safety. It's just too important. So, that's it, back on bans, everybody! Zack, just follow me today. I'm with your peer group on house chores. We'll save the wood corral for you until tomorrow."

I looked at Keith and tried to understand what he was. If he was getting paid, I never had a teacher like that. Maybe he doubled as the lacrosse coach? In my experience, team sport coaches and gym teachers were even worse than the Latin teachers and math tutors I'd met. If Keith's a student, why did he have any authority? I wasn't offended by his vulgarity but I was perplexed that he'd used it, when it was obvious he was acting from a position of authority. None of the adults had lifted an eyebrow to Tess's cursing either.

All the Papoose kids peeled themselves off the floor and rose from the couches and black plastic chairs. My peer group separated from the rest of the family. It had been only about two hours since I'd arrived in this place and I wasn't sure whether it was a work camp, teen ski lodge, some kind of jail, or just a really weird boarding school where I wasn't allowed music or long hair – but could smoke and curse and touch. I followed my new peer group up to the main lodge for chores, while the rest of the family suited up in work boots and gloves and went to the wood corral.

Doing chores sounded kind of easy, but at RMA, I found that the business lasted the entire morning. I scrubbed sinks and toilets. I took out some twenty small bags of garbage, loaded them into bigger bags and then into a massive bin behind the house to await whatever happened to discarded garbage. Five of us then swept the dining room until dust was gathered into piles and scooped into a double-sized metal dustpan. Along with Wally Gold and Jamie Durant, I vacuumed the floor of the entire house, including a pit-fireplace thing, and the offices.

In one room I noticed a telephone with blinking lights. The phone stood out, because it was the most modern thing I'd yet observed in the whole place. The phone's blinking lights made me wonder what building housed the people talking on those phone lines. Storing the knowledge that there was a phone in that room – they called it "the Bridge" – became the first in a series of actions designed to create a contingency plan. I made a mental note to check this door later to see if access would remain open at night. During chores, I found out that the Bridge was a staff headquarters. *Like on Star Trek.*

At precisely twelve noon, kids from all the different families arrived back up at the house. With Ernesto, and three other dudes who'd been down at the wood corral and in the Papoose room earlier in the day, I sat in one of the clusters of wooden furniture that littered the big house. It was clear that working in the house for daily cleaning chores was preferable to shifts at the wood corral. Along with their heavy work boots, the rest of their clothes were dusty and covered in tree particles.

"I know, it sounds like someone spanking a cat – God, I hate this music," Ernesto was ranting. "Can you believe this tape has been playing since before I went to first light? *Hijo de puta, madre,*" he added under his breath.

Tim Chalmers, the sharp-featured fellow who'd given me the orientation tour earlier, called my name and approached us. He was at the head of a mob of older students. As he came closer I immediately recognized the smell of animal feces. Tim had evidently come from the farm.

"Hey, I went to the commissary for you. Here's a pack of reds. You have another three packs of Marlboro's to last you until Sunday. Make 'em last. They're on your bunk down in La Mancha along with a toothbrush and some other shit you'll need. Make sure you let me know how your rap with Tess goes. Paul'll take you over there after rap sheets are read."

One of the kids in work boots shot me a devious look. "Won't that be nice? My first rap was with Tess, too. Good luck with that, Blood."

"What's a rap?" I countered.

Tim tossed the smokes to me and started laughing as the rest of the students flooded past him, filling the nooks and crannies of the furniture, pillows, and floor space.

"You'll find out soon enough. Just make sure you piss first, they can seem kind of long sometimes."

"Sometimes," Ernesto laughed, "try 'always eternal.' I'm fucking starved," he added for all of us.

But we had to wait until one of the self-important staff called us up. Warrior family followed the Summit people. Then we got to line up for lunch after the kids called Brave.

SEVEN

[Continued] The atmosphere in the family was made intolerable by your behavior. Even Sunday, when I saw you spitting, I thought, here's a law that you won't follow. Then too, your vulgar and obscene language, was turning you into someone not able to take part in civilized conversation.

As you know, we tried everything to get you back on the track. But the slide that began in seventh grade got worse at the Hill School, and led finally to the public school saying you couldn't be in regular classes. Let's forget for a moment your horrible academic performance and just look at the behavioral problems – insubordination, obscenity, breaking rules, rudeness to teachers. At home, you stayed out later than the agreed upon times, went to places we didn't allow you to go, slammed holes in the walls, argued with your brother, cursed your parents. At the same time, you gave up all the things which were healthy and at which you could have been successful – sports, school activities, even being a friend, and having good friends.

—Letter from author's mother, 11 July 1988

†

Tess Turnwell was the "facilitator" of my first rap at RMA. Stellar Annex was the name of the room where I would spend the entirety of my first afternoon in Idaho. The event was so apocalyptic, anything else would be forgettable by comparison if it hadn't already been the freakiest day in my life. I didn't know what to be nervous about. But so many kids during lunch asked me if this was going to be my first rap, and then when I said that it was, I could see they were anxious, too.

"My first day was a rap day, too. They don't usually do that anymore." Paul Rensselaer remembered aloud at lunch, staring off over a half-consumed portion of macaroni salad. "Grab the tray, Zack. We get to skip razz around the pit since Tess already told us to head to Stellar Annex. We can tighten up in the dish room first."

With that he led me into the dish room where we spent ten minutes organizing the hideous wood patterned bowls and plates.

I didn't know what was in store for me next. Paul escorted me from the house, and steered me across a path with a rock border, up the hill from the dorm La Mancha. I could see the lake and the mysterious sauna standing alone – *unless there was a Hedwig inside.*

Many other people were moving from the main house to their assigned rooms, and a sense of foreboding pervaded. Kids weren't playful now. I didn't know how to identify everyone's age, rank, or issues yet, but I got a strong whiff of reluctance when we sat down for that afternoon's rap.

A circle of more of those black plastic chairs was interrupted by one upholstered blue one with arm rests. Nobody went near that one. I sat down in the chair next to Paul and watched and listened as the room filled up with the rest of the anxiously tittering occupants. The

38

inhabitants of the room they called the Stellar Annex exuded fear. I was wearing the aroma thickly. It lingered like a mouthful of peanut butter.

Tess came in with a cup of tea and sat in the upholstered chair. She was next to Paul, two down from me. The room went silent. Tess softly breathed over her tea, and told the group that this was my first rap and would someone please inform me of the "Agreements." A boy with terrible acne – not as bad as the acne I was soon to get – quickly chimed in with the first Agreement:

"What is said in a rap stays in a rap."

OK. I don't think I'm getting this. What is a rap?

Thankfully, Tess translated: "Zack, a lot of people are going to be sharing things about themselves that are very private. Raps are our safe environment to clear up our differences with one another and clean up our dirt, and talk about our problems and take care of our feelings. When someone says something in a rap, we discuss it in raps, but to keep the environment "healthy" we don't need to bring it up in conversation outside of raps."

A foppish looking dude with shiny red lips – *he must be a staff –* reiterated Tess's assertions. The two of them would mimic each other many times that afternoon.

"Like, up in the house or down at the wood corral. Raps are safe, and one of the most important ways we ensure this safety, is by staying within that Agreement. Whatever gets said in here, stays in here."

Back to Tess for a spell: "Also, and this is really Agreement numero uno, and it really should go without saying: there is no violence here. This includes threats of violence. You can say whatever you want, but if you said to me 'If I wasn't in a rap right now, I'd grab a knife and stab you,' that'd be really unacceptable. We'd have to find another place for someone who threatened violence like that...And we can safely air our dirty laundry here without that, um – punishment. Unlike at another place, see?"

It was obvious she didn't have the word at her disposal for the repercussions of threatening someone in a rap with a knife. As for her quips about other places, any other place in the world seemed like it would be a better place than where I found myself right now. The attempts at translation helped some, but my overall feeling was that this room had been flooded with childhood nightmares made real. My mind ripped briefly to Andrew Oswald, the freak lemur-man, and his abrupt wrist control that morning – like he was one of my wrestling coaches back home. It was always about the wrist.

For the next Agreement, Tess nodded to a girl near me.

"Don't say anything people can't change." A very timid voice that hadn't wanted to share.

With more confidence and focus than I'd seen out of Paul all day, he contributed to the circle: "Alright, like if someone seemed sloppy, or you saw them around the house with their shirt untucked, comments about that would be acceptable. OK, you know umm, you can't say I think you're an asshole because you have a big nose."

My attention started being sent around the room like a ping-pong ball.

Ironically, a boy with a big nose interjected, "But you could say you're a slob when you walk around like that, or put your feet up on the furniture. Or you're an asshole when you break the Agreements or act without safety at the wood corral. But you can't say I don't like black people or like, you know. Do you understand?"

"I understand this," I said, and, feeling diplomatic, added, "I always support a specification against racism. I think the rule makes sense."

Several weird glances shot around the room. I had said the correct thing, I thought. For the umpteenth time today I felt threatened. This was a novel feeling for me. People here knew a lot more. They knew my name, where I was from, where the hell in the United States we apparently were. Idaho. I didn't know shit. I felt way out of my league.

"No leaving the rap." This boy was staring at me.

There was a little pause. I waited for the next regulation. Instead, Paul stood quietly up from his seat next to me, and switched chairs with a kid on the opposite side of the circle. Now I was sitting next to a pretty girl with brown hair tied back in a tight ponytail.

Paul had moved across the circle to speak to me.

"We get up and move when we want to indict somebody, that way we won't be spitting in their faces. If you..."

Tess cut Paul off in mid-sentence and swiveled her dark mop in my direction.

"Let's show how we use our voices here. Zack, this can get a little loud. So let's hear from a couple of people that have work to do today?"

Two or three hands went up.

"Let's hear a couple of you count to ten."

Tess encouraged six willing participants. By the time they'd gotten to FOUR the room was so loud it rang. By the time the voices reached EIGHT they were strained and breaking. Girls had begun crying at TEN, and from there the rap seemed to begin to take shape. With a disarming smile, Tess switched her focus to a boy sitting a few faces down.

"Now, Evan, tell the baby and us what an indictment is. I don't think you're a baby, Zack, you're just the newest person on campus."

I looked at Paul, but he was just waiting for Evan to pick up where his own definition of an indictment had been interrupted.

I had already noticed Evan. He had a little leather holster on his hip for his cigarettes and a lighter. His shirt was tucked in so deeply that it pulled his shoulders forward. He was about as thin as a cane and crooked over a bit like he might need one. He reminded me of driftwood. He searched for the correct words, but not fast enough, evidently.

Evan: "Well, I guess...."

"You guess what, Milton and Bradley....?"

Tess Turnwell roared suddenly, at the top of her lungs, about four feet from my cochlea.

It was as if a helicopter had just crash-landed in the middle of the circle. I jumped out of my seat. Then I realized her way of showing me the significance of this business of switching chairs was by "pretending" to scream at Evan about board games. I hated yelling. Or getting yelled at back home.

Screaming matches with my mother and father had become a daily occurrence. They always seemed to be mad at me about something, and recently they had grounds for complaint. Their near constant displays of disappointment and anger over the last several years always reduced me to tears, fight, and flight. When I was with my friends or a girl, I didn't care, so I started not being at home. In the year's time since I'd come back from France, I had been thrown out of the Hill School for smoking and kicked out of public school. I'd been a runaway from home, and summer camp.

I began to know something bad would happen – every day. I felt like that again here in Tess's rap: Something bad was going to happen, and I was way out of my league. I didn't want to stay in the room. I sensed danger.

The lessons that Tess wanted to instruct me on were already taking: move across the room, tuck in your shirt, don't talk about The Clash or The Doors, don't hit or punch, don't smoke anything but cigarettes, or write or carve on yourself, or chew gum, or call the Agreements rules, or run away, talk back, or complain about anything.

I was starting to understand quite well. *This was a joke.* It simply had to be. These several hours had introduced me to several lifetimes.

This was an elaborate act…Why would anyone carve on themselves?

OK, I'll bite, what's in the next act?

Tess fidgeted purposefully with a piece of paper in her hand. She then fiddled wildly with the band of her wristwatch, and then her shoelaces. Paul explained: Anything that could be fidgeted with absentmindedly would constitute a "rap toy." There were to be no distractions from the work we would be doing.

Also, there were to be at least "five feet on the floor" at all times. Demonstrating, Tess tried to push her chair back on two legs, but she just didn't have enough bulk. Essentially, there was to be no tipping of the chair, and you were not supposed to curl up in it, either. I came to understand that a student or staff could call you out for this at any time, but the Agreement was largely ignored. It was another good indicator of how a staff felt about you if you got "pulled up" for hiding in your chair. By the same standard, it would be pretty "needsy" if an older student pulled you up for playing with a rap toy, say, a rubber band – or a paper clip.

Hours after the Agreement explanation part of the afternoon, we were still in the circle of chairs. We hadn't left the room. Nobody asked to take a cigarette break. Piles of used tissues, from people crying, grew under some of the seats. At first my interest in what was going on in the room was enough to keep my focus. Then the distracting force that usually ripped my attention from subject to subject didn't intervene. I kept my focus on the rap session and didn't turn away like I did while watching a stupid movie or taking a test in school.

Numberless times, voices escalated to high-pitched, aching screams that pierced the air of the Stellar Annex. Quiet moments with kids talking to themselves, or staring at the floor and vocalizing in mysterious Pidgin English interspersed. Once I thought violence would ensue. A girl, whose face had gone completely red, grabbed a fistful of her hair and yanked hard on it, pulling three times at the spot until some thin blonde clumps of her hair floated off of her sweaty hands and into the middle of the circle.

She only stopped tugging because Tess brushed the hand away.

Each kid became a very important character over the afternoon, but Evan and Tess left the biggest impression with one baffling exchange. The blonde girl kept shrieking. I felt my mind trying to tear out my brain, to escape the room. I didn't want to sit anymore and I kept actively looking to the door or the windows. But simultaneously, my focus could not be pulled from Evan, now sitting next to me, who began to overflow like a flood overcoming a dam, acting out the terror that was going on between my ears:

"Oh my god, I'm not going to make it, I'm going to fuck up out there! I'm SO FUCKING SCARED. ME IS SCAAAAAAAAAAAAARED. WHY I? Why do you make me hurt every fucking day?"

I tried to take in Evan and block out the girl, still angered and wailing only six feet across. Tess was with her, but looked in our direction and exploded. "WHO IS RUNNING EVAN? Who's RUNNING THE SHOW RIGHT NOW?"

I looked behind Evan's chair for entertainment, or a threat, but the space was empty.

"I am! He always is, he's always TELLING ME WHAT TO DO! ME CAN'T WIN! I'S ALWAYS TELLING ME, ME CAN'T WIN! MOTHERFUCKER!"

"WHAT'S ME SAY?"

"FUCK YOU, I'll KILL YOU. I FUCKING HATE YOU! STOP! FUCKING STOP. STOP! STOOOOOOOOOOOOP!"

"That's RIGHT! KEEP GOING, EVAN! GIVE ME A VOICE!"

"AAAAAHHHHHHHH I'M GOING TO KILL YOU, I! I FUCKING HATE YOU, LEAVE ME ALONE! GIVE ME A VOICE, GIVE ME A VOICE, AHHHH GIVE ME A VOICE! GIVEMEAVOICE GIVEMEA VOICE!"

Evan's yelling, over the girl's wailing, made me plug my ears with my fingers. Tess gave me a hard look, but I closed my eyes and hummed softly under the unfolding noise of disaster.

EIGHT

[Continued] Zack, it's clear that you needed some major intervention to stop this horrible slide. I hope that Rocky Mountain Academy will be that for you.

When I think about WHY all this happened to you I come up with two or three explanations – but none of them really explain your problems entirely. You do have Attention Deficit Disorder, which just means you have some differences in the way you focus attention and the way you learn. In itself this wouldn't cause your problems. Then you became depressed (who wouldn't be depressed at being a failing student, in trouble all the time?). But the depression doesn't explain it either (Besides you refused to take the medicine which might have helped even though you promised to do so.) Another problem was having a successful older brother, but lots of kids have success-ful older brothers without having the problems you have. Dr. D believes it makes it hard to have an early adolescence and that's true too. You began to mature physically before other kids. All of these reasons explain a little bit but the real explanations may never be known.

Luckily, WHY isn't so important now. The point is YOU CAN CHANGE. YOU can learn how to take responsibility, how to study, how to accept author-ity and how to talk in a civilized way. Your gifts are extraordinary. You have a bright mind, a good feel for literature and language, a sociable and caring nature. You also have a family that values learning and kind-ness. Zack, everything you need for success is within you. It's just a matter of shaping it.

—Letter from author's mother, 11 July 1988

✝

The sounds of my dorm members' snoring dissipated through the stuffy night air. I was awake and I was asleep.

I was living with my family in Charlottesville, Virginia. I had my really cool rat-tail again. I was pretty happy with its length. I had been back from France for just a few days, and I was supposed to attend a boarding school called Hill the next week.

It occurred to me that I was dreaming, a foreshadowing dream that morphed into a flashback. Irony was not lost on me.

I sat in the sun on our back stoop, contemplating my ever-changing social position. My mother came outside. She had been looking at me through the window. Something was up.

"Well, what is it?"

She had already ruined my concentration by sliding open the glass door behind me.

"You have this one hair longer than the others."

"Why can't you just leave me alone, Mother?"

She was holding a pair of large metal scissors.

"It's just a flyaway, and it looks ridiculous. It'll only take a second."

She assured me, promised me, and finally swore to me that this was not a ploy to cut off my rat-tail. I acquiesced to her offer to groom it for me after her incessant yammering about how there "really was just one" longer hair deviating from the deftly trained twist and twirl of my punkish hairdo. I made her promise one last time not to separate her seeming nemesis of the last few months from my precious dome.

I turned on the steps to allow her the benefit of more precise sight. Then, with one, smooth, frighteningly natural motion that my mother and Kelly Grainger surely must have learned in a secret matriarchal ritual under some haunted lunar eclipse, she betrayed me. She cut off the whole fucking thing. So, I ran away. It wasn't the first time I had run away and it wouldn't be the last. But that time she had simply made me.

†

I woke abruptly to find I was surrounded by wood. I was on a bunk bed that was fitted to the wall. Resembling a pine coffin, the bunk was more like a shelf than a bed, and I was still in Idaho. Shower stalls in the bathroom shared my wall, and water rushed through pipes in short intervals, jarring me from sleep. I had had another haircut because of the laughable job that Kelly had made of me the first time around; I rubbed the short soft bristles and stood on the little wooden ladder that took me down from my dream-manufacturing shelf.

Every kid here had been through their own intrinsically memorable orientation ceremony.

Like it or not, I was enrolled in this bizarre place. I was a member of a community with a classification, a schedule, and a routine to which I was impelled to adhere.

We rose without fail at 6:30. I realized a shower was essential – a hot shower, lasting less than five minutes, was one of the few times I could be alone. I emerged from my shower amazed that none of my dorm mates resisted being up at such a blasphemous hour, or "agreeing" to such a short shower time. I pulled on the cardboard work jeans I'd worn since meeting Scissors Kelly and Andrew the lemur.

It was cool in the morning, even in July, but it was going to get pretty damn hot if it was anything like the preceding day. It didn't have the humidity of home, but that was just another unfamiliar new detail.

One of the older students in the dorm, a tall, ungainly boy with bright red hair, named Crosby Rohrback, waited for me to walk up to the main lodge for breakfast. Crosby was dorm support under Jasper Browning's peer leadership as dorm head. He mentioned that I wasn't allowed to walk up to the house from La Mancha alone. This was what Tess had meant when she said I didn't have my "ups and downs" yet.

I would have to wait until I was out of agreement to learn what many of the Agreements were. However, one of the first things I learned was that we didn't call the Agreements rules...which they clearly were.

Crosby remarked about the little lump of a mountain that framed the view of the entire campus as one looked east. "That's Forty Thirty-two."

"What's that?"

"That's what that little mountain is called. My peer group had its Brave quest up there."

"How far away is it to the top?" I asked.

"Dunno, about eight or ten miles, maybe."

I would find myself staring at 4032 quite a lot. It was a number designation by the forest service, in all likelihood, but for me it was the gateway. I committed to memory the contours and situation of 4032. I focused my viewing and longing in its direction. It was a long, rolling, sweeping set of hills, not huge, not steep. It separated our campus from the beginning of the very steep and mysterious Eastern Mountains. The majestic Selkirk Mountain ranges to the west and north were also impressive obstacles. This range could be seen from many miles away, and unlike 4032, those peaks were obviously impassable.

Little 4032 looked like a bored god had left it there. It looked so out of place. Topography by number – 4032 was stuck, seemingly unattached, about the shape of a Mr. Potato Head nose, and off to itself, surrounded by monsters on all sides. Clifty Mountain towered above it next door, directly south. I imagined 4032, my little baby mountain, longed to be with its maker as bad as I already wanted to be home.

Crosby and I climbed the steps by Big Ben, a Ponderosa Pine in Idaho, not a major tourist destination in England. The enormous tree cut through the wooden framework of the deck to burst up into the light. Crosby and I ascended to the main lodge for breakfast.

It was 7 AM. The kids flooded in, dressed for work. The older boys dressed for classes were obvious with their clean collared shirts, name-brand clothes, and the rank smell of aftershave that it was their privilege to wear. Older student girls could wear perfume on Saturday nights, and only if they were in town wear. Most girls complained frequently about the forbidden status of cremes, perfumes, and makeup.

I didn't care because I still smelled like last week's sweat, and I could not even walk up to a morning meal by myself. I only owned a couple of shirts. I knew I wasn't impressing anybody. My feet were decked out in the boots that I received the first day. They were so heavy that if a falling anvil had dropped on my foot, I'd only have noticed a little pressure. I felt indestructible in these boots. They weighed five pounds each and reminded me of ski boots.

Some non-logo T-shirt – most likely blue or red – adorned my hairless torso, and it was all topped off with the latest fashion of the area: the tucked-in flannel. Shirts stayed tucked in when you were indoors. I soon noted that most kids would take their shirts out of their pants first thing when walking out of the house, or the old Kootenai lodge. The un-tucking of a shirt was as casual a motion as an executive loosening his tie at the end of a workday. Perhaps it was the only gesture of resistance sanctioned at Rocky Mountain, this tugging and un-tucking of the shirt.

Image was everything at RMA, and the program worked to destroy any image that you might already have of yourself, or that you might just be developing. We had matching flannels and kept our shirts buttoned correctly – no Latino gangster "cholo" front for the California kids.

†

> Frequently, our students dress in impractical or "imagey" types of clothing before arriving at RMA. Our goal is to assist our students in creating relationships with others based upon who they are rather than how they appear. Therefore, students and faculty dress in practical, durable, non-imagey clothing that facilitates both work and various other activities. We ask that you work closely with the parent communicators in adhering to their clothing requests, which will include washable, non-black, non-imprinted or silk-screened items. Shoes should be sturdy, low-heeled for girls, and practical for the weather variations we experience. Inappropriate items will be returned to you. If you are uncertain as to the appropriateness please ask your parent communicator before mailing.
> —RMA New Parent Handbook

†

Trying to keep up, I was acclimating to the routine and integrating the social dynamics, learning a code still undeciphered. What's a "propheet"? Or a "facilitator"? Riddles everywhere: New words, new perceptions of me, new representatives of this new authority. The people who "ran" raps were so revered by the staff and students of the campus that it seemed like they must have specialized knowledge of everyone on the campus and everything that went on.

I still couldn't shake the thought that none of it was real. This place, the program, the customs and terminology, and these people had become so important so fast! Papoose family staff told us when to work, talk, eat, sleep, and clean. More staff and older students told us where to get supplies, how to do chores, how to dress, and what the rules – er, Agreements – were. I yearned to wake up, as if from a bizarre and freaky nightmare.

I tried to sense how any of this shtick applied to me. Each day I would ponder a different puzzle piece. I knew that all of the content

48

here had something to do with what everyone called "propheets." The term remained mysterious. One thing we babies to the program knew was that our "Truth propheet" was the next propheet to "go in," and that it took place overnight. It wasn't scheduled for a few weeks. As days went by, and I went through more raps, my anxiety about the upcoming Truth propheet grew, since nobody would tell us what would happen when we went in the propheet – or even define the word.

Each day was long.

The house bristled with a more normal life in the mornings, mostly because human bodily functions needed attending to and most staff hadn't arrived yet. Breaking free of the overprotective dorm head or dorm support who escorted me, I gravitated over to a table with some more familiar Papoose faces. Terrance Whittlemore, a chess-playing dude from Brave family, was in conversation with Ernesto about their dreams.

They were in the same dorm. Terrance was in a peer group two above mine, so had been there nearly a year and was approaching the crux of the emotional program. I'd heard he would be going through something called the "I Want to Live" propheet soon.

Terrance was from Atlanta, and commonly known to be one of the most athletic kids on the campus, and the best chess player. He'd been a jock before getting sent across the country. If he was good enough for Ernie, he would be good enough for me. I saddled up to their picnic table and nibbled on some unsweetened granola, while Terrance trounced a girl I didn't know at chess.

"What's for lunch, is it going to rain, is James Taylor still alive, and how do you think we should kill him?" I looked at the blisters forming on my hands, half proud and half perturbed at earning them.

Work camp drug addicts, we usually smoked inordinate quantities of cigs before the entire early shift arrived. It was a priority, getting as much "streetsyness" in as possible. This also applied to our ritualistic ingestion of coffee. While we lower-school kids were allowed only one cup, the upper-school students had earned the privilege to drink two. The coffee was boiled grounds that the kids all referred to reverently as cowboy coffee. It was not unusual to start sensing grains of coffee beans on your tongue at the first sip. Cowboy coffee was otherwise remarkable as probably the worst tasting breakfast beverage in the world. Most people on the planet would have masked the bitterness – I won't even call it taste – with sugar. We had honey. Milk was unavailable, unless an older brother would drop a spoonful out of his own powdered creamer from town. Indicators like that taught me which kids were senior enough in the program to receive those privileges.

One daily occurrence lent each morning enough authenticity to convince me that the staff and kids weren't just robots and actors. Cowboy coffee cleaned my intestines out as efficiently as a syringe being emptied. I never took a crap in my dorm that first year. One sip of boiled coffee grounds in the morning acted as the greatest laxative in the universe. I was on the gastric equivalent of a sundial, so precise that I usually had the same person next to me in the cluster of two men's stalls by the mudroom. Terrance Whittlemore and I took a shit, at precisely the same time, every day. The beautiful thing was – if taking a poop can ever be described as beautiful – the meetings were always serendipitous and authentic. There was nothing fake or subversive in expelling bodily waste after cowboy coffee and a morning chess exercise. Because no staff or "look-good" older student was there to cop us out, Terrance and I could plot and plan, meditate and philosophize, while our heart rates increased in anticipation of farm work for Terrance, cleaning chores or the wood corral for me.

> Through daily work activities, students can explore their interest in the vocational curriculum. Here, the academy's farm plays an integral part as students care for the animals and learn the many aspects of farm management... Woodlot management and wood technology are also taught, along with a construction program that develops carpentry skills, logic and pride in workmanship.
> —RMA brochure

I was not allowed to use any tools except the wheelbarrow and the broom down in the wood corral. I spent the first weeks in a daze, carrying wood all over the campus in a wheelbarrow, or doing chores in the house, still not sure why I was in this place. Soon I was awarded the task of working the two-man saw, which made me feel special for about forty seconds. We had to be checked out for proficiency on every tool. Just like authentic lumberjacks with wavy, whiskey-stained red beards, we stood on either side of the giant sawhorse that supported the log we were cutting. We cut the log into three-foot lengths using a discarded broom handle as a measuring stick. In our matching lumberjack wear, we would guide and thrust the six-foot blade into the meat of the log. The teeth of the blade shot out shark-tooth-shaped wood chips in both directions.

Though it was called the two-man saw, it really favored three laborers. Our sawhorses were hand-made by Brave family, and were not anchored to the ground. They would sway under the rhythm of the blade, making things dangerous and unproductive. A third laborer needed to sit on the log to slow the bucking sawhorses. Log rider was generally a girl's job, so at first, it was a reason to work – to show off for the girls.

Vera Cruces, a Papoose from the peer group above mine, was the girl from the smoking porch my first day. The tan one who'd hissed the word "Bans" at me. She worked with my crew in the log riding position. I admit I lost concentration while watching Vera wiggle on the length of dead tree dancing in its trough, and may have been responsible for the sudden bouncing of the long blade. It vaulted out of its groove and popped onto Vera's broken-in work boot.

"Oh my god, did you hear that?" Dylan, the other sawyer and member of my PG, exclaimed as the steel blade ran skidding across rubber.

"Holy shit, Vera, are you OK? Are you bleeding? Did the blade go through your Sorel?" I grabbed the pretty girl's boot. I tugged, only to see that the blade had bit the rubber toe just enough to roughen it. Her foot, encased within the new vocabulary word – Sorel boot, was fine.

"Umm. Bans. I just got off of WD's this morning, so please lay off?"

But I held on, and she didn't move for a moment. And in those three seconds was the awkwardness and excitement of flirtation.

While work crews were daily, and you did them with your family, WD's – Work Details – were for when you fucked up in some way. Like Vera must have done.

That got me thinking: *Maybe I'm here because of girls: sneaking into girls' houses, getting caught once doing so, getting wickedly depressed when one stopped liking me, forgetting her after meeting a girl with a car, and hitchhiking all the way back from Camp Minnehaha to see her.*

One time the police had called from two counties over when they saw me on a bicycle at 1 AM. It perturbed my family that I didn't let the lack of a car stop me. My brother hadn't laughed that time the police brought me home. And then splitting from Minnehaha had been a last straw for Mom and Dad. They were all done with me and my quest for independence.

Starting in the wood corral, we were in the approach phase of a thirty-month expedition. While RMA named our families with Native American descriptors, it also used the language of mountain climbing. We heard that little pieces of specialized knowledge would accompany the major changes of terrain. Whether we trusted our older brothers to be "on belay" for us, or not, was a significance that took me almost a year in Idaho to appreciate. Whatever I would learn when I reached the next RMA family, and started to reach the "crux" of the program's metaphorical mountain, was in the future. Meanwhile, surely some unique aspect of the school would reveal itself to support my hypothesis that the program was simply too weird, too fake to be real. My findings of fakeness ranged from *"This can't be real,"* to *"These guys have GOT to be acting – that's the only explanation."*

A large percentage of the energy used to heat and cook food was produced on campus. We, new kids in the first family, Papooses, did all of the sawing, axing, bark-peeling, mauling, and hauling of wood. We seemed to do all the cleaning of the buildings, too. Papoose, my new family, was named to remind us that we only had a baby understanding of the bravery we would need at the summit of the mountain of CEDU's study in human behavior modification.

The next family up in the RMA program was called Brave. They cut down the trees and landscaped the enormous property. Warrior was the third family, followed by Summit. Warrior family, perhaps the most visible students on the campus due to their leadership responsibilities in the lower two families, also worked all the chores on the farm. Summit Grads had classes with some Warrior students – called Leadership – in the newly built upper school academic building called Skinner.

The smell of freshly sliced and diced wood was strongest there.

The Papoose family headquarters was in the old Kootenai lodge, the place where Tess Turnwell expected her entrance hug on the first day, but our family also had to take care of a tipi, our secondary, outdoor family room. Brave family had an Ernest Shackleton-inspired lounge called the Quest room. Brave family was in charge of deforestation, and kept our department of the wood factory awash in wood to measure, cut, and haul. They dragged tree after tree to us in the wood corral from the densely wooded area behind the tipi.

The tipi was built on a wide platform in the woods on a path past the Stellar Annex, where I'd had that freaky rap on my first day. The tipi was large. I had never been in one before, but didn't think they were supposed to be this permanent. It was the last structure to the east that I could see, before the border with dense forest and Mount 4032. It was one of our responsibilities as Papooses to keep the tipi area clean, and make sure the pathways were pretty.

One morning after breakfast, we cleaned the tipi's canvas with scrub brushes dipped in little buckets of bleach and water. We swept the wooden stage it sat upon, too. Keith and Tess called the group together. We made a circle around a freshly built outhouse nearby.

"Look at our new addition that the Brave kids just installed! That's some great craftsmanship, right there! Not craftsmanshit, get it? I'll tell you, George Daughtry and Chet Lively are doing great things with those kids. See that everybody? That's what we call ownership!" Keith beamed.

The Brave family had installed a funnel into a wooden box that housed a small pit in the ground, and gave it to the Papoose family. Here we were, standing in a circle – worshiping it. *Whooptidooda for Brave and Papoose!* Tess stressed what ownership and legacy meant at RMA. We had special standards at CEDU, she droned. I stared into the privy, which would soon be filled with human waste and scoops of powdered lime.

I went back to picking up trash. Unlike campsites I'd seen near the Appalachian Trail back East, there were no crushed cans of soda or beer, and no discarded plastic or faded aluminum cans of Mellow Yellow or Tab. I took the chance to wander off from the group for a moment, and noted some manicured trails wandering deeper into the coniferous foliage. The paths switched back and forth up the south side of campus, far back into the woods. One wound up a long steep hill.

Poking around on the paths near the tipi, wandering in and out of sight of the group, seeking bits of paper and out-of-place sticks, I looked up to see another student. It was Ivy Larrabee, from my peer group.

"Hey." I saluted her German style.

She pointed to herself and did a side-to-side sweep. Slowly, she gave me an "Are you really talking to me?" wave.

"Isn't this smurfy? Being a slave?"

I got a little eye contact, but Ivy was mostly focused on the woods in the direction of the base of 4032. Maybe she was contemplating like I was – getting the hell out of this place already. She stared deeply into the woods. I didn't know if she was one of those people on bans. Like I really cared. I just needed information, and I knew we were on the same wavelength.

Why did she stay here? What made her not run? What did she know that I didn't know? Was all this for real? Or was she in on the act? Did she have any answers for me about this place? I mean why shouldn't I be allowed to talk to her?

What had been done to these kids? Bans? Was this code? Bands? Like rubber bands, or bands like music bands?

It occurred to me to ask Ivy just that, and where I could find a map.

I spoke in a subdued tone, avoiding any ears that could've been out in the woods.

"You want to tell me why we're here? What is this place? I mean, what is going on here? How far away is Bomber's Fairy?"

She opened her mouth. Then she glanced over her shoulder toward the rest of the family scrubbing and sweeping the tipi area. It appeared to be the wrong time to ask. Evidently, she had changed her mind about speaking to me because she gave the curt one-syllable response:

"Bans."

Perhaps I had been too spontaneous. I hadn't been called but I had shown my cards. My heart raced in a familiar pitter-patter of mischief. I wondered if I had just been jilted or if she would have spoken to me if she could have. *And she could have.* There wasn't anybody else around, and weren't we still in the good ol' United States? *What was there to be afraid of?*

I had been confident I could talk to her, and received a subtle confirmation as she raised a cute eyebrow and sashayed back to the tipi and the Papoose group. Just an hour before, I asked one of the guys in my family if he knew what time it was. He'd given the same response, exactly: Bans.

What had been done to these kids? Bans? Was this code? Bands? Like rubber bands, or bands like music bands?

Bands are when you cannot talk to anyone. And everyone ignores you. There's a lot to it but believe me
it sucks SHIT. If I am forced to stay the whole program
like just about everybody does I won't be home until
2 ½ YEARS from July 11. I would only get to go home
once after 1 ½ years. I hate this joint. It is a freak
house they try to convert me into something I'm not.
In fact, I really don't think I should be here. Because
90% of the people are here or at a mental institution
or Jail or Juvie because they were pushers or addicts
or – Shit I've got to go.
  —Author journal entry, 20 July 1988

†

I had waited until that moment alone with Ivy because it was
already obvious there were "spies" among us, at RMA. I was conclud-
ing that the entire area – the tipi, the family rooms, the dorms, the
rap rooms, and the odd hiding places in the house-lodge thing – all of
them were bugged. I wasn't sure yet about the use of surveillance, but I
became absolutely convinced of it after my next rap.

NINE

What are raps?

Raps, generally 3.5 hours in length, occur 3 times a week and are designed to facilitate personal growth. Student participants, (numbering 12-15) and faculty facilitators and supports (usually numbering 3) discuss and confront personal issues that are both current and past. Acceptance and resolution are two primary goals that are achieved. Relationship building, bonding, values clarification, and goal setting and achievement are discussed. Closer, more honest relationships with peers, adults and family occur as a result. Daily life experiences are processed through the rap, thereby creating learning opportunities inside and outside of the formal classroom.

—RMA New Parent Handbook

It was still July. Eternally July.

That afternoon, the door to Papoose room closed. Darlayne Hammer sat in the rap circle in a regular black chair instead of the one puffy, cushioned chair with armrests. As facilitator, she could sit in it at any point she chose. She didn't need the rap sheet that was folded up in her hand – she already knew the names and hometowns of every kid in the room. A few older boys and girls, unknown to me, sat in the circle too. Darlayne called out each name with a colorful and flippant remark about each kid. When she got to me, she pretended to pull fake guns from her porky hips and pointed the finger guns at me.

"ZAP Bonnie. From the wilds of Camp Minnehaha, hunh?" That reference to the summer camp I had run away from couldn't have been known to anyone but me.

She went on: "Oh shit I'm busted! How did she know that?"

Darlayne was subtexting my thoughts!

My parents never said anything, but I was pretty sure they had taken marijuana from my jean jacket after I hitchhiked home from Camp Minnehaha a month and a lifetime ago.

I never considered the ramifications of that incident.

OK – perhaps life had gotten pretty turbulent before I arrived in Idaho. The perpetual fights with my parents had come to be normal.

OK – it wasn't perfect; I wasn't perfect – I had run away a lot, not just from Camp Minnehaha, but from home.

OK – my parents might have grounds for a change, to show they were in charge. Maybe this place was supposed to make me listen to my parents – restore me to their good graces – pole vault me back to into education system – make up for the fact that I needed Ritalin, was depressed, and had better start to take school more seriously – all of these things, OK.

But this? The lessons here were supposed to surpass the education I'd be getting if I were still at home? This was the *first step* to compensate for all the fucking up I did before, but this was over the top.

My parents hate me now.

"So, why are you here, Dr. Bonnie?"

Did Darlayne know I'd been drinking at my cousin's wedding in Baltimore? "I don't know."

"No really, it's OK, we want to know, right?"

"Well, I got kicked out of a few schools. Had processing issues, like I couldn't pay attention."

"Uh hunh. That's what you think. Why do you think you couldn't pay attention?"

"I don't know."

"So everything at home was perfect then?"

"I'm not saying that."

"Well say it then."

"Say what?"

"You see how babies need you to do the work?" She smiled around the circle. "He can't even see the lack of honesty.

"Zack, I was a kid just like you at CEDU a few years ago. You didn't know that, did you? Well, I know you're here because you're a fuck up. Just like the rest of us. That's how you got here, and until you take some accountability and take a look at yourself, your resistance is going to work against you. I know you don't quite get it yet, but I love you, and I'm going to help you."

I waved to the group and pondered my overall situation.

Darlayne went on to the guy next to me.

"ARI CORKPOPPER!"

"Korta." He stared up at the ceiling fan as he corrected her. Ari, a Brave family kid, sat in very dirty jeans and I realized he was the kid I'd seen with the clanging wheelbarrow on my orientation tour.

"Yeah. I'll call you whatever I want. You wish we could be outside today? Too bad. Yup, 'I fucked up again!' Well at least there's all these pretty girls and boys. Hmm, what should we talk about? Girls and boys, boys and girls, boys and boys?"

Darlayne addressed the group as a whole, but it was plain she was continuing her response to Ari. She gazed back at him. Her already unusually expressive face melted into a look like pure love: a huge goofy smile accompanied by wide-open, sparkling eyes.

This was the fakest, most obvious look of disdain I'd ever seen. I got the feeling this woman was more dangerous than an anaconda! I had heard it was a snake from the Amazon that can't see its prey, or sense it, per se, but will know you – and strike you – only when you see them! Darlayne seemed as capable as an anaconda, smelling the fear in this rap.

"I had the coolest dream last night," Darlayne continued. "I love dreams. Dreaming is a gateway, you know, but in this dream I was on this train. Sol used to read our dreams at CEDU – I wonder why Nat doesn't take that on. No, anyway – the train. Or a car, maybe the wind was blowing. And I felt SEXY! Sexed up, and wanting some AC-TION. Come on girls, act like it, you know my rules, you've all been in my raps before. That's it, Fiona! NAUGHTY! YEEESSSS."

At the word "sexy," the five girls in the room blushed, but ran their hands over their breasts and undid their hair, making poses like cover girls. My thoughts retracted. Still behind the eight-ball on understanding, I wondered how this moment had even begun.

Suddenness had become a character in itself. There never seemed to be any shift from one important thing to another. If Darlayne's face was the anaconda, Suddenness was like a savannah gazelle in the moment when it realizes its primitive nemesis has caught it vulnerable. It can't help but flick its ears and tail. And bring on the dark, crushing, doom – just for being there, alive, still breathing.

Wrong place, wrong time. It was inevitable. The realization was itself a shift. Something dangerous was stalking us.

Like the teenagers they were, the girls in the rap shifted in their chairs and cooed sisterly with Darlayne's ooohh-ing and aaahhh-ing. It was hot, and unexpected – but demented and contrived. Was I supposed to watch this spectacle? I didn't know any of these girls; only one or two even looked familiar. Some of them, including a girl named Jennifer who was a little bit on the rotund side, continued their spotlight moment with embarrassed smiles and smirks, making sparkly eye contact with all of us in the room.

"Yeah, that's it, Shirl, get INTO it. Ha, look at Zack. He thinks he's died and maybe gone to heaven. Or hell. I love raps. Ari! Do you like raps?"

Darlayne zeroed in on him again as energy continued to flit around the room like a pesky housefly.

She hadn't been sitting still, either. Pushing her hands around her body and into her hair, she began doing skinny supermodel poses. Darlayne moved her fanny to the very last edge of the chair. I could see her leg muscles under her sweatpants compensate for the weight adjustment that thrust her massive bust halfway into the center of the rap circle. I'd never seen anyone use such a small percentage of chair to take all of their body weight, and I wasn't sure her chair, which seemed to be melting, could manage the strain.

During the performance, Darlayne tried to make intermittent eye contact with Ari. She took her time morphing her body into suggestive positions, even pinching her nipples through her baggy sweatshirt. The rest of the girls stopped, as the nipple pinching seemed to cross some invisible line. Pouting and generating a randy energy, Darlayne demanded the attention of everyone in the room. I noticed that she kept looking over at Ari even though he had gone back to staring at the fan that twirled and droned unevenly overhead.

"I was HIIIIIIIIGH and on top of the world in this dream, girls!" She began fanning herself. "And in this dream, from the, like, convertible train, there were fireworks going off, and the stars were all lit up. I love the moon, the moon was definitely there.

"What about you guys? Anyone else here want to tell me if they had good dreams last night? Hunh?" She was still smiling. "Kath, how about you? Yeah? And Jen? Go on."

Darlayne's gazes back and forth had stopped. She was now totally focused on Ari.

Jennifer took the pause, since she had been encouraged, and began to recount her most recent dream.

"Well, for me, I had this dream last week. My stepfather had taken me and my sister to the movies."

As soon as Jen opened her mouth to continue, Darlayne turned away and ignored her, interjecting loudly to Ari: "You don't fucking sleepwalk, Ari! Do you fucking sleepwalk when you dream or something? Or do you sleep-split?"

I saw Ari's eye muscles instinctively twitch in the direction of Darlayne's voice but his retinas were still glued on the spinning fan. He was stone still. The anaconda and her prey. Two people sitting near Ari popped up almost simultaneously and switched seats to flank Darlayne on her side of the circle.

Oh shit.

That suddenness – the change of content and pace in the room – threw me for yet another loop. I'd have to be ready for surprises around here.

Darlayne's voice sharply escalated to another level.

"Ari, what the fuck were you doing out of your dorm Saturday night? Lights out means lights out! Not lights out for everyone but you, dickhead. You're in Brave now! You've been through the Brother's! That's an important propheet and I know you fucking know better. USE THE FUCKING TOOLS HERE, NUMBNUTS! It's like the rest of your peer group left you behind. Oh well, fuck Ari, he can't keep up. He's not worth it! RIGHT?"

Darlayne shrieked the final syllable, then needed to refill her hefty chest. Jen, one of the older students, took the slight pause.

"Ari, I saw you down by the pond when you were on WD's yesterday and you were skipping stones."

Jen's voice warbled up at the end, with incredulousness. Her high notes perturbed the atmosphere further.

Ari was already in trouble before this, if he was on Work Details.

Jen continued. "I mean, what the fuck? You're supposed to be thinking about your life and whether or not you still want to be here and you're just fucking slacking off. I care about you. When I see you skipping stones when you're supposed to be introspecting it pisses me off. I take that personally. You act like you don't care what happens to you!"

I don't know about Jen, but I've often found skipping stones to be relaxing.

"I was on my break! George gave me twenty minutes break, JEN!"

Ari reacted for a moment but quickly reined it in. As he seemed to consider whether to expand his rebuttal, a third voice added to the mix:

"And I filled out a rap request for you, too!"

That booming male voice belonged to the oldest person in the rap. He was small and stout, and sported a patchy, untrimmed beard.

"You're supposed to be on bans from Papoose girls, and that includes Ivy. Darlayne told me that you copped out in your dirt list to cutting up the streets with Ivy. That pisses me off, kid! You're just one step from getting sent to who knows where for splitting!"

"For the tenth fucking time, I wasn't splitting!" Ari said. "I wanted air. It's fucking July. I said I was sleepwalking because I didn't want to get in trouble!"

"You know what I think? I think you wanted attention! That's why you didn't really even leave the campus! You're a wimp, man! It's the same thing as when you were a Papoose. I was always on you for attention games. Remember? Playing with the fire in the pit, cutting up Judas Priest, and breaking bans. Remember that shit? What's changed? You aren't growing, Ari."

A healthy pause saturated the rap circle before Darlayne reiterated what the short bearded dude had said.

"You're through your Brother's Keeper propheet now and you're supposed to be in middle school. You're supposed to be getting ready to be a big brother and instead you're on a restriction. I want you to stay away from Ivy and Zack and the rest of my fucking Papooses. I don't trust you! It's too easy for you to get brought down by their bullshit. And I'm worried about them. You are George's problem. You know how it WORKS! SO!"

Darlayne's voice became sugar coated. "So, if I see you bringing them down, I'm going to recommend to George that you be put on a full-time. I'm about as serious as a heart attack! If you're not going to take your emotional growth seriously here, I damn sure will, you little fuck!"

Her voice wasn't sweet now. "I hate having to see your peer group taking up your slack!"

It was loud. I didn't like the pitch. And the threat of a "full-time" was big. A kid on a full-time was on bans from everyone. And was stuck in isolation, facing the wall in a booth in the dining room, and on indefinite solo Work Details. A kid on a full-time wasn't allowed to smile, sing, or talk to anyone – except in raps. A full-time could last many days, until your family head or Hedwig decided otherwise.

My first rap with Tess had been shrill and weird and wet with tears and snot. This one was going to be of a similar intensity, but in Tess's rap there had often been a smack of pseudo-kindness. Darlayne wasn't giving any quarter to Ari this afternoon. She wiped spittle from her chin. I could see she was gearing up for something more.

Someone's voice casually slipped in: "Exactly, Ari, I've never trusted you and whenever I see you my gut flips. You still hold on to your image. It's a FUCKING FRONT! I know the truth in you and I know your little kid! What are you doing to let that little Jocko shine? It's not right that you still haven't decided what the rest of us in the peer group have: that I do want real friends! If you're jailhousing with Ivy and cutting up music with Papooses what does that say about MY fucking peer group? I'm working hard and you are bringing me down, dude! I want my little kid to shine and you bring me down!"

This yelling seemed like it would go on for some time. I now knew where Ari Korta was from, based on the accusation made against him. If he had been "cutting up the streets" with Ivy, he had to be from San Francisco, like she was.

It was in raps that we all learned the lurid details about one another. Everything about everybody was on the table in a rap. Though I still only understood a fraction of the vocabulary – who or what the hell was "Jocko"? – some communication nuances, and the cast of characters, were becoming clear.

"Jailhousing" was bragging about bad stuff you had done. "Cutting up music" was talking about unacceptable music.

I was learning.

Now I needed escape. I needed it quickly, and unconsciously I shifted my weight so I was leaning toward the door.

Since I couldn't leave the rap until the facilitator excused us, I would avoid the world inside this circle, by actively not paying attention. Usually in school, it had been the opposite. I would have to rein my thoughts back into the classroom, back to what the teacher was saying. But in Idaho, after those first raps, I gave myself permission to let my mind wander.

Mind: Go! Wander as far as possible!

Using my imagination as an intentional, dimensional time zone to actively self-distract, became a semi-conscious escape. Even when I became aware of it, when my personal growth depended on this awareness several months later, I had a tough time not letting myself drift into the safety corridors of my non-RMA mind.

> While our structure contains a measure of deliberate stress, it is designed to build student confidence and self-esteem. It is our belief that the balance between challenge and success is the key element that nurtures growth.
>
> —RMA brochure

✝

I didn't want to be in the same room with these people. Yet I had to sit.

It was torture already. I was imagining I was back in Virginia puffing on a joint behind my neighbor's fence with Don Roff. I called him Done Rough. Done, like he was – all done. Eighteen years old, he'd been emancipated from his parents when he was sixteen. He was the coolest friend from home, and the only kid I knew that had their own place. Eventually, I knew, he'd help me launch a successful and permanent escape.

I was fading a long way from the room that was, in fact, only nineteen miles from another country. *Done comes driving onto the campus with a group of my friends from home. They grab me. We're speeding away in a van, the familiar music of my life playing. We're going to make it somewhere else.*

Some time must've passed because Darlayne startled me out of an imaginary bong hit in the back of my imaginary breakout van.

"Hey, new guy!" Darlayne had the uncanny ability to smile and raise her voice by 75 decibels simultaneously. She used that trick a lot.

My periphery twinkled into focus. My ribs were pinned to the black chair but I was still turned toward the door. It was like being woken abruptly from a dream, though I hadn't been asleep. Teachers before RMA had accused me of frequent daydreaming, but this felt different. This feeling – that I was confused about who I was, where I was, why I was really here, and all the things that had been going on around me – never stopped during my time in those mountains.

I was hearing inside information about everyone. My mind raced around inside itself in a frenzy until it landed me back in the chair. I didn't want to be there, in my contorted body and sitting in that black chair. And raps happened every Monday, Wednesday, and Friday.

Four hours of raps three days a week. One of the worst things ever. Ever.

Something from the first rap with Tess two days before settled in my spinning brain like a roulette ball dropping into its allegedly arbitrary number. When a kid had moved me out of my chair so he could begin to yell at a guy he dormed with, I noticed that the boxier black chairs were much more comfortable than the ones with rounded frames and feet. I realized that I had scored a slightly more comfortable seat than Darlayne's. The one I was in had a brace in the front. Darlayne's chair was still melted down and drooping. The mass of my body only became heavier in the squarely molded, black metal-framed chair as I returned regretfully to a very real room.

July sun sent a searing light into the center of the circle. The blood ran to my face, and all eyes shifted to me. *My ears are glowing – my eyes cannot look at fifteen people simultaneously.*

Being woken up abruptly out of a guilty and pleasurable daydream left me feeling disjointed. I couldn't yet think of looking at Darlayne or the numerous eyes now turned to the freshest meat in the whole place. I turned my weight back toward the middle of the room. I kept my eyes situated on the row of shoes and work boots across the circle.

"You can't ask a girl in the woods to run away with you, OK? You're the baby so I will baby you and just do the work for you. Just telling you there is no splitting, no splitting contracts. No sex, my little horndog, no fucking the girls, GOT IT?" Darlayne roared.

"No, I don't have it? I'm confused."

"What's fucking confusing?"

"I didn't proposition that girl. I wasn't – I didn't for a minute think..."

"You weren't propositioning! What the fuck do you think this is? Were you going to make an appointment with her? Were you talking to her because you support her little kid? Or were you talking to her because you want to split?"

"No, I guess I just didn't know she's on bans and..."

"Just shut up! She talked to me, Ivy did! So don't bullshit me! I know you broke bans and tried to get her to split. She copped out because she's starting to take a look at this shit that GOT HER HERE."

I didn't say anything. I gulped and tried not to let my eyes remain wide.

"I need you to validate me. Say 'OK'."

"OK." I flinched at my instinct to hit her with my chair, for the betterment of group safety. I had gone from being critical, to feeling outright violent.

I was still an obvious foreigner here. These customs were upside down. No one I knew at home would let someone talk to them this way. A year before, I had learned that people were "meaner" in Paris, France, than they were in Charlottesville, Virginia. But this was at a completely different level than being cursed at in the streets in a foreign language.

Darlayne's voice softened just a tad. She warned me that she was already close to putting me on bans.

Seemingly out of the blue, Ari, doubled up on his chair, his body folded in such a way that his hands held his opposite ankles. He raised his posterior up out of the little dimple in the chair where asses went. He began to shake his head, muttering at first. The louder his voice became, the more he started to rock.

"Motherfucker, motherfucker, why can't I do anything right? I still fucking hate it here. I do! I don't care about people, I fucking hate them. You know, my parents, my peer group, my fucking self! I hate myself. FUUUUUCK! I shit all over my little kid. All the time, all the time! I can't I can't. I fuck up every time. I'm a shitty friend. I do want to split, but I wasn't. ... I really wasn't the other night. FUCK ME! I hate my life. I fucking hate doing this. FUUUUCK! I don't have any faith. FUCK TRUST FUCK TRUSTING! God it does hurt. It does fucking hurrrrrt!"

He may pop.

The bearded man yelled from next to me, "That's right! Say that again! YEAH! It does hurt me!"

I suddenly had to fight the urge to use the bathroom.

Ari repeated the last words suggested by the little bearded dude a few more times. Then he launched into new territory. Sudden bursts of physical gesticulation punctuated many of his thoughts. He pointed harshly to his clenched eyes with his thumb, or lifted tight fists toward the ceiling.

"I don't want to be here, I'm still mad at my mom. The Brother's only MADE ME FEEL FUCKING WORSE! Fucking hated the Brother's. More fucking worthless shit. I'm worthless shit. I'm fucking worthless."

"LOOK AT THE LUGGAGE YOU MAKE JOCKO CARRY!" Darlayne switched seats to be next to Ari, whose face was noticeably swelling and reddening. "I'm fucking worthless! SAY IT AGAIN, ARI! I AM WORTHLESS! That's right! It fucking hurts doesn't it? My REAL parents don't want me, my peer group doesn't want me. SAY IT!"

Ari, his eyes starting to spill tears, sweat forming between his shoulder blades, took the cue: "My parents don't want me, it's fucking true! My real parents didn't want me, nobody does. MY stepmother HATES ME! THATFUCKINGBITCH! NO! IT'S ME GOD I AM WORTHLESS! My peer group hates me. WHAAAtheeeeeFUUUUUCK!"

Ari's hands rushed to his face. He was sobbing. His fingernails were gross, with dirt caked beneath them. I could see the pores of his face clogging as he clutched and wiped at his eyes. Darlayne pulled her chair right next to Ari, and was pressing and rubbing awkwardly on Ari's back in an upward-only motion, over and over. She leaned over him so closely that it looked like she was nuzzling him. She had switched roles and was pretending to be his third surrogate adopted mother, the tenderest, most platonic saint of a nurturer there ever was.

She spoke softly into Ari's ear. Then she closed her eyes and began making stage whispers for the rest of us to hear.

What an act!

"Just feel it. Yeah. Slow down and go into that place. You know the spot, don't you? You want to tell us about that special place? Let Jocko come out and tell the rap?"

"I guess. When I was young, before my stepparents moved to the Bay Area, we used to live on a farm in Arkansas."

"Arkansas?"

"Ye-Yeah. And well, we used to have this barn. I used to play in there. It was like, you know, a place I could bring the dog...and it was just a nice place and yeah...I guess I just felt safe there or something.

"You felt special in the barn."

"It was my special place." Ari had been whimpering through the last bit. I had already stopped trying to understand why things that seemed insignificant, or banal, should be so prominent up here.

Darlayne began again: "It's OK to feel hurt, isn't it? To feel worthless? Are you still in your special place? Yeah. Who is in there? Jocko? Jocko, that's right. That's right – Ari's in the barn? Yeah. Is it OK to be hurt? For Jocko to be hurt? It is, isn't it? Say it. Yeah. Go on. Again. It's OK for me, for Jocko to be loved. It's alright for me to be loved. Yeah, that's right. Say that again!"

Ari broke into a continuous sob and nodded his head, babbling a babyish gibber-jabber.

Was there a dog? Was that Jocko? What did Jocko have to do with whatever was making Ari freak out and speak in nonsensical tongues?

I imagined the expression on my face. That brought me to an outright laugh which I turned into a polite cough: I must look like a dog having geometry explained to him.

With breathing labored from his physical position, Ari snorted, and a clot of mucus shot out of his nose onto the carpet. Darlayne, ignoring the projected bodily fluid, continued to rub on Ari for the next several minutes even as she turned toward the girl named Jen and began a fresh indictment:

"Jennifer Oyama, would you suck Ari's dick for a gram of cocaine? You would, wouldn't you? Do you really think you'll be ready for a home visit next month? I fucking don't, not the way you still shake your ass around here. You do know you shake your ass, don't you?"

Darlayne was back to smiling insanely and brutally, though her hand still rested on Ari's back.

There had to be about two hours left to go in this CEDU therapy session in Idaho. I already knew that raps lasted four hours. They always got loud, and felt apocalyptic.

They were the glue that held a system of anxiety, paranoia, and fear together.

✝

[Continued] Zack, everything you need for success is within you. It's just a matter of shaping it.

I hope you'll throw yourself into your new school and get as much from it as you possibly can. Your new life is beginning and every day I'll be thinking of you, missing you, and wishing you well in becoming the fine person I know you can be.

I love you,

Mommy

—Letter from author's mother, 11 July 1988

TEN

Bans were explained to me by members of my dorm.

"Well, when you're on bans, you're probably on bans with someone you were contracted up with, in some way."

"Maybe for music cracks. Or because you're not supporting what really matters in that person. Five minutes until lights, fellow gentlemen delinquents." My dorm head rolled over for sleep.

"If you're on bans with someone you should respect them," Crosby Rohrback, my dorm support, put in. "Don't talk to them. Don't communicate – don't make cracks, alright? For example, you know you can't sit with them at a meal. That's a typical Papoose crack in the Agreement. If you want to talk to them that bad, you can fill out a rap request."

Bans, like most things at RMA, were a little extreme and a lot confusing. For example, black clothing was forbidden, and even black paint and magic markers were missing from art supplies. And nobody had ripped jeans – once they got faded to the point of comfort, they were snatched up by your family head and discarded. If you were on bans from someone, and you wanted to talk to them, you could put your name and their name on a rap request, fold it up, and stick it in the slot of the door to the facilitator Bridge. Then the staff would decide whether to honor the request.

If I saw someone on bans approaching, I was to go to the other side of the room or hallway. There was to be no sitting in the same vicinity; you weren't to signal or gesture to someone on bans. Even if their shirt was untucked or they were out of agreement, you weren't supposed to pull them up. Obviously, writing notes about unacceptable music to anyone on bans would be "out of agreement" on two counts.

The school, the people, the agreements, the bands the courses the food the work Everything here sucks. AND the music. Oh the music. Oh by the way in case you're wondering this isn't any normal boarding school. There is absolutely no drugs or alcohol on campus. Trust me I know. They do everything to

insure this including feel every stitch in all my clothes
and even look up my Asshole! More later.
—Author journal entry 23 July 1988

†

One entertaining morning, Ernesto was using his spoon and
bowl of oatmeal as rap-snot for Terrance and me when Keith, Tess,
and Darlayne came parading toward our picnic table. Wasn't it too
early for staff? Darlayne should have been on a leash the way she
approached Ernesto and me, teeth and torpedo-tits first. Keith was
flashing his eyes in a look he reserved for when he was angry or demanded extra respect. Tess was the "good cop" this morning. Darlayne
launched into accusations as soon as she was close enough to be heard
over the dining room din:

"Two turtle drugs, right where I thought you'd be. Listen up! One
of you gave Ivy money. Having any money is out of agreement. Which
one of you butt buddies gave it to her?"

Ernie looked at me gravely, and enunciated slowly, perhaps just
because it was still early in the morning: "Ivy has money."

I tried not to laugh. Biting my lip and waiting just a beat, I couldn't
resist a nicely timed punch line, "Massah sho' don'lahk that!"

Ernesto burst out laughing. I contained it for about two seconds
before exploding with my own naughty raspberry of a cackle. It was
the first time I had really had a laugh in Idaho. It couldn't be sup-
pressed, or repressed like all the other aspects of me since arriving in
this shitpit. The constant pressure had finally ruptured a small seal in
me. I knew that the more I laughed in the three staff members' faces,
the more trouble I was going to be in, but I couldn't help it. This was
a real emotion: unexpected, momentous, and serendipitous joy! The
practiced deadpan staff stares prolonged our hysteria.

When the moment finally did subside, Tess smiled at us saying
quietly and simply:

"OK, well you two are obviously now on bans. Bans for both of
you. Brave down. Ernesto, you've had enough oatmeal. Why don't you
go with Darlayne down to the wood corral? I think a day of WD's
is in order while you two think about what we're doing here. I came
over here to tell you that Ivy split last night and was picked up by the
sheriff. We're trying to decide what to do with her. Why don't you two
think about...what's the matter, Mr. Bonnie?"

"Is Ivy OK?"

"You just worry about yourself," Darlayne hissed from behind Tess. Darlayne turned away, driving Ernesto by the shoulder into the dish room. That left me facing Tess and Keith. Tess spoke.

"Darlayne is right. You know, I can see that you spend a lot of time worrying about everyone else, but you gotta start worrying about what's going on with Zack – you know what I'm saying? Time to stop worrying about home, or about Ernesto. It's time to focus on you – inside."

I nodded, because I did worry about myself, and because I was supposed to respond. That didn't end it.

"Darlayne told me about your rap with her on Wednesday. You got a rap pass because you're still a baby, but I'm still going to put you on female bans. I don't want you talking to any more girls that aren't staff. And if I found out you stole or brought money in, or contracted up with Ivy in any way, I'll be fucking pissed."

"Tess, I didn't know Ivy was leaving and she's on bans from me. I've hardly ever talked to her. Where would I get money? I don't have that ability. You know, why ya askin' me anyway? What grounds! Just because you accuse us doesn't mean..."

"Enough!" Keith boomed, and slammed his fist on the table. Even the picnic tables nearby went quiet.

That shut me up.

"Just clean this stuff and get your boots from your cubby in the mudroom. I'll set you up on your WD. I don't want to hear more of your weaselly intellectualized shit."

Keith made air quotes with calloused fingers around "intellectualized."

"You have no choice," he added. "Unless you want to sit at a booth."

Sit at a booth? That meant a full-time.

Keith hitched his thumb over his shoulder at the booth. Half his thumb was missing, I noticed. Hmmm. He looked like a jar-head Marine. With big teeth.

Fuck this place. Would I follow these stupid Agreements? Did I have a choice? Keith was a douchebag. Why would anyone who'd been a student here ever come back? What a loser!

I imagined that all of them were actors, Keith Rios and Darlayne

Hammer especially. They both behaved like they were on stage all the time. Or maybe in film – they beamed their exaggerated expressions. Keith flashed his eyes like he was in a Chinese opera. He was young, and several of the girls in Papoose flirted with him, which fed my growing distrust.

Could all of this actually be some elaborate script to get me to fall in line? Were all these "kids" playing roles – being subservient look-goods? Or were they really evil, telling on one another persistently, and following rules that ran contrary to almost everything I'd learned since kindergarten?

Also, the rules – Agreements – in the place countered all that I knew about why civil law existed. I mean, what was the meaning of the Constitution if it only protected my parents' right to lose me here? Keith, Paul, Tim, and Tess all seemed jubilant to remind me that I had no rights. I had no privileges – my parents had signed them away. I couldn't conceive of my father doing that, and even though I made requests, I wasn't shown any documentation. Not until after my splitting. My inevitable escape.

When I was little, my mother and father encouraged me to memorize texts, particularly historical speeches. My "Give Me Liberty Or Give Me Death" presentation as Patrick Henry in the seventh grade had won me prestige at school. I remembered, verbatim, the preamble to the List of Grievances of the Thirteen Colonies. I knew most people erroneously referred to it as the Declaration of Independence, and celebrated it two days too late. I knew that Mr. John Adams, the father of that document, set out July Second as the day of celebration, not the Fourth, as is commonly observed.

In my real family at home, we discussed the tenets of Madison and Jefferson as if they were Jesus and the neighborhood minister. Our Ten Commandments were the Bill of Rights. That's what my world in Charlottesville had been: Monticello and philosophy. I was just entering a new world of rock 'n roll, getting an idea of what I liked, not what my mom or my brother liked. I was making friends that were older. With their cars came loads more freedom that I'd starting insisting on. My friends back home – or at least the fact that they weren't at my parents' home – had become important. Well, I just couldn't for the life of me understand what force would demand that everyone tattle on one another and snitch on themselves. I had so much to learn.

Compliance with senseless regulations seemed contradictory to the very idea of free will.

Wouldn't there be an underground? Where was the booze and weed? Surely, no boarding school would be complete without some sneakiness? Who's in the underground? Did that girl, Ivy, seriously RAT on me just for talking to her near the tipi the other afternoon? Did she tell Darlayne that I tried something inappropriate? Is that why Darlayne had attacked me and put me on bans from girls?

✝

All of this just HAD to be a ruse that my parents were in on. There was no law that I had gotten caught breaking, no police problems that I hadn't skateboarded away from without incident. I had more experience with real drug users here in the last few days than I had ever had back in Virginia. I didn't believe it was possible to control speech. Not mine. Scare me some, I figured, that's the game. I just couldn't yet believe the stakes were as high as the place insisted. Like I'd die, or go to a booby hatch if I didn't stay.

Being on a work detail didn't scare me, because I didn't know what one was. I didn't yet understand how I could be punished after not doing anything wrong. I hadn't any money to give Ivy. I did not know she was going to split. Why should Ernesto and I be punished for the actions of someone we couldn't communicate with? So, OK, Ernesto and I got a little smart, laughed too loud. That's what our crime had really been. A lapse of impulse control.

It's what makes me, me.

I was pleased to have laughed in their faces. I looked forward to another go at it! Then I countered my previous thought: Maybe a break from house chores and the wood corral would do me good.

I was separated from the rest of the Papoose family. They were some of the only people whose names I even knew.

"You gonna stay in line after this work detail?" Keith asked.

Nah, probably not.

I couldn't help protesting a little more when he dropped me at the site of my work detail.

"I didn't do anything wrong. I swear I didn't do anything wrong."

Keith spoke quickly. "I don't really care whether you broke bans or not, or whether you did smuggle money in here. OK? The work has to be done, you're going to do it. You already show you don't like to work with a group so you can work by yourself. You're the one that set it up that way. Am I right? You're working against me, and the work I'm trying to do here. When you're ready to take responsibility for your actions, introspect yourself some, and say something of substance, we can talk some more. You're not worth my time as you are."

Keith had indeed been a student at RMA. My first suspicions confirmed, I eventually got the skinny on him. He had been in Peer Group 1. I was in Peer Group 31. He was among the founding members – a pioneer. We had already heard the stories how RMA's pioneers came from the California campus in 1982, six years before, and with hardly any structure standing on the land, built the hallowed campus where I stood.

Being a pioneer, former student, and staff made Keith an anomaly. Darlayne Hammer and one other dude, George Daughtry, family head of Warrior, had also been students, either here or at the original campus in California. They came up here with Nat and Hedwig, the adult pioneers. Even though George, Darlayne and Keith were younger than many of the other paid staff, I noticed that their CEDU pedigree came with a passport to be even more familiar with everybody about everything! In Keith's case, not only was he a pioneer, but he'd also been a student at both CEDU schools. The trio always demanded a deferential respect from the kids, and received a slightly different treatment from the rest of the staff. They had special license to touch us, and were more brutal and cutting than many of the other power staffers, in and out of raps.

Those three really did walk around like their shit didn't stink, as if they owned the place.

Clearly, the current student body was here to continue the physical improvement of the grounds. Somehow, RMA's master, Sol Turnwell, had hatched the perfect plan to convince my parents that it would benefit them for me to cut wood and milk the chickens.

I spent the first twenty minutes of my work detail sitting in the wheelbarrow looking at my impossible task. A pile of branches about eighty feet wide rose thirty feet in the air. There were hundreds of branches as long as twenty feet. I was to strip off all the biggest sticks that were still attached so that each branch was about the same length, and bald of everything except bark. I was supposed to make an organized pile of readied timber.

Other than a shovel, I wasn't allowed tools. I climbed, examining my work area. I scurried around the pile, occasionally slipping, one of my legs falling into the darkness below. Branches intersected and seemed to continue growing and bending around me. The smell of pitch and dirt was heavy, and millions of insects traveled the decomposing landscape.

I tried to move one of the branches to the side from the top of the pile. It wouldn't budge. I took the shovel and started to whack off the attached limbs. When I had done this, I assessed what was left and went to the part of the branch where it tapered down and got thinner. I began to stomp on top of it. I stomped through it. I had a length about fifteen feet long that I could barely move. I felt like a moth trying to swing a baseball bat. Eventually, I managed to swing it a few feet off the pile.

"One," I said to myself, mildly pleased. I looked around to see if anyone would see me sneak a cigarette. I sat in the wheelbarrow behind the pile so I wouldn't easily be spotted if any staff or older students passed by on the road. I freely puffed on my cig, happily singing "unacceptable" songs to myself.

Darlayne and Keith emerged from a trail that I didn't know existed. I popped up and stuck the cigarette butt under my boot, spinning on it a little to make sure it was extinguished. The wheelbarrow tipped over.

The little cuts and blisters already on my hands from the wood corral began to grow. The sores stung. My work gloves felt slimy against the blisters, and the smell inside the glove would have made a yak covered in its own poop gag. It took months before hard calluses formed on my hands and the open blisters stopped being painful. The gloves would never stop being smelly and they had to be replaced every season. The fingerpads always disintegrated first.

I tried to make the songs I'd been singing seem more like work grunts. But I hadn't done anything for at least ten minutes. I wanted water.

"How 'bout a water break?" I asked, sounding upbeat as they approached my clearing.

"Can you believe this kid?" Keith said to Darlayne.

It was lunchtime, anyway.

†

I make my phone call tonight. I'm going to ask Mom and Dad if I can go home. They will probably say NO but I hope not. If they do I might really split. This place is trying to make me into something I'm not. Oh! Get this I think this is pretty funny. They don't let you wear black, right so we make cards and they took out all the Black Magic Markers. Pretty stupid hunh? You know whats cool though! I'm up in these woods all by myself and I'm loving it. Shit I'm having suicide thoughts again. I'm afraid one day I will really do it.

Sometimes I wonder if I would really be better off dead. I might, but then again I might not. I wonder.

Now it's 6 ½ hours later AND my parents said that if I split All State Authorities will be put out on me & when I'm caught I will be locked up. Pretty shitty huh? I really think I want to Die Now. I really can't cry anymore. I Really Wish I Were Dead. Shit I gotta go.

—Author Journal entry, 28 July 1988 (17 days at RMA)

ELEVEN

[Continued] P.S. I had to fight with myself so I wouldn't express any anger I might feel, but I lost. Zack, I was angry that you thought your poor behavior would have no consequences, that you could treat me and Daddy so horribly, the camp people so irresponsibly, the teachers so disrespectfully and NOTHING would happen. A person's actions always have consequences. But even though you were getting negative feed-back you weren't changing for the better. I believe now that you are in a school where other kids have had similar problems and learned how to deal with them. You will learn too. Good behavior and hard work bring success; negative behavior and laziness bring awful consequences. Remember my half-joking rule: "do good and Avoid Evil." It's true I DO LOVE YOU.

—Letter from author's mother 11 July 1988

Right on schedule. Almost a month in Idaho!

The novelty was fading. I was physically tired of being alert. Other than the letter from my mother that Tess had given me the first week, I had not had any contact with my parents. I was mad at them for obvious and more obscured reasons. Although kids were allowed a fifteen-minute phone call to their parents every two weeks, staff or older students routinely monitored all calls. We Papooses joked about the obvious implications of "big brother" listening to our conversations. I was disconnected from my parents prematurely every time, at first. The first and only call home before I split went like this:

"Hello?"

"Hello, Mr. Bonnie? This is Tim. Uh, Tim Chalmers from RMA?"

I could hear my mother's fake excitement through the phone's earpiece. They were both on the line. "Richard told me that you and Paul are showing Zack the ropes with all the other big brothers. Is that right?"

"Uh, yeah. He's hard-headed, but if he's making a phone call, he must be doing OK, I guess. Shit, well, let me put Zack on, then."

"Dude, don't be a dick." Tim whispered at me and lifted his eyebrows in a last ditch plea. I took the receiver.

"Hi Dad, it's me."

"Zack! We've been waiting for this call. Your mother and I feel sorry that we had to lie to you. But we could no longer control you! Please, LET ME FINISH! You were not going down the path to success, running away from home, running away from camp, being disrespectful to your mother and to me. We could no longer tolerate it. We won't! For right now, you're going to stay there."

"No I'm not!"

"Yes, you are. Your mother and I do not want you back here. We don't want you at home. We want you to change and we want real changes. Maybe at some point in the future, if your family heads give you good marks, we'll talk about it."

"But they're always yelling and cursing, and they're spying on me right now! I'm trying to tell you I'll be good. I understand. I get it now! If you don't let me come home I'm going to run away! You've got to at least let me try again?!"

"You will stay! The police can have you, Zack. We don't want you home and that's final. You're out of tries."

My father had spoken slowly. I knew from experience that when he bothered to contain himself, he was holding in an explosion. At least his threats were consistent. Nothing in this place was predictable. My parents sounded resolute and said they were never budging, or being manipulated by me again. It sounded like someone had been talking to them, implanting these seeds so they'd be ready for my desperate arguments. My stories would sound invented.

This feeling was infuriating. I felt like my arguments had been undermined and nothing I ever said to them would matter. They had forced me again to run away.

No more friends from home, no more food out of the fridge and into the microwave whenever I felt like it. My world was shrinking to nothing but RMA, and my thoughts began to fold inward on my turmoil. But I didn't notice my collapse until I died in my Summit, over two years later.

Because much of the business is unregulated, it's difficult to know what actually goes on inside many of these facilities. Since almost all claim that all teens' stories of maltreatment or abuse are simply the lies of troublemakers, most complaints are dismissed without investigation. After all, if these kids told the truth, they wouldn't need to be in the program, would they?

——Maia Szalavitz, *Help at any Cost: How the Troubled Teen Industry Cons Parents and Hurts Kids*, Riverhead Books, New York, 2006, page 5.

We were ready when it was "razz around the pit" time, the few minutes before raps where we found out which room to go to and who would be facilitating that day. Even if you were straggling in the adjacent dining hall, or outside, all it took was one reminder to come quick. I never saw anyone intentionally late for anything at RMA. Everyone came straight to the house's pit, a recessed public area in front of the fireplace in the house's huge main space, when it was time for the raps or for announcements. The pit was the central focus after our well-earned lunch.

Fridays were the worst day of the week for several reasons, not the least of which was that the monotonous routine would still not be broken. Most importantly, Fridays were lame because the raps that heralded the end of the week lacked the Summit students. This older RMA brood always took lots of time for themselves – ranting and hysterical, yes, but not focused entirely on calling out the shortcomings of younger students. They would not be in attendance.

"Introspection," as the older students' "work" was called, wasn't just looking inside yourself, or prying into someone else to see what made fucked-up kids tick. Introspection was also about identifying self-deprecating thoughts in yourself or others. The expression of this inner turmoil is what the Summit and Warrior kids were always talking about. The Warrior kids also added a lot of screaming at the floor angrily in tongues I didn't yet understand.

Performances by Summit kids during Monday and Wednesday raps often included round after round of self-induced hysterics in Pidgin English. Watching older kids perform the freaky ranting and screaming at their own "thinking" really made the time fly by, like watching

Evan regress during my first rap with Tess. By the time a week had passed, I saw that Evan and Ari weren't the only older kids to talk this way.

Almost all of them seemed to break into the schizophrenic talk in raps, or at last lights. Their "ME" and "I" special vocabulary was enough to pique interest and intensify the creepiness. It was weird to witness this behavior, and not know what was really being said. These older kids spoke a forbidden language. It felt like I was being invited into a place I shouldn't go.

On Fridays, though, Summit students had Truth counseling sessions. Whatever that meant. So, Friday raps generally involved a lot of needsy Papoose, Brave, and Warrior indictments. The staff had to make up for the time that upper schoolers normally filled with hours of introspection, and so things tended to drag on, even more so than Monday and Wednesdays. There was no more hollow feeling for me than realizing that more of this was going on in other rooms nearby. Other kids were sitting in chairs experiencing raps for themselves. It certainly wasn't an act for my benefit.

How silly I'd been. How fucking naïve.

TWELVE

Keith held a handful of rap lists. He stood just off center in the pit. The stone he stood on, though it wasn't in the corner and didn't have any visible markings on it, was revered as the corner stone. The masonry pit, with the enormous fireplace and chimney, had been built by his own peer group when they arrived from California to construct the Rocky Mountain Academy, eight miles north of Bonners Ferry, Idaho. It was his turn to read off the rap lists; I had noticed them in his hand as he paraded with the rest of the staff out of the Bridge.

I hovered to see if the door got locked as the staff exited. If nobody noticed, I'd be one of the last out of the house, and I'd know if the Bridge – the room with the phone – would be unlocked during raps. I didn't know exactly what to do with this information, but felt like a daytime attempt at an unmonitored call could be better than trying to elude the night watchmen. These guys didn't usually talk to us students, weren't expected to interact with staff, or go through propheets. I strongly suspected they were armed when they skulked around the campus late at night.

Keith started with George Daughtry's rap. Ernesto was at the top of the list and George, the head of Brave family, chimed in loudly from the back of the lodge, "Your ASS is mine, Ernie!"

I was guilty by association just for being his friend. I was getting paranoid, but nobody noticed me at the back of the house yet, or knew my intentions to see if the Bridge was locked up when Keith was done razzing the house. The rest of the students jeered at Ernesto and laughed along with the staff. Yeah, he was going to get reamed today. Keith went through more names, and tossed off a couple of remarks meant to be entertaining. Keith got to the final list – his own rap. Shit, my name hadn't yet been called so I was in that one.

Keith took extra ownership for his rap. He began by doling out an unusual compliment to one of the upper schoolers in front of the entire house. "Jasper Browning, where are you? Hey! I hear you've been doing some solid work lately down at the farm. That right? Come on up here and give me a hug. OK, no no no, don't go anywhere. Let's just stand here together for a second. Good. OK. You got any rap requests in here? I see you've got one of your little brothers in here. You wanna read the last rap sheet? Go ahead."

Keith shared the list with Jasper. Jasper had been inching in on me, trying to adopt me as one of his little brainwashed disciples. So I knew they were talking about me. I tried to remain flat and still by the Bridge. Why had Keith invited Jasper up there? Was that code for Jasper to be pseudo-staff now? Having a dangerous upper-schooler in your rap could be as bad as having a rap with a power staffer. I still couldn't always be sure which older people were staff and which were students, but the general rule I observed was not to trust anyone I didn't know to be a Papoose. This staff hazing was a clue that I was going to have a bad rap. It was time. There were newer kids.

At RMA I became superstitious. Because I'd worn a red shirt, or someone had been nice to me. Or it had been raining on a particularly bad day. I'd be waiting for something horrible every time it rained after that. And nobody warned me about the weeks of spring called mud season, which reminded me of every rainy Vietnam war movie I'd ever seen. In several months I'd actually be relating to those film actors who always had water dripping from ponchos and helmets, or struggled to sleep while slapping at bugs on their necks.

My general view when it came to questions about god and the cosmos changed, too. I started to become more pessimistic. There would be a lot to explore, maybe at RMA, about life with Mom and Dad, and about death and god too. It would take time for me to comprehend that their expectations were more important to my whole life than the choices I'd already made for myself. Without any personal accountability for my parents' decision, I was trying to rein in what I was supposed to say and feel about their decision to put me here.

So far, I hadn't learned much from my passive reconnaissance by the door to the Bridge. The room didn't seem to get locked, but as I followed the last students out, I saw that two adults stayed in the house, and used the Bridge for clerical work.

The name before mine on Keith and Jasper's rap list was Paul Renssalaer. Paul had become my older brother de facto after that tour my first day, but now that Jasper was moving in, Paul would have to prove his worthiness – being older and more senior in the program.

"I'll see you in the Stellar Annex, Zack. We're going to push those Daddy buttons in my rap today."

The expectations were great and the penalties painful if you could not perform all the intricate rituals correctly. While this applied to every aspect of life on campus, everything was magnified in raps. You had to participate. Sliding by silently for four hours of this, even if it were possible, would have been bad enough. The demand that we had to participate really made the three-per-week ordeal feel like torture.

Vera, the girl with the saw-sliced boot, walked ten feet ahead of me to the rap room. Her peer group had gone through the Brother's Keeper propheet the previous weekend. Taking my seat, I looked over the other kids while Keith read off the participants' names. I had a pretty good idea, based on the way people sat, and how old they looked, what program family they were in. Sometimes, though, I could still confuse the Summit boys with younger staff, because they were interchangeable.

When the rap list was handed to that day's facilitator, it mystically transformed into a "rap sheet." We had just finished sitting in our chairs when Keith looked at the rap sheet, turned and said, "Zack, I'm going to start the rap right off because I need to talk to you."

A goofy grin emanated from my face and a guffaw passed my lips. I had never ever been shy, and here I was almost pissing my pants from fear! I was in a room with Keith and Hedwig. They were both power staff. They were the pioneers, along with Darlayne, George Daughtry, and Nat, Hedwig's husband. Anything could happen in this room.

Keith's voice was still nagging at me ten minutes later, though I'd grunted and nodded through a lot of our conversation in the beginning.

"...So other than running away from camp, and being a dirtbag, why do you think you're here?"

"I don't know." A pause slipped by. "For the same reason as most of us, my parents were sick of my shit, and I have a little sister so they need to focus their attention on her."

That was true. Of course there was a lot more to it. I knew Hedwig and Keith wanted it all decontained, unconstrained. Hedwig nodded.

"And what's her name? Your sister. How old is she? Do you remember the day she was born? That must have been a wonderful day. What do you think has happened since then? Hattie has been talking to your mom a lot, you know that?"

Hattie was one of the parent communicators. She seemed to be the resident expert on all things Zack.

I answered each of Hedwig's questions that required a response.

Then a male staff from Warrior who I met at the farm one day started to pick at the questions.

"Let's go back to the getting here part and work backwards? What do you say? Tell me more about why you think you're here, in this seat today?"

"Because I ran away and was disrespectful to authority."

"That's the real reason, you think, that you're here?"

"Yeah, I guess mostly."

"But you were a straight-A student and paid them rent."

"N-no..."

"NO, I didn't think so!"

Hedwig bared her incisors in a disturbing fake smile.

"Do you think that none of this applies to you? Do you think you're above the work we're doing here?"

"No, I'm just still a little pissed at them."

"I would be too. Having a little prick like you for a son."

"I wasn't talking about them – "

"EXACTLY!"

"I know you don't have any respect for your parents, do you?"

"Of course I did! My father is a great man – "

"What do you mean you did?"

I laughed at the staff's mincemeat semantics.

"Don't fucking laugh. It's not funny. It's NOT! YOU'RE the ONE that's HERE NOW!"

"Maybe but he wasn't a very good father, or you wouldn't have to be sitting in that chair? Agreed?"

"I don't really know why I'm here, then, I guess?"

"Maybe because you failed and ran away from every other place they sent you! Yeah. You think that could have anything to do with it? You were one step from no options, Zack! You were this close to not having a home to go home to. You're here, and you may not understand this now, but this is the right place for you. You should trust me, and the people in this place – we're going to pick apart the steps that

84

got you here. It's your life! Right...so? Hedwig?"

"Let's have a rap!"

Silence. She added, "Who is going to start? Who filled out rap requests today?

"I did."

"Yeah, me too."

An older kid spoke. "Fine, I'll start. Dylan, I filled out a request for you. When I was in Papoose I tried to refuse the program, like you were talking about the other day. I know you aren't, but just talking about it is fucking bullshit, man! Isn't that why Hedwig has you on writing assignments?"

"She didn't give me writing assignments, she just said I could take a WD or an assignment, so..."

"You are missing the fucking point!"

Hedwig zeroed in, "Tell everybody, what was the writing assignment?"

Pause.

Dylan spoke quietly, "All the lies I cover up my truth with and what I will do to support the truth in others."

"And what did you learn, DYLAN?"

"Well. I don't know."

Softer from Hedwig: "And do you remember when you gave up on being a star football player? You really needed that dream to stay alive in you, didn't you?"

Keith picked it up. "Dylan, I know you have something you can relate about that? Share that with our papooses."

The kid went from wanting to be a linebacker to telling us all about his scrambling around on all fours picking up crumbs of pot, or stashing stolen booze around the neighborhood for later consumption. This led Hedwig to eventually reach her hand to the kid's stomach and repeat how lonely and empty he felt at RMA, and in life. Then after the moaning continued for twenty minutes or so, when he was doing the shaking-crying part at the end, Hedwig rubbed his back and told him he was special.

Watching a kid dump his guts out in a rap always led to more kids talking about how rotten they thought every one else thought they were, and how they believed their negative thinking. I could feel myself get riled up every time a staff would try to bring me into the therapy session with a line like, "Zack, don't you have something going on right now watching Jamie work? It's alright to talk here when you're ready. Let's just give you some space."

That really meant, Nobody's gonna talk until you say something monumentally embarrassing or painful about someone else or yourself.

Vera's legs twined around the legs of her black chair. Her jeans were broken in, so they had a greenish brown hue. For some reason she was looking right at me. She started talking to me.

"DUDE! You HAVE GOT TO slow down around the house, man! You've got to be aware of people who've been taking care of their feelings. My peer group just got out of our Brother's and you were being so obnoxious in the house on Sunday, and man, I know it's Sunday and you guys had the spades tournament, but for real!"

"Vera has a good point!"

"Yeah, I mean I know you're new here but, seriously, do you think you could try not to make such a mess in the bathrooms in La Mancha? Clean up after yourself. I get so tired of talking to Papooses. I was in there last night, after I ALREADY filled out a rap request for you, and I was watching you floss your teeth. You LEFT like, FUCKING WHATEVER THAT SHIT is ALL OVER THE MIRROR."

"I'm on mirrors in the morning, so I always clean up."

"THAT'S NOT MY POINT, BRO!"

"Seriously, it's like a typhoon in there every time you guys are done in the bathroom. You're supposed to clean a sink or urinal every time you guys use it. I mean I know we don't always do that so this is a bit of a projection. Still, try to be aware of it."

"Yeah, you're pulling La Mancha down. That's MY FUCKING DORM, OK?"

"It's my dorm too."

"Not FUCKING YET, IT'S NOT!

"Yeah, just because I'm a girl doesn't mean I can't hear what's going on in the house, and I think I always hear you and Sebastian making little cracks in bitches and music."

Vera flung another dagger toward me.

"Wait a minute, Zack, you're on bans with ERNESTO! AREN'T

YOU?"

"Well maybe it was Jamie or Dylan but I could definitely tell you were there!"

Keith spoke up, and kept the focus on me. "YOU ARE ON BANS. You make cracks all the time. You make cracks in music too. I fucking resent that shit! It shows a lack of respect for me, and for MY FUCK-ING HOUSE! THIS IS MY HOME, MOTHERFUCKER!"

"I do follow the Agreements, I DO! You're staff, you know what THE FUCKING RULES ARE! I am TRYING!"

"You're on bans because you're a dirtbag. Also, I don't know what you were doing with the wedges at the wood corral the other day during clean up. What's up with that?"

"I just dropped them on the ground, man, it's not like I was throwing darts with them, Keith."

"Don't DEFEND! Just DON'T! Stop defending! You've been here a month now, asshole, time to grow up. You're not even supposed to touch the fucking things, SO! Get with it, Zack!"

"I was just tightening up the shed like you told me to."

I knew I shouldn't say anything, but this was a tad off. Keith was the one who had put the wedges in my hand with instructions to put them in their assigned spot.

"And you did a shitty job of it too! The shovels weren't clean! They weren't. I asked you nicely to do it, twice, before I practically had to blow you away by the Papoose fire pit! You're always getting smart, and one of these days you're going to have to slow down and just look at why you do the shit you do. There's a reason that you're here, buddy! Don't act like your shit don't stink!"

Jasper casually stood and walked across the circle to the chair next to Keith. He sat directly opposite me in the circle.

"Yeah, that's a game. I mean I don't even know what happened in the wood corral, but I've gotten to know you from the dorm, and I'm fucking sure that you and Ernesto are contracted up. You were popping off at breakfast just this fucking morning! Aren't you two on bans, anyway?"

"I wasn't popping off, Jasper, I was just whistling."

"YOU ARE ON BANS FROM ERNESTO. THAT MEANS NO FUCKING CONTACT, SHIT FOR BRAINS!"

"We weren't breaking bans, Keith. We were facing opposite directions and sitting in different booths."

"Oh my god you are so full of shit and I'm not buying it. Do you understand you're struggling here? You're on bans from like half the fucking program.

Melanie, do you want to say something to Zack, right?"

"Yeah. Zack, you and I are in the same peer group, and I know we're going to get off of bans eventually, and that's just not going to happen if you keep trying to break them."

"Oh. Please! I forgot we were on bans, and it was work related. I thought that was within agreement?"

I was not full of shit. I was trying. It seemed like the harder I tried to live by their fucking Agreements, the dirtier I got. The more I tried to understand what this place wanted from me, the more confusing and exasperating the demands became. That reminded me of life at home with Mom and Dad.

Paul needed to get in a few words to retain his position of oldest and official big brother. He moved across the room, too. I tried not to roll my eyes.

"I know it sucks being here but we've all been through it. You can get your shit together here, but it isn't going to be any easier with you contracting up, and getting on a full-time. AND I DON'T WANT TO HEAR THAT YOU SPLIT, OK. You can come to me, man. Let's make an appointment after dinner for some time on the floor. I'm committed to telling you my story, so you can know me better."

After a few more indictments from Jasper about my dorm space and how my bed wasn't tight enough and the clothes hangers in the closets weren't spaced properly, my indictments ended. It was humiliating but nothing too heavy had been slung in my direction. I mean nobody really knew anything about me, did they? I stored away Jasper's betrayal, and noted that I should be appreciative of Keith and Paul for not escalating further with a third or fourth louder wave of indictments. I was still a new guy, and there were other troublemakers.

They moved on to a girl in Brave family. Her parents had just told her that they were getting a divorce. Didn't she feel like that was her fault?

This rap wasn't even close to being over.

Hedwig channeled the frenzy of an orchestra conductor as the indictments started to fly. She motioned one way, and the girls on that side of the room would let me have it. Hedwig pointed to a boy on her left and he would trumpet a nasty blow my way. Though I tried to obey the survival instinct to remain bone silent, not "closed off" or resistant, the railing continued. They needed me to admit I felt hateful, unlovable, and angry.

Vera wasn't done with me. "What's your name? Zack? Zack, I AM ON WRITING ASSIGNMENTS! I don't want another fucking FULL-TIME, OK! Stop playing attention games around me! During Saturday crews I swear I think you were trying to break bans with me. You're supposed to stock the kitchen, not be touching the rocks FOR MY ROCK WALL. I'M WORKING MY ASS OFF UP THERE! SO CUT IT OUT!"

I was developing a guilt complex. I began to speak, but was interrupted by Hedwig's hoarse diaphragm thunder normally reserved for Summit people.

"YOU ARE SO FULL OF SHIT." Her muddled Nordic accent had been mildly entertaining at first. A throaty "h" preceded words like "are."

"You walk around here like some kind of macho man. You always put yourself on the OUTSIDE. You're living a lie! Man, you're like one of my DOGS. I doubt you're going make it here. AND THAT IS GOING TO BE YOUR FAULT! Don't you see how sad you h'are? I heard your Truth propheet was very important, kid. You better learn to h'use those tools, OK?"

I didn't see any need to correct her inconsistencies. Jamie and Dylan and I were all Papooses, but Dylan was one PG ahead, and had been through his Truth propheet. Like other senior staff, Hedwig sometimes would confuse members of my PG with the one above us. Keeping track of peer group members remained a point of trivia for us. After a graduation ceremony or when a Summit got out, we always knew who was in which group. And we could refer to the class photographs archived for future advertisement in the RMA library if we needed a refresher.

"I always feel bad, ma'am," I said. "I fucking hate this place, and I'm tired of acting like I love it half the time. I don't understand why everyone acts like they love it here."

Keith Rios shot suddenly across the room, "WELL, VERA, MAYBE YOU SHOULD SPEND A LITTLE MORE TIME CON-

CENTRATING ON YOUR WRITING ASSIGNMENTS! Instead of falling for the attention games of the Papooses!! Trying to hear if babies are cutting up music? That's not concentrating on yourself, is it?"

Perhaps inadvertently, the staff had come to my rescue. Instead of tackling me with his mean beak, Keith opted for the weakest of our group that week. Having the indictment flipped on her, Vera immediately gave up on any designs she'd had on deflecting attention from her own full-time of writing assignments and school-wide bans.

The rest of the horde followed Keith's lead, with the instinct for an easier kill.

"Yeah VERA! What is up with you? You've been on work details for a week."

"How many work details and raps are we going to watch in the Vera game? You pointing at Papooses is just needsy, since you KNOW YOU'VE GOT SHIT GOING ON!"

"Seriously, Vera are you so in your shit, you can't see how hypocritical that is?"

"Why do you insist on shitting on your little kid?

"Whatever. I don't know what the 'Vera game' is."

"Yes you do, Vera, don't even try to DENY it. That's just another RESISTANCE GAME! You're like Milton and Bradley or Parker Brothers or some shit!"

Time for the pros, Hedwig and Keith.

"I can't believe we are still having this conversation, I mean haven't you been hearing the same shit since you got here? You haven't been learning anything here yet? Do you miss drugs that much? Is that really it? You NEED DRUGS TO ESCAPE YOUR ISSUES HERE SO MUCH?"

"That's all there is to Vera!"

"NO! THAT'S NOT ALL THERE IS! THAT'S NOT...fuck it. And fuck just fuck. I'm not going to do this."

"Do what? Look at YOUR FEELINGS?"

"Well you must have something in the way. There's some THING – SOME DIRT, some GUILT stunting your growth here, and I WANT TO KNOW WHAT THAT IS! What are you still holding on to?"

"Why are you yelling at me? I haven't done anything wrong, bitch!"

"Ooh. That's exactly it, you haven't DONE ANYTHING. That is why you were put on a booth. I know you're a strong headed little woman, and I respect that, but you've got to get honest with these feelings and the anger that is driving your negative decisions around here."

"You've been here long enough to know what you're doing."

"What am I doing?"

"You mean 'Do the work for me'!"

"No, it's not. How am I being resistant? I'm sitting here, I'm listening to this."

"You're asking everybody in this room to do that work for you. I'll bet your manipulation games have gotten most everybody in your life fooled, but not me. Not here! I can see though your bullshit, Miss Priss."

Other students got in the spirit.

"You know, Vera, I thought the same thing before I got put on my full-time for stagnating. Like how it wasn't a choice being here, I totally remember that feeling. And how I thought I wasn't resistant. But I was. I was totally in my head all the time. Can you look at me please... thanks. Um."

"Well, I don't know you really well, Vera, but I've been in a couple of raps with you, and it's always like this with you. I mean you always get the same feedback and nothing ever changes. I'm sick of listening to the 'Vera game.' I know this was before your Brother's but I couldn't get you in a rap until now: How did you even get on a full time anyway? I thought they were just WD's?"

"Hedwig put me on the full-time after I carved in the booth."

"YOU DID WHAT?"

"WHEN was THIS?"

"What did you CARVE IN A BOOTH?"

"OH MY GOD THAT IS BULLSHIT!"

"YOU TOTALLY SHIT ON WHAT I'M – what we're ALL FUCKING DOING HERE! That's the kind of shit that makes this place unsafe!"

"...and I know that we will have the I Want To Live soon, so."

"Why don't you tell us a little bit about what's going on with you at your booth?"

Vera sat up. "Well, in the Brothers, I did work with George, and really remembered a lot of things that I just...don't know how to deal with."

"I don't like your fucking attitude and I'm not going TO TOLER-ATE IT ANY LONGER. THIS IS MY HOME! I CARE ABOUT IT HERE! IT'S YOUR CHOICE TO BE HERE! WHEN I HEAR YOU WERE CARVING ON the FUCKING FURNITURE, THAT HURTS ME."

"That's like one of the biggest red flags, Vera. What were you thinking?"

"It was a month ago, though! It was. I was thinking how I'd like to get another tattoo."

"ONLY BECAUSE YOUR LITTLE GIRL IS IN SO MUCH PAIN SHE NEEDS TO ILLUSTRATE THAT ANY WAY SHE FUCKING CAN!"

"TIME TO TALK ABOUT WHAT'S REALLY GOING ON IN VERA!"

"Like the thing with your step brother."

"Pfff. Yeah. I HAVE BEEN! I guess that's one thing, and another is..."

"Well, let's not just brush that off. Tell every one here what kind of friend you are."

"Uh, honest. I'm an honest friend."

"And tell me about the luggage you're carrying?"

"I am in hate with myself, Mommy."

"I want you to just put your hand where you feel the struggle in you is taking place. Be in the conflict. What's your thinking saying to you? What's that thought right THERE?"

Hedwig had sidled up to Vera. She reached out her hand to press near Vera's belly-button. Very intimate. I wasn't sure what Vera must feel, or what the rest of us should be thinking.

"I feel trapped! I feel angry! I don't want to be resistant all the time! But I hate it here. I FUCKING HATE IT HERE. I HATE HOW I FEEL."

"You're GOING TO FUCKING FEEL THIS WAY FOREVER IF YOU DON'T JUST SURRENDER. IT IS OK TO BE ANGRY, OK?" Hedwig withdrew her hand like she'd been taking a scientific reading.

"That's the feeling right there." Hedwig's whisper was an urgent cue to Vera. A rupture was expected now.

"I DON'T KNOW WHAT TO SAY!"

"WHAT ELSE? LET IT OUT. JUST SURRENDER!"

"I FUCKING HATE THIS CHAIR, THIS PLACE, THESE UGLY FUCKING CLOTHES. I WANT TO WEAR MY HAIR HOW I WANT. I DON'T WANT TO BE A FUCKING LOGGER OR A FARMER. I WANT TO WEAR MAKEUP. I DON'T THINK THERE'S ANYTHING WRONG WITH THAT! I DON'T WANT TO WORK ANYMORE. I FUCKING HATE PUSHING THOSE FUCKING ROCKS AROUND. FUCKING WHEELBARROWS. I WANT TO BE WITH MY FRIENDS. FROM HOME. THIS PLACE IS FULL OF FRUITCAKE FUCKING MOTHERFUCKERS."

"MOMMY ISN'T BUYING YOUR BULLSHIT ANYMORE. TELL HER WHAT IT'S LIKE TO BE HERE."

Support staff du jour started their therapeutic facilitator relay.

"IT ISN'T FAIR. IT SUCKS. IT FUCKING SUCKS HAVING TO BE TOLD YOU'RE A SLUT OR A BITCH ALL THE TIME. YOU'RE THE FUCKING BITCH."

"YEAH, TELL HER."

"NO! FUCK fuck it...no."

"YOU'RE JUST GOING TO GIVE UP ON THAT LITTLE GIRL?

"I'M not GIVING UP, I just don't want to fucking cry...

"LOOK AT HER, SHE'S SO FULL OF FEELINGS THEY'RE LEAKING OUT."

"LET'S GET REAL, VERA!"

"I just don't feel like it."

"LOOK AT ME AND TELL ME!"

"I NEVER FEEL FUCKING BETTER. It NEVER FUCKING WORKS."

"YOU HAVE TO KEEP TRYING. DON'T QUIT NOW, YOU'RE RIGHT THERE!"

"OK! I HATE IT, I HATE YOU. YOU'RE ALWAYS MAKING ME FEEL SO ASHAMED HERE. Hedwig is ALWAYS MAKING MY FUCKING LIFE HELL. YOU PLAY SO MANY FAVORITES, YOU BITCH. WHY CAN'T YOU JUST LEAVE ME ALONE. I JUST WANT YOU TO BE NICE TO ME. TO FUCKING LIKE ME IF YOU CAN'T LOVE ME!"

"TELL YOUR MOM NOW!"

"WHY'D YOU LEAVE ME? WHY'D MY DADDY LEAVE ME HERE. WHY DID MY REAL MOMMY LEAVE? I FUCK-ING WISH I COULD FIND HER. I HATE HAVING TO THINK ABOUT BEING ADOPTED. I'M NOT WHAT THEY WAAAAAAAAANT!"

Vera pulled her flannel shirt down over her hands and wiped at tears while making an effort to oxygenate her brain. With a gulp of breath, she gave a final long wail. I clenched my teeth as Hedwig and Keith started working on the other girls in the rap, now that Vera had discharged. She could dump the tears and snot while the next person got indicted.

"WHO ELSE IN HERE IS ADOPTED?"

Hedwig raised her raspy foreign accent over Vera, now sounding soft. "Yeah? Come sit over here. Talk to Vera. That's it. Tell her you understand. Let's see what comes up."

Hedwig needed more scabs to pick. Three people, like synchro-nized machines, began to work with issues of being adopted. Hedwig's support staff busied themselves for a few minutes scratching at the adopted ones. Hedwig sprang out of her seat to the other side, next to a sobbing boy. She whispered in his ear, and a few minutes later he was talking about being adopted and having acne. Hedwig placed a comforting hand on his head as he got into his feelings.

With her hand still resting gently on the nape of his neck, she start-ed to blast another guy who'd been too quiet about being adopted. She railed at the dude.

"Get honest! Let's tell Danny what he represents to the community. He's terrified around here, isn't he? Why don't you get honest with which way you're facing. It isn't toward life, is it? LOOK AT THE FEAR."

"Danny, I agree. For me, you're facing death here, you don't work your program, and face your struggle the way I always have to." Another helpful student.

Danny shocked me a bit with his response: "I wish YOU were adopted! I FUCKING RESENT THAT. YOU GET TO BE COASTING HERE! I WORK MY ASS OFF, AND YOU HOLD ME BACK. FUCK YOU FOR THAT!"

He was just begging to have staff come back with: "And who does THAT remind you of?"

"My FUCKING STEP-MOTHER! GREEDY FUCKING BITCH!"

"THAT'S IT! GET RID OF IT!"

Here we go. Shit.

While Hedwig demanded the older students in the rap to get honest and tell Danny more, the guy who spoke stopped to breathe, so two other older kids and a junior staff took up the slack.

"Don't you need to do some work in here with that?"

"If not now, when?"

The older students saw a double opportunity. First, by focusing on younger kids, they could stave off the humiliation of being indicted, as long as they put on a convincing show of being upset. Second, if they played their cards just right, they too could have the comforting hand of Hedwig upon their back or shoulder – if they were a boy. Boys had to take care of their feelings even more than the girls, it appeared to me.

I guess I saw some truth in that; we were going to be men, and obviously there were primate instincts raging to get out and go to war. The staff, even those who had been in the military, seemed to subscribe to the principles of the American armed forces, but without the worldwide wars. I'm not exactly sure. My mind swung around the room trying to allow my face to reflect the right thing if any staff questioned me directly.

It was finally over.

"OK, who is going to make sure the room is tightened up? Thanks, James. Zack, why don't you stay and help, too, would you? And thank you. Let's all give some hugs."

This meant everybody had a chance to hug the people who'd been

95

yelling, and then race to the bathrooms.

†

Elementary School Faculty Feed-Back Form

25 Nov 1980

Problem: Zack was sent to my office by Mrs C.
for having used foul language. He was angry with
another boy for having taken his place in line, and he
expressed this anger in four letter Anglo-Saxon verbal
form.

Result of Conference: I told Zack that there is
nothing wrong with being angry; there is something
wrong with expressing his anger in this form. Teachers do not use those words; I do not use those words;
he will not use those words. This is a school rule, and I
am asking his parents (through this memo) to help us
reinforce this concept with Zack.

—Principal's memo to parents, when author was in
first grade (age 6)

†

Along with the rituals, we had our own language and code of
ethics.

Indictments in raps would surprise me for a long time. I couldn't
get used to the fact that every rap day I was going to witness something that I knew, inherently, I did not want to hear. Even as rap days
became the norm, they always shocked me.

The uncertainty in a rap was one of its interesting characteristics.
You didn't know what was going to happen. That I could become
desensitized to the rap atmosphere as I moved through the program
is testament to its purpose and logic. Hell, I would eventually look
forward to raps, and feel that their existence – as a place to "take care
of my feelings" – was something I needed, and that without them I
would be deficient. Raps would come to be the place where the school
reinforced our life lessons – the messages of the propheets.

"Words can't hurt," we were frequently told. Sometimes I believed
that; but during some raps and propheets, when words mingled with
action, I knew it to be false. Words hurt more than almost anything
else, and I came to wish I'd never learned English. The staff claimed
that the harder we pushed ourselves to use words to identify our

deepest regrets and thoughts, the more we'd understand ourselves, and through this knowledge, a secret understanding of every other human on the planet would be available to us.

OK, that could be true.

Lessons at RMA could be universal, if they could get everyone into raps and propheets! I could not have predicted that I would become dependent on the loathsome, introspective "work" done in the emotional program.

At first, however, I felt before each rap that I was about to witness a terrible act of cruelty. Raps were very aggressive. Physically, not just emotionally, I mean; sometimes I thought a person was just going to snap and kick the living shit out of the person laying the indictment on them. If that did happen, at least one person would be off the campus permanently, perhaps to the program called Survival where they allegedly starved kids into submission. Or to a lock-up with plenty of beatings, or ultra-violence, as my friend Done Rough at home would've called it.

The staff tried to get us to go off of the deep end. Then they could say or do anything to you. If they threw you out, they assured us, you'd be dead, insane, or in jail. If you split, and went to a lock-up, or perhaps a mental institution, your life was over. The best you'd have would be a vacant existence, worse even than death. You'd be a waste. Being a waste, thinking I was a waste, started to catch up with me after enough reinforcing statements that smacked of absolute truth:

"Your parents don't want you. They're sick of your shit. They already hired us. They trust our regimen and therapy to show you the way to be. Here it is."

At first the purpose of raps was lost on me. I could see no logic behind having them so often. The only reason I could invent as to why raps existed was to allow them to scream at us until we popped. Staff and older students, with their emotionally charged antics, kept the anxious feeling of uncertainty and fear alive in every rap, every week, every month.

In my rap with Tess on my first day at RMA, I had thought Evan was going to implode from his shaking anger. I couldn't believe she wanted him MORE upset. How was it possible for him to become more upset? *Why would he do that to himself?* He just started blubbering and talking to himself while two other indictments were going on. After a few moments the other indictments had cleared up and with a few of Tess's words, the boy screamed at the floor some crazy shit. Tess yelled something like "OPEN ME UP, just surrender to ME! THAT'S IT!" and he broke into shoulder-shaking sobs. I know that from that hour, my memory began to self-wipe and strip the gloss of detail away. The sounds remained.

Raps were not the only means of control at RMA. We spent about as much time on work crews or work details as in raps. The work details served two purposes. They were excuses for getting routine labor accomplished, and they isolated and excluded people who acted out of agreement. To coerce them to stay in agreement. People like me. Sometimes kids would be punished for dirt that staff just *thought* they might be considering.

✝

The key to understanding why these controlling, humiliating regimens work to produce apparent compliance and how dangerous they are to mental health is social neuroscience. It turns out that the human stress system is modulated by social support. That means that what turns off—or on—our stress systems, is mainly other people.

In fact, keeping one's stress hormones balanced requires the comfort of others: Even short periods of forced isolation can make them spiral out of control.

If in addition, you deprive someone of all physical affection, further overload the stress system via temperature extremes, low calorie diets, and physical stresses like over-exercise or confinement, you have a perfect storm of traumatic experience.

—Maia Szalavitz, "America's Tough Love Habit," *Mother Jones*, May, 2009

THIRTEEN

If I could just make my parents see the chicanery, they'd get me out of here.

That didn't seem like a hard sell. This program wasn't a drug rehab – a few kids had described their time in and out of those. It wasn't a loony bin – some kids had seen them, including Horatio from my PG, who had been in a hospital for manic depression. My eighteen-year-old friend at home had that same diagnosis.

Donald Roff, who I called Done Rough, had been at one of those hospitals for a few weeks when he emancipated himself from his parents. Except for my guidance counselor from seventh grade, Done was the only person I knew who had heard of this child-driven divorce from parents. Unfortunately, I remained ineligible for emancipation until I turned sixteen.

Maybe my parents had dumped me here because I mentioned the term to them?

I no longer thought that this place was merely an act. It felt like RMA was a storage facility for kids whose parents had given up their unruly teenage children for slave labor. I was trying to remain out-wardly calm, while writing frantically in my journal at night in the laundry room while the rest of my dorm slept.

If I let all of this get inside of me, I really would break a seal.

I had reason to be scared at the way people REALLY yelled and ranted. I knew no one had done that to me yet, only because I was still new. After the upcoming Truth propheet we would exit the grace period that being the baby peer group allowed us.

I was taken off of the two-man saw to make room for the members of my peer group who were just arriving. We had several more new kids:

"Horatio Seguro, I'm from Las Vegas, Nevada. I'm sixteen. I like playing piano and video games."

"I'm Craig Felder. I'm from Albuquerque, New Mexico. I used to play baseball so I guess I like that. Alright?" He seemed normal enough to me, a little country. I liked that because I wouldn't be the only one.

"My name is Yu-Yu. I'm from San Jose. I like to read. Oh yeah. Pacheco. Yu-Yu Pacheco."

She seemed to be half Asian. She had had pierced ears with several studs in them, I heard. Also, the rumor mill produced insight, based on the black and white Gothy mime make-up she had been spied wearing on her "tour," into the unacceptable bands she probably listens – er, listened – to. She didn't seem too upset, yet.

"Galen Terzian is my name. I'm from Minneapolis. I like my girl-friend."

"I'm Narissa Lorenzano, I'm from Jersey. I like my life just the way it is, thanks. No. No, that's all."

"Hello. My name is Daphne Skaggs. I'm from Boston. I like the Grateful Dead."

Just about everybody in the room dropped their lower mandible on the cheap, snot stained, salmon-colored carpeting.

"Yeah, we don't say the names of music or bands that we deem to be unacceptable." Tess had to intervene quickly before we all start-ed shouting out the names of bands: The Cars – acceptable or not? "Didn't your new big sister tell you that? Who did your tour, Daphne? Do you remember their name? She should have informed you of the basic Agreements."

"Yeah, it was a girl named Fran. I don't remember her last name, Ms. Turnwell."

"Tess is fine. Well why don't you tell us your favorite color then?"

Daphne and the rest of the program babies had the same confused and betrayed expression I had worn.

"Sledge and Wedge forces it all apart."

I arrived at the wood corral after my bitter coffee and morning purge. Keith informed me that I had moved up in my responsibilities at the wood corral. He gave me a two-foot sledgehammer and a set of the wedges that he'd yelled at me about the previous week.

These wedges were made from solid iron and when pounded into a fissure in the logs, they would split it open a bit. It was here the second wedge was placed and rammed in, to widen it further. Repeat until log is split. *This is progress?* I had to wear these dumb-looking goggles, but I enjoyed the task more than any other down at the wood corral because I was left on my own to do as much as possible and I didn't have to interact with the inane conversation makers of my group. The rewarding and resonating ping from the hammer hitting the wedges delighted and isolated me with its exalted ringing. It probably deafened me, too.

There was nothing to talk about with my new "family." We couldn't talk about home, music, sex, or drugs, so frankly, I had nothing in common with them.

The Truth propheet was scheduled for the following week. We knew we wouldn't be able to write or call home for at least two weeks after the overnight ceremony thing. Maybe we'd receive an award that showed our parents we'd changed and were a step closer to coming home. Through osmosis, things overheard in raps and last lights, we had learned that we would receive metaphorical "tools" to somehow help us with life's problems. The progression of the propheets was mysterious and confusing to Papooses. Rumors were all we had to go on.

One of the chief Agreements of RMA was that you weren't allowed to talk about the propheets with anyone else unless they had also achieved the group of tools from the same propheet. Hence we were not told anything about what would happen in the "Brother's Keeper" or the "I Want To Live," or any other propheet. But after we did this nighttime event, we would be able to talk about the Truth propheet with almost everyone in the place. Only kids that came after and formed the next peer group, PG 33, would know less, since the Truth was the first of the propheets.

For some reason our peer groups at the school only had odd numbers. We were told that even numbers were for all the kids that ran away before the end of the program. Staff and older kids were always telling Papoose to be "odd keeled," in opposition to even keeled canoes and even numbered peer groups. From all those blinking lights on the phone in the Bridge, calls must have been adding filing cabinets full of information about us. I was sure whole wide drawers were filled with the lists of kids who had split – the absentees. There were probably lists of our current odd numbered peer groups, and lists of our deceased or divorced parents' names, and whether or not we had a twin. They probably had a full inventory of spy equipment that they used to record and monitor raps and the campus, as well as our calls home, of course.

I suspected that the information contained in even-number PG lists included how far along in the program a kid had progressed before becoming an even-keeled, never-to-have-existed, absentee. What happened to the absent kids was just hearsay. I imagined they tracked whether the kid really went to a worse place, disappeared, was dead, or in a mental hospital. I had never before understood the anatomy of a lie, nor how to be duplicitous with my thoughts or feelings. It didn't occur to me for a long time that maybe a few of these kids had gotten home and were just fine.

When a kid became an absentee, regardless whether they'd been pulled or split, the staff would inform us that the worst had happened. The kid was almost always going to some lock-up, or on Survival. We could ask our questions, but after that, we'd be back to focusing on ourselves. We knew that sometimes kids died when they left the program, because the staff said so. They never gave out proof; we had to take their word that the absentees were fucked.

Sometimes, the worst really had happened. Staff would stand up before raps and tell everyone that a former student had died. Some had split, some had graduated; it didn't matter if they were the victim of disease or a drive-by shooting. They were obviously loved by the staff, and a ripple of screaming and crying would move around the room.

"Only a few of us here remember Jacob Reed who died of a drug overdose...."

I was less worried about dying when I split, and more worried about angering my dad.

Why would someone who was nearly graduating decide to split, knowing they'd go somewhere worse?

Eventually, around the time of my entering Summit, I came to understand the pressures some of these older brothers and sisters felt. But for now my new-kid journal recorded my fears and slender hopes.

> Dear god or devil, please take me away. I had another phone call tonight. My parents said they would consider letting me come home in six months if the family life is ok and I get c's or better, if not, back to Northern Idaho.
>
> In my rap yesterday they wanted a secret. I tried to bluff my way out but it didn't work. I had to tell them about my fascination with death. Now counselors are watching closely because they think I am going to go hacking people up!

I love keeping people on the edge of their seats.
Congratulate me it is my 24 day!!!!
—Author journal, 4 August 1988 (24 days at RMA)

Mom and Dad come up on Sept 1 I think. I have to
write Mom & Dad I keep forgetting. I am really getting sick of James Taylor and it's pissing me off. I am
beginning to go around the track and I want to quit
smoking.
—Author journal, 7 August 1988 (27 days at RMA)

Our peer group was fully formed. Just like at home, I was in the middle, by the order in which the academy had collected us. My PG had already lost six kids, so our number fluctuated depending on how many incoming kids got their "orientation tours." There were sixteen of us now, and I was the only fourteen year old. In this new RMA world, there was only one younger kid, Kano. He'd arrived a few months before I did, and so was in the group ahead of mine. Most kids got here at fifteen or sixteen.

We weren't supposed to talk about people who left the program – in fact, we weren't supposed to talk about anybody who stayed in the program, either! Talking behind someone's back was against the Agreements. So it all came out in the raps; anywhere else, that kind of talk was unacceptable, because it was anti-team gossip. We were allowed to "bad rap" the shit out of people in raps, though.

In raps, we found out whose parents were famous or super-rich – each RMA family had a kid or two from what Keith called "big horn" families. We found out which dads cheated on moms, did drugs, or had other step-kids. In this way rumors stayed rumors until confirmed by staff or by kids in raps.

From what I understood of the CEDU program, we were here to expose thoughts and feelings, not contain them – for to do that was to lie. Weeks before the actual overnight experience of the Truth Propheet, the word play in raps instigated my peer group's curiosity.

FOURTEEN

AUGUST

During the early months students receive structured support and guidance...The emotional growth curriculum consists of group sessions, individual counseling and a series of workshops designed to assist students in their self-discovery process.

—RMA brochure

†

What was the Truth propheet all about? After we went through this ritual, we were reminded, we would truly be part of the school. The all-encompassing mysticism, the inner workings of the place, were beginning to be decrypted.

Tim told me the day of my Truth to make sure I got a nap during "nap time." "Dude, this is a pretty serious experience."

"Well, can you tell me if it's like a rap?"

"Yes and no, Zack. Don't worry, you'll understand once you experience it. I'm excited for you. I wish I could be in there with you. I'll represent to be in your Brother's propheet, if I haven't graduated yet, and you're still odd."

"And Tess said we didn't have to go for raps today!"

"Yeah, if you weren't so new you'd get to go to the dorms for the propheet nap, but instead you guys are going to be in Denali, right?"

"Yeah. So, it really is just like...nap time?" I thought "nap time" had to be code for something.

Tim laughed, remembering his Papoose days before the Truth. "Yeah. Definitely get a nap in, if you can. I never did and I was a wreck all weekend. Oh, and Zack, don't drink the water."

"Fuck you, Tim!"

Being told not to drink the water during the propheet had lost its hazing luster – we had all heard it so many times. Maybe at the propheet they'd get us drunk, or they'd tempt us, at least. Maybe that was what the joke was about.

"You'll see. Anyway, I'm looking forward to knowing the truth about you, so. Go for broke in there, amigo! Don't be afraid to show yourself."

I felt SO happy that I was going to escape from that afternoon's rap. In fact, I actually looked forward to the propheet. I didn't see how they could shell out anything worse than a rap. I knew I really "wasn't ready" to be here yet, to use RMA lingo, and I was still formulating my probable escape plan, but I felt I owed it to my parents, shrink, guidance counselors, and the staff to investigate the Truth propheet. To get a better idea of what this program was about would help me make my decision.

My PG was constantly reminded to go for broke, which in RMA vernacular had an emotional connotation. I was supposed to deeply invest myself in my emotional growth. Incidentally, nobody I had met knew the correct spelling of the word propheet, but "putting feet under the words of the prophet" is what we were told, that first afternoon when we were a bit scared to drink the water, and would be made to stay awake all night in a bright room with creepy, foreign music blasting and people implanting messages into our brains.

Because we were untrustworthy, we weren't allowed to be alone in our quarters to sleep the afternoon away while most others were in Friday raps. Instead, for nap time we were taken to Denali where the space had been reserved for us. We took turns reading from *Winnie the Pooh*. Stupid, but that's what Darlayne demanded. She watched over us like we were her stegosaurus eggs. In one room at Denali we all had to make at least three greeting cards for older brothers and sisters. The smaller, northern room called Canoe would double as a quiet space for napping. No blankets or pillows, though, I noted.

I wrote cards to Tim and Paul, and a girl named Mariah, who Darlayne suggested when I couldn't think of a third program influence. I included sentiments that supposedly would let them know how much I appreciated them or wanted to get to know them. How I loved their kindness and openness, and how I wouldn't have even gotten to my Truth propheets without their support. Making cards for kids I hardly knew felt like kindergarten crud, especially since I didn't actually make friends with Tim and Paul so much as I was thrust into my older brothers' nests. But Darlayne's overbearing expectations of mush blew over my shoulder with minty breath.

During the warm-up in Denali we were encouraged to drift off to sleep, or draw, or write, but to be silent. After Pooh had been read, and the cards had been filed away for later delivery to our adopted, example-setting "siblings," most of us slept during nap time. I didn't, because I kept hearing little bursts of loud vulgarity and Pidgin English waft into our room from nearby raps.

> For some reason I am on Bans. Fuck I HATE this place! We go into the Truth propheet today. What is this place? It's scary and I won't be able to talk to my parents afterwards for almost a month! I shouldn't be here, the staff are crazy, junkies, and pervs. They are trying to convert me into something I'm not."
> —Author journal, 8 August 1988 (4 weeks at RMA)

We were put on bans from all kids Brave and lower when we woke from our naps and filed back from Denali to the house: We wouldn't be joking with our friends who had been in Idaho for less than a year. It didn't matter to me since I was already on those bans. I watched the rest of my peer group cope with the newfound silence. They weren't very good at shunning and being shunned. I still wasn't allowed to talk to almost any girl in the school! My peer group, now restricted to the house, was not allowed to play sports or chess. My parents, like the rest of the parents and stepparents of my peer group, were forewarned that we were on bans from them, too! We wouldn't be calling home after propheets for at least two weeks. My parents had simply written, "Maybe your feelings about RMA will change after this experience."

After dinner we were to "smoosh" with our older brothers and sisters and listen to their stories. When somebody told their story at RMA, they told a version deemed acceptable by the school. Deep Meaningful Talks, or DMT's as they were called, were expected virtually every night. The older brothers and sisters had been showing us this process from the beginning. We usually made appointments after raps to exchange our stories in the evening. Basically, you had to follow up with one of the people who had yelled at you in the rap; staff would set up appointments for you if you didn't do it yourself.

Smoosh circles abounded every night, and staff strongly encouraged participation. The idea was to lie down on your back or side and lay your head on another person's thigh or stomach. Then someone would lay their noggin on your stomach, and so on. A daisy chain of bodies networked its way across the house floor. The nightly main meeting place, half smothered in bodies, was where we listened to one another's stories and had DMT's with "house music" in the background at all times.

Guys walked around with their arms spread across each other's backs. The girls held hands and nuzzled each other in smoosh circles where older boys would latch on. These older boys, walking the tightwire between quality time and "copping" a feel, had to be careful to think and act as if every girl was old, ugly, or unattainable insofar as their imaginations would allow. Smooshing and mandatory hugs at the end of the evenings created a bizarre, tight knit environment into which I was starting to be invited. I was pretty sure I didn't really want to be part of it, but I wasn't even allowed to act asocial. There was no option except to do what I thought was expected of me at all times.

Tess had lifted my bans for the express purpose of listening to

Mariah tell me her story. I guess Darlayne and Tess determined that Mariah was senior enough in the program for me to talk to, without the fear that I would sexually or philosophically corrupt her. Mariah and Jasper were in the same PG as Tim Chalmers, and after the next graduation, they'd be the Summit students on campus. Mariah Verdera was seventeen and I was fourteen. She was practically a woman, and I was still a boy. I mean, I could see that. Mariah Verdera was out of my league, in every way possible, I knew, and enlightened emotionally, compared to Papoose wastoids such as myself. Our DMT appointment was one requirement, so far, I was OK with.

I rested my head in her lap. We were in the middle of the house and Mariah stroked my hair softly. At first I was alarmed, because I thought I felt a rush of warmness to my privates, and I wasn't sure if I was smooshing right. Alerted to the possible embarrassment getting a hard-on would have caused, I willed the potential liability away by concentrating on her story. First, her birthday and where she was from, and what her parents were like, where they were from, what school and life at home had been like before RMA. Mariah skipped ahead to tell me of abuse by an uncle on her father's side. After an hour of this personal history, her tone changed to very serious.

I could see it was not easy, but she began an extremely detailed account of everything drug related and sexual that had EVER happened in her life before she came to Idaho. Together we stamped out any normal feelings that talking about sex would have produced. I wasn't a priest, and though I wondered what was really going to happen later tonight, I also wondered why she was telling me so much private information, and what it had to do with me or the Truth propheet. I didn't even know how to do some of the drugs she was copping out to me about.

"Copping out" and "copping a feel" were different terms. If Mariah was copping out, it could be said that I was copping a feel; I wasn't. I wasn't doing anything that wasn't sanctioned by Tess, my senior counselor. None of the floor staff seemed to take any notice of us from their own smoosh piles. I wasn't doing any touching with Mariah, but just being there and being the focus of each other's attention could be easily misconstrued. I was already at heightened alertness. Mariah had completed the meat of her story, replete with confessions that were normally reserved for last rites.

"I'm telling you my story, because I know you don't judge me, and there's a lot of things I did to hurt me, Rock Bottom. You know what I'm saying?"

As Mariah said "rock bottom" her hand went instinctively to her belly button but my head was there. She patted my head a moment, gently roughing a few strings of hair. I stopped listening for a minute.

What's a "rock bottom"?

And what the hell was a propheet, and what's up with the water?

Virtually every student from Brave to Summit had already contributed to my angst, telling me and my peer group to not drink the water, a clear attempt to haze us before our first propheet.

At last light, Mariah and her peer group, next to the most senior group on campus, asked the entire house to think about their own Truth propheets. The staff shared, too, mostly that when our peer group "got out" the following evening, we would be part of the community and that we would really need for people to "slow down." More older brothers and sisters we'd acquired in the past few weeks also were invited to share for a few minutes each. The whole last light was about my peer group and the evening ahead.

Tim Chalmers, a member of Mariah's PG, stood up, and the eyes of the student body shifted to him. He was looking at and walking toward me. My big brother's eyes were glazing over and he was sniffling.

"My Truth was almost two years ago and it's still one of my favorite propheets. I'm so glad that you'll know the truth and we can uncover together more of the tools for you guys to use. You're really special to me."

Tim had gotten to me and pulled me up off the floor. Um. I made sure my shirt was tucked in. He had his arm around me now and was staring into my left ear while I gazed at all the kids lounging on themselves and between one another's legs. Tim started to get really weepy. I scanned the room to see if eyes could read my thoughts. Most eyes were focused on my big brother. My discomfort increased steadily with Tim's profession of love for me in front of everybody assembled.

"I'd really represented to be able to support in this Truth. I love this peer group, so I applied to support facilitate, but I got passed over. Anyway, I know it's going to be an incredibly special experience for you like mine was to me. Mine..." He had to pause as his lips started to quiver. I could feel his breath on my cheek and the weight of his arm around my shoulder.

George Daughtry, the wet-lipped head counselor of the Brave family, addressed Tim from across the populated house. "Yeah Tim, that's right. That's right, isn't that the truth? Just feel it. You really care, don't you? Go on and tell Zack how much he means to you? I'm sure you mean a lot to him. This is part of your legacy, isn't it? Remember? Yeah. Be there right now."

Tim nodded and breathed on me some more. "Zack, I know it's hard to be here, and I think after the Truth, you'll see how...how..." Another stifled sob and the rest of what he said spilled out like a punctured water balloon. "Fucking hard to just fucking surrender. But we are all on the same team here. I am so proud of you. It's going to be awesome, I swear. You just gotta go for broke. And remember not to drink the water, just kidding! Give me a hug!"

Everybody clapped. *How could I have refused the hug? Why should I?* This place was so weird, it defied ordered thought. We sat back down while a bunch of the rest of Mariah and Tim's peers rushed to us for extra hugs and more public sharing.

My whole peer group had to keep standing, with the older PG's arms around us, and be publicly proselytized to about this initiation. Some were crying as they talked about the Truth propheet, and its place in the program. This thing about crying at RMA was so weird. I knew they were going to pull out all the tricks tonight, but I still didn't know how to identify the weaponry.

I wasn't a closed-off student. I knew I wasn't perfect, and that life could be risky, especially if your parents threw you out on the streets. But I wasn't a pushover either, ready to do whatever was asked of me and believe everything these freaks said to me. I was expecting to be taught something quite valuable. I needed to know why these new people and my parents were so gung-ho about me being here.

Propheets (based upon the book "The Prophet" by Kahil [sic] Gibran) are emotional growth experiences that are thematic and sequential. These introspective experiences assist the student in looking at their past behaviors, thoughts and feelings. They address such issues as: What's true about themselves, the child inside, friendship, dreams, values and choices. These propheets assist in the forgiveness, acceptance and trusting process and allow a youngster to replace feelings of unworthiness and distrust with feelings of self-love, self-reliance and true friendship.
—RMA New Parent Handbook

FIFTEEN

THE TRUTH PROPHEET PART ONE

The sappy last light session ended, and all who were not on bans exchanged the nightly ritualistic hugs. Staff hugged my PG especially close before their departures, too. Except for my Papoose peer group, the whole populace went to their dorms for a night of sleep. Walter Nemecek, the Brave staff who was in charge of floor duty, told my group to join hands and walk in a line, silently, to the tipi. With obvious trepidation, we followed the two older student "supports" who were scheduled to repeat the propheet with my PG.

Jon Garner and Micah Mortemer, two of the dudes in my PG who arrived after I did, were obviously and happily breaking bans, exchanging looks like we might be in line for an amusement park's roller coaster ride. They appeared to cheerily accept the unknown. Then again, many of us looked as if we were going to the gallows. Ivy had her stoic, disdainful frown and kept her eyes on her padding work boots. I resolved to remain fair, even though part of me could see that this objective – to remain balanced in my interpretation of the evening – was impossible as long as we were captives.

We clunked up wooden steps to the platform that the enormous tipi was built upon. Our boots disrupted the silence of the forest. A torch was lit beyond the tipi, and we instinctively approached the light. In the torch's flame I could see a couple of moths fight over which would be incinerated first. They bounced off each other's fuzzy bodies, flicking moth dust into the blackness below the torch. The flickering light revealed a face that I already knew: Chet Lively, the patchy bearded shit-midget from Darlayne's rap a few weeks ago. Instead of work boots and dirty jeans, he was decked out in dress slacks and a white shirt, and a plastic brown belt. To be fair, his beard was tamer than when we'd been sitting in Darlayne's rap circle.

"Hello, Tess is waiting for us. Follow me."

The two older students and my peer group, still holding hands in a long row, followed Chet's torch into the dark woods. We stayed on a path for a long while. I didn't know where we were going, or if Chet should necessarily be trusted. How did I know he hadn't arranged a kidnapping? But lo, something was finally coming into view. More fire? I wondered if the secret of the Truth propheet was that my PG would roast marshmallows and hang out by a campfire all night.

No, probably not.

A large building was up ahead.

The building must be named Walden, we discovered, because white light leaked out of it and threw photons on a simple wooden sign swinging from a beam on the porch. WALDEN, the sign pronounced, like "wooden," like the building itself, I thought. *Maybe we are entering a small town, or another dimension.*

What was in store for us, if they had to bring us to a building separated from the rest of the campus? Chet unlatched a big metal handle and weird music flooded out of one of the rooms as we entered. One door was open – to the right. *What was to the left?*

We entered the room to the right with the music – through a small hallway with bathrooms. Inside the darkened room, two large white paper signs were attached to the walls with white-headed pushpins. One sign proclaimed, "THE TRUTH WILL SET YOU FREE." The second, as a sort of play on the first, pronounced "TO THE DEGREE THAT WE FEEL SORROW, THAT SAME DEGREE WE FEEL JOY!"

Were we going to feel joy tonight? Were we going to feel sorrow? I found each option equally bothersome, under the circumstances. An indescribable feeling of apprehension accompanied me as we found seats.

The windows to the room were covered with large cardboard slats cut to size. *What the fuck? Aren't we already in one of the most underpopulated North American states, in the middle of the woods, in a building hidden far from the nearest road? Why did they have to cover the windows, too?*

I didn't feel free, I felt more imprisoned, and to me that equaled unsafe. Call me resistant. The dark room was also bathed in whooshing and murky sounds. The whooshing eventually turned into singing and then finally wailing. After the yearning voice of the lady was done yelling "somewhere" for the fiftieth or sixtieth time over the speakers, the whooshing, windy music would fade and she would begin the redundant chant again. It took repeats of the tune until I realized it was not one drawn-out horrible song. It was one drawn-out, horrible song, being played multiple times, over and over.

This made me think I'd better listen carefully, and not make the decision to block the miserable music out – yet. Kids at RMA had a word for songs that were prominent in the propheets. I'd heard the term "snot rippers" several times during the weeks leading up to this night.

Over the hours, I couldn't figure where my first snot ripper song ended and where it began. Under normal circumstances I wouldn't have even considered this repetition of an ugly, stupid song to be music. Air from the singer's lungs whooshed the sound into vibrations that flitted around the room until they became much more than just bad music in the ears. The song took on an identity. Barbra Streisand's whooshing and screeching snot ripper was a hyper sensory presence. Not even the artist herself could possibly have enjoyed it.

In raps, the chairs had always been in circles, not in a horseshoe shape like tonight. Also, these black chairs were uniform, whereas in raps, the circle could be part chair, part couch or bench. Tonight my peer group would all sit in boxy black chairs. I took my seat next to Jamie Durant.

Large, and clean of course, the room clearly was special. The carpet was less cheap and stained. The carpets in the house, rap rooms, and family headquarters were matted and stained in table-sized places, threadbare in others. Carpeting in Walden was brown, and while it wasn't lush like new, it wasn't matted. This building seemed newer than most of the others. Attention had been paid to setting up the room. There were plants in the corners. A rose scented candle and a worn book sat obtrusively on a little table behind the stereo cabinet. A pot with a phallic flower crept up a popsicle stick in the soil, and a flickering candle sat on Tess's side table. From here she could control the music in the room without getting out of her upholstered white armchair. Her candle leaked waxy, flowery essence into our air. Overhead track lighting buzzed with noise, while the dim light it shed struggled with the single candle to illuminate the entire room.

Tess appeared freshly showered and brightly dressed, beaming a frozen yet warm benign smile. She hadn't made an entrance on campus all day, until manifesting in the big, white puffy chair, waiting for us in the horseshoe. Next to Tess and her cushy throne, on a giant pad of paper affixed to an easel read the words "Welcome to your Truth Propheet." So that's how you spell it.

Walden West was cold – traces of the summer day's temperature disappeared. At first it was pleasant: coming out of the muggy darkness into a fresh, clean open room, with a magical feeling. Maybe this whole evening was going to be a good thing, maybe like a Bible study. My mind continued to search for a non-existent parallel. Peer group girls were clinging to stuffed animals, and some caring older sisters of theirs had had the good sense to tell them to wear a warm layer. Melanie wore two flannels, while Ivy wore an oversized sweatshirt with no logo. Soon they would also be shivering in black chairs from the cold night, yearning to sleep, and struggling to stay awake.

Tess opened the ratty old book to its bookmark. She read a long passage. Tess's voice and the content of the work read like scripture.

> Then Almitra spoke, saying, "We would ask now of Death."
>
> And he said:
>
> You would know the secret of death.
>
> But how shall you find it unless you seek it in the heart of life?
>
> The owl whose night-bound eyes are blind unto the day cannot unveil the mystery of light.
>
> If you would indeed behold the spirit of death, open your heart wide unto the body of life.
>
> For life and death are one, even as the river and the sea are one.
>
> In the depth of your hopes and desires lies your silent knowledge of the beyond;
>
> And like seeds dreaming beneath the snow your heart dreams of spring.
>
> Trust the dreams, for in them is hidden the gate to eternity.
>
> Your fear of death is but the trembling of the shepherd when he stands before the king whose hand is to be laid upon him in honour.
>
> Is the sheered not joyful beneath his trembling, that he shall wear the mark of the king?
>
> Yet is he not more mindful of his trembling?
>
> For what is it to die but to stand naked in the wind and to melt into the sun?
>
> And what is to cease breathing, but to free the breath from its restless tides, that it may rise and expand and seek God unencumbered?
>
> Only when you drink from the river of silence shall you indeed sing.
>
> And when you have reached the mountain top,

then you shall begin to climb.
    And when the earth shall claim your limbs, then
shall you truly dance.
    —Khalil Gibran, "Death," The Prophet

Tess intermittently made poignant eye contact with us between phrases from her sacred book, and attempted with her California accent to make the words divine. They were a jumble of metaphor and proverb. The imagery in the writing made it difficult for me to identify a through message. Looking around the room I could see I wasn't the only one who didn't get it. As Tess read, the Barbra Streisand music bled into the mix a couple of times. Tess closed the cover of the book and held it up for us to see. The Prophet, by Khalil Gibran.

Wait, did he go to CEDU?

Tess Turnwell put her ratty book away and nodded toward the door. Chet Lively shot out from behind our chairs where he'd been lurking, went to the hallway door, and opened it. Waiting in the dark were two more adults. I felt ambushed. I wasn't expecting to have three older students and Tess AND two other staff.

Keith Rios, the staff member who'd once been a pioneer student, first came into view. He seemed out of his element in a button-up oxford shirt and slacks, instead of the usual flannel and jeans. He had also cleaned his boots. Standing meekly behind Keith, weighing in fifty pounds lighter and dressed shabbily, was Kelly Grainger, the little woman who'd hacked off my hair the first day. I don't think I'd ever seen her since the orientation and slow moments of my move-in.

I was immediately even more on alert. Kelly and Andrew Oswald hadn't hesitated to put hands or blades to my body during my orientation. What was to stop the staff now, if Kelly or Keith wanted us all to strip or get haircuts?

What was Kelly holding this time?

Kelly carried a jug full of Bazooka bubble gum. Keith strode into the room and stood behind my peer group. My very fucking creepy meter started to register again, and I didn't know where my eyes were supposed to go.

"Who's the baby of this peer group again? Remind me, Zack." Tess locked eyes on me. I looked to the baby and lifted my eyebrows. It was Micah. He'd only been here for two weeks. Micah was from New York, and he wouldn't stop reminding everyone of this factoid.

"Well, Micah, come on up here, and – oh, thank you Chet, can you and Kelly go get us three more chairs? Thank you. And uh...yeah Micah – tell your peer group, if you'll be so bold, what you mentioned to me Wednesday in our rap. No, come on up here. That's it, right in front of everyone."

Micah took his place in front of Tess's puffy chair.

"Um...I don't know. I guess that I was missing my girlfriend in the city. And that at home I'd be a senior this year? Is that it? Oh, yeah! I'll be eighteen right around the time of my first home visit. Is that it?"

The baby of my PG, Micah was actually the oldest among us kids. If I were eighteen, I'd have been back home yesterday! I could hear Micah force his voice to sound lower when he talked – an obvious front that clearly came from some insecurity, not that I'd be the one to point it out.

Tess waved a piece of bubble gum from Kelly's tub. "Micah, take your hands out of your pockets. That's it. Do you want a piece of gum? Get on your knees if you want the gum, Micah."

Tess wasn't asking Micah if he wanted gum. She was telling him to get on his knees.

Micah dropped after giving us all a pitiful and comic roll of the eyes.

"Hands on your hips, that's it. OK. Open up wide. Chew." Tess unwrapped a piece of gum from the comic strip inside and plopped it in Micah's open, expectant mouth. The baby of my peer group reminded me of a baby bird.

"Now I want you to go around the room and do the Peter Pan song. You know the one. You know it. 'I won't grow up...I don't wanna go to school...' That's it. We'll give you a minute to chew. What? I don't give a fuck, make up the words. The point is go out of our comfort zones."

From his knees, Micah scooted around the room singing and chewing with exuberance. We laughed at the spectacle. After a few minutes watching him, Keith and Tess pulled another one of us out of our chairs to join in. First one, then two, now me. Until we all, on our knees, drooling and singing and chomping, paraded around the room. Chet and Kelly got really into it, growing their eyes as big as possible and leading the song. They knew more of the words. The room stank of gum, and the smell reminded me of my childhood and school holidays like Halloween and Valentines Day.

This feeling of having to do something embarrassing and out of my "comfort zone" was similar to that of watching my first rap. It was like an archetypal dream that both Sigmund Freud and the poet Shel Silverstein described: You go out, ready for the day, get on the bus in the morning, all without realizing you weren't wearing pants! A racing, acute sense of doing something I didn't want to do – was this stage fright? I was on the spot, chewing and chomping, overproducing saliva in my mouth.

My brain unleashed its imagination. The taste in my mouth was hot lipstick – I wanted the gum out. I wondered how long the box of gum had been sitting in the building and how long until I could get up off of my knees. It was as if I was being undressed by a giant's hands, or like a house cat must feel when rubbed backwards. I was embarrassed for myself, and then for my group. My level of discomfort with the performance heightened the longer it went on. What would happen if I just got up and sat down in a chair? Or walked out? Keith's voice boomed to "keep it up" when we started to get out of breath. Then the song began playing from the cassette player, morphing over our own efforts.

"I won't grow up! I won't grow up! I don't wanna go to school! I don't wanna go to school!" Julie Andrews or Mary Martin delivered the song in a playful whine. The choir's chorus flooded my noggin to the brim. A different auditory stimulation than the "Somewhere" song, this number fit with what we were doing – what I was seeing and hearing.

Keith barked constantly over the song as it played. We didn't know the song or the script or why we had to do what the hell we were doing.

"I can't hear you, Ivy. What was that, Blaire? Let me hear that again, Horatio? Let's see you move, Jon! Look at Melanie, nice work! Keep singing! I WON'T GROW UP, I DON'T WANNA GO TO SCHOOL. I DON'T WANNA WEAR A TIE! That's right, Zack, isn't it! NOT ME, JAMIE? NOT I, RIGHT, Kelly?"

The newer names stuck out at me, since I didn't know much about the newer kids, babies that I'd been on bans with since their arrival. Hearing Kelly and Chet's names inserted into Keith's litany made me wonder more than ever what kind of place my father had left me in. Keith was younger than Kelly! What did he know about her youth, or anything about Chet, the short woodsman who worked on the farm?

We did this song over and over. Tess and Keith had us add our own lyrics.

"I DON'T WANNA BE HERE! I DON'T WANNA CUT WOOD! THAT'S OK, NARISSA – SAY WHATEVER COMES INTO YOUR BRAIN! DON'T THINK, JUST BE IN THE MOMENT! NICE WORK, ERNESTO! GET INTO IT, IVY. Let's see you blow bubbles, too. Can you KEEP MOVING!"

We were supposed to now blow bubbles with our gum. Tess got on her knees and did it, even though it was usually unacceptable, like blowing smoke rings. I knew upper-schoolers were allowed to chew gum, but I saw one older girl "blown away" – half the room screaming at her simultaneously – in a rap just two days prior, for allegedly blowing bubbles with her gum in the academic building.

I'd had enough of this song; my knees and jaws were starting to ache. The rest of my peer group was still singing and laughing. The gum would shoot out of singing mouths, only to quickly be replaced. Chet or Kelly flicked the waxy paper from the candy, flung gum into any empty mouths, and picked the discarded, chewed up gum with their bare hands from the carpet. They stayed on their knees, participating in the spectacle, going back and forth to Tess's chair, where they stored all the Bazooka wax-paper comics.

Tess let the cassette player's volume rip while we slobbered, hands on our hips, waddling on our knees around Walden. Peter Pan's theme ebbed in over it. The taste of boiling lipstick in my mouth and the discomfort in my brain and body were driving me toward an edge. I didn't know what it was the edge of, though. I looked for signs from Tess that we had fulfilled her expectations, and that this would soon end. She just continued clapping along to the song and smiling between repeating snippets of our ad-libbed lyrics. She used her fluffy white chair as a base from which to watch us, and occasionally jumped up and joined Keith in conjuring up more energy from us. It was odd to see the two adult passengers, Chet and Kelly, perform in the embarrassing entrance ceremony.

They shouldn't be here. As junior staff, did they know more than my peer group about what was to come? Aren't all these old people receiving a paycheck?

I took part. Madness was beginning. We had to keep going around making eye contact with one another and singing made-up words while the Peter Pan music whined from the suspended speakers. I was starting to learn the bratty words. My creep-o-meter was moving from about four, where it had been since I stood with Tim in the front of the house, toward five or six – where it had been frozen during my first day. I'm guessing a ten on my creepy scale would be where I died of a fear-induced heart attack. Fear, stage fright, the apprehension, the new room, the suddenness, some anger: the creepy factor moved upwards.

Another freaky aspect was seeing the members of the community, like the oldest lady in the Truth propheet. She was a "parent communicator," and it wasn't until I went home, much later, that I fully understood her role. The most innocent seeming, quietest men and women among us – were the implanted spies. They were the ones that communicated with Mom and Dad about me, though they hardly ever saw me.

Watching the old man and old lady wobble around stiffly while chewing gum and trying to keep up was like seeing old people naked. It was the vulnerability we were all feeling, but I could see it physically in the older people in our propheet.

Snap, crackle, pop! The gum and the smells of masticated sugar, the awful melted-lipstick taste, the pain in my knees, and that I could – but couldn't – choose to stop participating in the embarrassment, left me overwhelmed. Their mixture inside me that night made me think of volcanoes and plate tectonics, not for the last time. What I was feeling in these minutes was a new thing: apprehension mixed with paranoia blended into mild amusement and total self-absorption. I knew – as Keith and Tess still encouraged us to move, to sing, to blow bubbles with the disgusting gum – that we were going to do whatever they wanted us to do during this Truth propheet.

This bubble-blowing, singing bullshit loosened us up for whatever the master plan was. Tess had said as much at the beginning, with the "comfort zone" business. I strongly wished to skip, or see, into the future. I wished I had been paying more attention to what she said. That zone where I felt I had any control over my brain's world, and the zone of the Peter Pan song and the propheet's happenings, would now be forever etched together. After an hour and two hundred repeats of the girl's mocking voice, we wound down from what the program called an "ice breaker." Kelly Grainger came around with a trashcan and we spit our wads of gum out into an amorphous, masticated sculpture resembling a cross between dog shit and Cyndi Lauper-inspired fashion. The room still smelled like mushed roses and boiled lipstick.

We finally sat back in our horseshoe, and started bantering like we'd do at the beginning of raps, about our pre-RMA lives. What druggies and thugs, hot stuff and studs, we thought we were. Soon, we were to be converted into the thieves, criminals, stoners, surfers, or whores that the staff thought we really were. Keith seemed to be the ringleader of this round. His harsh voice boomed when he hit his punchy lines. One stereotype they could always target: Our parents or guardians couldn't or wouldn't deal with us and our antics, and CEDU education would.

"I would never ask you to do something that I wasn't prepared to do myself," Tess stated. "You're all so lucky that you're not on the streets tonight. Who here has spent a night on the street or in the woods because he ran away? Who here ever got kicked out of their own house? It's a rough place – the world out there. RMA and CEDU Campus is a two-of-a-kind environment. This is a unique place, with unique individuals who care. No one here will be asked to do something that we would not do ourselves. Remember that tonight, OK? You can trust me. You're here, whether you see it or not, by agreement."

"But you still don't know shit about shit, do you?" Keith's harsh tone had already injected the phrase into the horseshoe twice.

Yeah yeah yeah. I've been here four weeks, I've heard all this shit before.

Not only did we agree to be here, but RMA had chosen us. Platitudes like this start to root in when you hear them a hundred times a week. There were very few locks, true, but there wasn't anywhere to go either – if you did run away.

"This could be the most important day of your life. Don't squander time here tonight. We're here to go for broke!" As Tess spouted adages, she popped Barbra Streisand's twin ninety-minute cassettes back into the Sony tape player's dual slots. Again we were absorbed in mystery and whooshing from the overhead speakers.

She stood up from the armchair and flipped the page on an easel to expose the next giant leaf of paper. Tess drew a circle. Inside it she drew a little square, giving her circle a three-dimensional, spherical look.

"What do you think this is?" she asked.

Everyone looked daunted. In Idaho, rhetorical questions frequently were precursors to something bad. In a rap, rhetorical questions were a trick: you sometimes had to answer staff questions, but sometimes you were supposed to just sit there and let them vocalize. My peer group was dealing with their nerves by offering possibilities.

"Is it a ring?" I asked.

"How about a cue ball?" asked Jamie Durant.

"No. It's my asshole!" Ernesto volunteered to some laughs.

"Knock it off, Ernie!" Keith's bark was becoming familiar.

"Uhhh. How about a gumball?" asked Horatio, from Nevada.

Tess wrote the words "GLASS MARBLE" under the circle on the big pad and reached into the pockets of her sweater. She produced a big glass shooter marble and held it up between two fingers. Like a magician preparing for a trick, she drew our attention to it with her eyes and free hand. Tess huffed on her shooter marble, shining it up on her pink sweater. My peer group exchanged blank looks around the horseshoe. Alright, what the fuck is this?

Tess made a little mark on her drawing of a glass marble. "This scuff mark represents the first time someone said something to you that hurt you." She made another mark with her sharpie.

"And another, and another. All of the things that people said about you, and things that hurt you. Things your parents or relatives did to hurt you, they scuffed up your shiny shooter marble. And we are going to spend tonight shining up that glass marble. Your shooter marble is an analogy to the little sprout inside of us all. That sparkle inside of you all was made out of love, but it is hurt now. That little dooger in there, your core little child within, well, it can do hurt, too, but we'll get to all that. That core self, that little child, got covered up with shit. It tarnished. I know when I was little I was perfect; I know Ivy was perfect. And Blaire. All of you. You older doogers too, am I right?"

She smiled genuinely at Kelly, then at Ivy, who camouflaged a grimace with an innocent but perturbed smirk. Tess redirected her eyes toward Keith.

"Keith, I know when you were little you had a nickname, didn't you?"

Keith unnaturally enjoyed or hated any particular instant he lived. Now he was feeling joy, I guessed. "Yeah, you know it Tess."

Keith leaned back in his chair and locked his fingers over his head. "When I was little my mother ran a day care in West Virginia, and she used to call all the children 'doogers'. So, the first thing I ever remember being called by her was her favorite dooger. Her little 'do-gooder.'"

Keith was steaming up in the eyeballs, so he plastered a weird nostalgic smile above his chin.

"Thanks for sharing that with us, Keith. Kelly would you take these index cards and make Keith one that says "Dooger"? Thank you. My father always called me Princess. Melanie, what do you remember about your mom? She used to have a name for you, too, didn't she?"

"I guess so." Melanie Taylor picked up her cue from Tess.

"Yeah. What was her favorite nickname for that beautiful little tyke? Can you remember for me?"

"She used to call me Rainbow..." Melanie started crying. I wanted to start crying from watching Melanie, who I'd really never even talked to. Seeing raw sadness like that melted my heart. I felt it like a punch to the solar plexus.

Toughen up.

Over the next indeterminate amount of time – I'd guess about two hours – we each recounted one or two memories involving our early childhoods. Then a card with that nickname on it would be taped over our hearts. Except for me, everyone, including the staff, had a little index card. There was a Princess, a Peanut, a Buster, a Twinkles, a Monkey Boy, a Kissnose, a Rainbow, a Pig-bug. And Keith was Dooger. I had a hard time remembering anything that my parents had called me. When they returned to me the third time I remembered a name that my uncle used to call me.

"Zack, did you want to share with us what you remembered."

"Uh. Yeah, my uncle who we'd see for Christmas was always tickling me and called me Spider-Man. Uncle Kevin called me this because I would climb all over every chair and every tree I would come across."

"Go on." Keith's voice caused my head to turn.

"Well, one time my grandmother, his mother, caught me up on the counter tiptoeing above the dishwasher. I was seeing if circumnavigation of the kitchen could be done without setting a foot on the floor."

"Circumnavigation, huh?" Keith mocked, I suspected.

"My grandmother gasped words in a rush without a hint of playfulness, 'Get the fuck down off of there!' Yeah, I was going to make it too! And she said, 'Goddammit Spider-Man put your feet back on the floor!' So you know, after that my mom would sometimes call me Spider-Man. Is that OK?"

Truthfully, it had kind of bothered me that I didn't have a memory of a nickname that my parents had called me when I was younger. My mother was always mean to my uncle, the way her mom was mean to all of us when we visited New Jersey. Mom most certainly never called me Spider-Man. Most of the kids had names from their early childhood. Mine was a product of exploration: of growth, in fact. It stung a little, and I knew I might have to address that question to myself later.

How does that feel, Spider-Man? Take a look.

I reawakened a notch when the music stopped for a moment. Tess opened wide all the doors and turned the lights up a few settings so that the room became almost bright.

"I know you've already heard not to drink the water. There are cups over there and all of you will have a chance to drink water later and I promise you it will come from the faucet and it is perfectly harmless." She was obviously wise to the rumors about the first propheet. The older students who were "supporting" in the experience laughed along with the staff as Tess took a long drink of water.

One of the student supports, Jasper Browning, was in Warrior, and was also my dorm head. The other boy, Barry Galligan, had just entered the final phase of the school. This Summiteer was in my big brother Paul Renssalaer's peer group. As a Summit student, Barry would be graduating the program in a matter of weeks.

Tess let us want water for a moment.

Then she said, "It's time for a bathroom break. There will be no going outside, WAIT, when we take our breaks. Would our co-facilitators help stack the chairs? Yup, against the wall there is good. Let's get a lot of space in the room while we all get a chance to use the bathroom? Thank you. Now, ONE AT A TIME, you may silently go use the bathroom. When you return come to the standing circle we'll have in the middle. When we come back we're going to be ready to really get to work? Right? You're ready for this experience. Don't forget: 'What you put into this experience will be what you get out of this.'"

She pointed to the sign on the wall. "OK...any questions? Good. Commence."

We peed and drank water. When it was my turn to walk past Chet and go to the corridor toward the bathroom, I saw the door that we had come through before. Did I not want to just make a run for it when I was done peeing? No. It was the middle of the night. *Remember to stash a flashlight,* I had wisely thought to myself, but never followed through on that detail. Where could I procure one, anyway? We had eaten last at dinner. The sun had still been up. Where would I run TO in the dark, middle of the night, were I to split right now? The conflict nagged at me.

Chet corralled me back into the loose standing circle that formed. Tess urinated last. My peer group stood there, with the older supports, and waited. As she passed her console on her way back from the restroom, Tess turned the lights up brighter and the music a little louder. The little table and stereo cabinet had her Prophet book, the candle, magic markers, and other knickknacks. The circle my peer group was standing in now included Chet and Kelly. Tess came into the middle of the group to address us.

"Now as passengers in this propheet, we have to have a safe environment to do the important work we're about to do for the rest of the night. So, before we begin in earnest, and begin the next step in this important process, we're going to have a dirt list from everyone. Don't roll your eyes, Blaire and Galen!

Tess went on, "Don't you want to be clean for this experience? This is that time to come clean again. I want to hear everything. Everything. What you put into this is what you'll get out of it. This is your chance to come clean so you can experience this first propheet within agreement. Complete acceptance within agreement, right Chet? We are here, and you will be better to earn, to achieve honesty, than to keep living lies. There's a lot of liars in this group, isn't there? Keith, do you have anything you want to say?"

Tess had said it all.

It was our turn. We all said all the things that we had done out of agreement that we hadn't already "copped out" to in writing during the preceding week. People copped to breaking smaller Agreements first. Talking about partying with friends at home, or looking at the attributes of girls in the program, or talking about girls from before RMA, cutting up the streets – these were all included in the category of "jailhousing." Girls copped to having desires for a few of the older brothers who weren't in the propheet.

I had a crush on Ivy, but I wasn't going to say shit. Besides, maybe I only had a crush on her because we couldn't communicate because of our bans. For me, there was no one to cut up the streets with, since I was the only one from Virginia. Just talking about a local middle school or pizza parlor was enough to be construed as cutting up the streets, and also therefore jailhousing.

Jamie and Ivy copped to smoking in the woods, thus prompting another hour of more serious dirt. I had done it too – smoked off the porch – as it was called. Smoking anywhere on the campus was strictly forbidden except on the smoking porch back at the lodge. Just thinking of smoking made me want one. I wasn't the only one. Keith jumped down Ernesto's throat for impulsively having asked if we could have a smoke during the bathroom break. We probably weren't going to be leaving the building at all for the whole experience.

We all had dirt. Being new, Papooses were the ones that ran away, cut up "unacceptable" music bands, bad rapped people, and generally did most of the serious jailhousing and "getting dirty" on the campus. The staff frowned deeply upon any time we spent alone, especially in the woods. Copping to being alone in the woods was just about as bad as two Papooses getting caught smoking in the woods. After that, it was just logical for the staff to assume the two were hatching a plan to split. Therefore it was considered a split contract when two Papoose members smoked off the porch. If it happened to be a mixed sex, Agreement-breaking duo, it was automatically assumed to be a sex/split contract, by the same unsubstantiated criteria. This is what we learned, and how we learned it.

Micah Mortemer copped to telling Ivy, Yu-Yu, and Horatio how to get high a variety of ways. He said nutmeg, stolen from the kitchen, could produce a high like coke. He tried harvesting banana peels to dry and smoke, but his dorm head found the bananas and thought he was just hoarding food. We watched Micah squirm. He claimed he was presently beginning the fermentation of potatoes in his cubby in La Mancha. His interrogation went on for some time, giving me much more education in the illicit uses of everyday items than RMA probably ever intended. I was to learn a lot more.

Yu-Yu Pacheco was quiet, but Ivy was the quietest. She had to be verbally prompted for everything. Ivy seemed shy to the point of paralysis, and was clearly made uncomfortable by prolonged eye contact with Keith or Tess. And yet Ivy had the courage to split once during my first week, when they accused Ernesto and me of giving her money, and I got my first Work Detail. She seemed so shy, but she had already left another time, too. On her second attempt, she'd come back hungry and wet before breakfast without ever having been discovered. Under Keith's carefully loaded questioning, Ivy copped out that she had told Galen Terzian and Narissa, another new girl, that she had split. Not only had Galen and Narissa broken bans, but they were accused of having a split contract that Keith and Tess easily now represented as a sex contract.

"Mr. Terzian, why didn't you tell us about this contract with Narissa in your dirt list yesterday?"

"I don't have any contract with Narissa."

"Yes you do, don't contradict ME. IT'S A FUCKING CON-TRACT, isn't it, everybody? If Ivy splits and tells you two...Then you knew it! You didn't come to me or Darlayne or Tess, did you?"

"Ivy didn't split! She came back, that's not splitting, dude!"

"I'm NOT YOUR FUCKING DUDE, GOT IT? You're weaseling behind words. Being wordsy. You should just say 'I got contracted up with Ivy and Narissa, and we wanted to leave to make dirt.'"

"I didn't have the chance! I was going to cop out, honestly, when it was my turn!" Galen pleaded.

They must have given Ivy the money that sent me and Ernesto to Work Details.

"This isn't school, you already blew that! We don't have to raise our hands. You lied yesterday and today by not copping out! You don't have to wait your turn, Galen! You can come clean whenever you want. You chose to not come clean, to be and stay dirty."

Tess tried to sound reasonable. Keith came at Galen again from the other side.

"Oh come on GALEN GET REAL! You're so full of shit your eyes are brown. Getting contracted up with the new girl, hunh? Yu-Yu we'll get BACK to YOU. First, Narissa and Galen – we all know you're both dirty. Just clear this up so you can get something from this experience. Don't sabotage yourself anymore, kids! If someone tells you they want to split and you don't do something then that is a fucking contract... Did you tell whoever was on house duty? Did you come to me or Darlayne? She's your senior counselor. Jeez, take some fucking responsibility for your lives." Keith flashed his eyes menacingly at our faces.

Ernesto, my friend, then really shocked me. He admitted to huffing gas in order to get high. That WAS a big deal at RMA. Would they toss him out of the school right then? Nobody in the room was as surprised as I was when he copped out to it. When he had done it in front of me, offering me a potent rag to gas myself with, I had promised him that I wouldn't rat. I didn't "huff," but I had been there when Ernie did. He had turned greenish and appeared rubbery and unstable on his feet for a few minutes. I was glad I had politely declined. He did have a goofy grin across his face as he wobbled to and fro, but I just wasn't interested.

Now Ernesto sold me out. "Zack was there too."

"What!"

"GET THE FUCK...We're going to get to that. I am so FUCK-ING MAD RIGHT NOW!"

I could see Keith's face swelling red with anger.

I felt my face go white. Fainting was a physical reaction I had never experienced, but I am positive I was close to doing exactly that as I sputtered for words. "I didn't...I was there, I guess, BUT I DIDN'T INHALE! I didn't inhale, so I WASN'T HUFFING!"

"But you admit that you were there with him? Where did this take place, Ernesto?"

Tess flashed a quick look to Keith, and he stowed his fury for the moment. They had to work together to get the most dirt, and Tess's look had said it all.

Ernesto may have copped out to save the group from something. Or he did it because he didn't trust me enough that I wouldn't let it go, and would rat on him. Perhaps he had told other members of the PG or was protecting something else from discovery? I suspected chicanery. Maybe he just wanted to show off for Micah, Galen, Blaire, Horatio, Craig, Daphne, Melanie, Ivy, Yu-Yu, and me, or he really did want to come clean, but I felt betrayed. Keith and Tess had all night, after all, to determine whether we were getting honest enough.

Questioning could be indirect. These mini-encounters alternated between intense and unexpectedly quiet. During the dirt lists and interspersed among all of these questions came more questions from Keith and Tess.

"Where did you get it?"

"Who were you with?"

"Who else?"

"Where?"

"How many times did you go there?"

"Who else knew about this?"

"I don't believe that, you must have told someone?"

"Did you tell somebody in this room?"

"What did he or she say, exactly?"

"Is that all?"

And when it was my turn, I saw how my dirt came into Ernie's dirt. It was hard to not be honest. Maybe I was appreciative that I wasn't crucified for my inactive participation in Ernie's dirt. I did admit to smoking off-porch, going into the woods, and singing unacceptable songs on WD's. I ratted on the small stuff I knew about others in the room, since they were doing it to me. A culture of confession and attrition began to form.

"You and Ernesto were huffing gas? Is that what I heard! We're trying to help you little spoiled bastards and this is how you help? What if you'd gone blind, or died? Did you even know that there could be bad gas? I'd have to call your mom and dad and tell them you died from huffing expired gas. I knew there was something snaky about you from the get go."

When Keith lifted his finger to punctuate his feedback to me, all I could think of were the words snakey and gecko.

"I wasn't huffing any gas. Ask Ernie."

"Ernie. Awww. Isn't that fucking cute. So, you and Ernesto went to the farm specifically to siphon gas from the haybine? Whose idea was it, Hunhhunh? Yours, I'm betting?"

He had me there. "I don't know."

"You don't KNOW. Riiiighhhhht. Let's see a show of hands in this room that believe that. I know you're not being honest right now! Who believes that Zack doesn't know which one of them had the idea to siphon gas to get high and WALK down to the farm...?"

"That's NOT why we WENT TO THE FARM!" I pleaded to the room while Keith waved for the group to put their hands back down. He had seen who'd accommodated him in his poll of my dishonesty.

"That's not the point, the point is what you did when you were at the fucking farm. It's worse than that, you know? You should have pulled him up. You should have stopped him? You could have stopped him. You see?" Tess rounded out her argument somewhat more casually than Keith had. "I mean, unaware though you may be, you can see how this issue is real for Ernesto. We're taking this very seriously. Can't you see how you bring one another down, every day! You're supporting the nightmare in him, not the truth, not the dooger! Take a look at how you automatically use each other for crutches for your negativity!"

"How was I supposed to stop him? What, with violence?" I retorted.

"Bullshit, don't hide behind the Agreements! Look how defensive he is. Look how he's sitting, what he chose to wear tonight, with that shirt and those dirty socks. Zack, do you know what defensiveness tells me about kids, about you? That you're scared. You're scared of taking a real deep look inside yourself. You're afraid everyone will see what a liar you are."

"I AM NOT A LIAR. I've been nothing but honest."

I had played right in.

"Another lie, see how we touched a nerve? I think we've found our first truth tonight. Zack thinks he's honest when HE IS A LIAR! Get him a card, Chet!"

Tess and Keith were smiling in triumph.

"You're not going to waste our time any longer right now."

"You're wasting our time." I countered sullenly.

"You see how he just got! You are a headsy little lawyer's son, right?"

I nodded. "So?"

"So I bet you had to get really wordsy and headsy with him, but it ain't gonna work here, my little prince. You can't paint that dishonesty around this campus. That's NOT OK! Look at me, you little liar."

"What now?"

"Tape that card to your chest. Chet will take the other one."

Tess threw a roll of masking tape from her console. "You're going to wear that card right over your heart. Yup."

"Now Ivy! Just because you're one of my favorites, did you not think I was going to find out about you and Micah jailhousing about drugs? Isn't that what got you sent here? This is your chance to start changing, but you're just jailhousing the time away. Wasting my time and your parents' money. It makes me SICK WHAT YOU GET AWAY WITH AROUND HERE!"

Ivy spoke. "I don't know what you're even talking about. That's not what a contract is."

I could have warned Ivy about the futility of logic at this school.

"That's what it is here and you're fucking HERE, right? You got Galen and Narissa dirty. ADMIT IT!" Keith was punctuating as loudly as he had ever gotten. I wanted to come to Ivy's defense, but she was the one who copped out to it.

"OK." Ivy looked up, sadly, with a smattering of confusion. Her "OK" left an upturned syllable open in the air.

"'OK'? OK, I'll just fuck whoever comes along? I'm a doormat right?"

In watching these encounters between staff and kids in my group, I zigzagged between feeling apathetic and protective of their feelings. But during the all-night event, no one like me could help Ivy. It would only make it worse if one of us tried to stop a stream of staff and look-good older student indictments once they'd begun.

And they went on.

Galen Terzian was next, his indictment also followed by an index card over his heart. After about twenty minutes on Galen, it went to Jamie, and on to the next. We all wanted to look good, I mused. Perform right for the peer group we were supposed to be getting to know so well, and satisfy the staff with confirmations of our infidelity to their impossible rules. Where was the rulebook? Every boarding school I had gone to had made us sign a little book promising we wouldn't steal shit or do drugs or cheat. There was no RMA student handbook with bylaws in it.

Tess opened a door to the porch. Cold night air flooded in. Until the evacuation of the old, used, atmosphere, I hadn't noticed how stuffy the room had become. It had gotten quite warm in our standing circle. When the door swung open, it felt like a suggestion that we might be going back outside. It would be nice to leave the room for a few minutes, and get away from everybody I'd been forced to look at since coming into Walden. But we weren't going outside. We weren't going to even get to sit down.

Keith addressed us from outside the circle. His voice now had a new practiced quality that whispered empathy. When he used this soft voice I felt an undertone of fake seriousness that wasn't there when he yelled.

"OK people. Let's take another break. No leaving the room, except to use the bathroom. Jasper, make sure it's one at a time, thank you. Guys, this break time try to remember any more dirt you still haven't copped to. Use these minutes to really introspect on what you would like to get from this experience. The work we're doing is solid."

As we waited to take turns peeing, I looked at the cards taped over everyone's heart. There were two of us with LIAR cards, three

TAKER's, a DRUGGY, a BROKEN, two DAMAGED GOODS, a HEARTLESS, five FEARFUL's, a SPAZ, and two LOSER's. Tess and three other girls wore placards labeling themselves USED.

"Good job everybody so far tonight. Right, Keith?"

"Yeah, Tess, now let's go further, let's introspect a little deeper. Good idea, you think that they can handle it, Tess? I don't know. Let's try."

Like parents in front of their children, it was as if we were really bad, really young, or really not in the room at all. This quality in staff communications showed up frequently, when staff wanted to self-promote and validate a statement they had made. It smacked of condescension, like when they repeated everything back.

"Now I want you to remember all those times – all those times that someone said something mean to you, or said something bad about you. Because every time someone hurts us, we put a mark on our core selves. After a while that core self, that little do-gooder, that little kid – the person who you are, rock bottom, gets a little more and a little bit more scuffed up. Let's start this process of cleaning our shooter marbles. How was your little kid shit on? Look at that little kid. Really look into one another, see them for what they've been hurt by. What did that little girl hear? What did Mom say? Daddy? What happened to you when Dad left? When Mommy died? What did they say to hurt that little boy? Let's get started!"

I could remember from school and camp lots of negative things I was called. Some had had an impact. A hypnotic, bizarre feeling began to accompany me. I reflected aloud on things my brother and father had said to me, because they were the things that would get me in the appropriate self-loathing mood. I tried to keep my voice lower than others, and when reminded or urged by Tess or Keith to look deeply into faces across from the circle, I blurred my eyes so as not to feel the tears I saw. I honestly confessed being called things that I'm sure I had sworn never to make known. I did so, because the staff expected it, and because my peer group was digging deep into themselves this way. To not share would be to betray them and the confidences that they shared. I said the innermost things that made my voice tremble to admit, bringing an ancient anger and self-hatred to the surface. It wasn't just the situation; it was where it was taking me, inside myself.

"I'm useless."

"Who used to say that to you?" Keith's soft voice back at me.

"My father."

"Your father called you useless?"

"Yeah."

Had he really? Yes, he had.

"Say it again. 'My father said I'm useless.' Good. It hurt you? Yeah. You can say that again, that's riiiight."

Tess and Keith repeated what we said a lot. Just about every time a kid in my group said something, Jasper, Tess, or Keith was there to repeat it. This is how we always seemed to get roped in to going deeper within ourselves.

"I can't hear you, Melanie. A spoiled little bitch? Spoiled little bitch. LITTLE BITCH! Why did he call you that? That's right, let me hear you.

"Go for it, Wally...GET IT OUT, PEOPLE. That's RIGHT!

"A SLUT! Who said that to little Daphne? You really let that little girl down, didn't you?

"Yeah? When? After the abortion. Say that again, Narissa - you've got to stop being that girl with the reputation? Look at her!

"Here's some tissues, Melanie. Let it go.

"How old is that oldest sister, Blaire? She's 26 now? And she called you immature for your age? What did she mean?

"That's right, isn't it, honey? That wasn't right Daphne, was it?"

If bad rapping people – or saying bad shit about them – was par for the course in raps, in the Truth, it went up a notch. They encouraged us to talk trash about our parents and families at home. Keith would take on the identity of the teacher, former classmate, sibling, or former parent or guardian. Other than the raps I'd been in, I had never seen behavior this bizarre in my life. I'd been in a handful of schools, a couple of summer camps. I didn't grow up locked in a closet. I did an Outward Bound course, biking around coastal Maine, out-biking a group of older kids daily. I'd even been to France without my parents for over a month. I'd had sex. I'd been rejected, been in a fistfight, I'd gotten good grades and bad grades. I'd been voted into student office, and I'd mowed lawns, shoveled snow, and raked leaves for money since I was nine years old. I'd been to parties with older drinking people several times. I'd been thrown out of schools, and even had a pregnancy scare with the first love of my life, who, it turned out, I would never see or talk to again. So I thought I had a good, well-rounded idea of what people were – how normal people usually interacted.

Before the program, whenever I thought of "people in the aggregate" – Dad used that phrase a lot – I didn't have a fearful idea of their intentions. Then again, I wasn't green – I'd been robbed, beaten, and grabbed at by strangers. I'd seen a dead body, been betrayed by friends, and been emotionally hurt by my first serious girlfriend. I'd survived all that, and hadn't thought too much about the details of my emotions after I'd first felt them. I wasn't as firm in my beliefs as Martin Luther, or Dr. Martin Luther King, Jr., and non-Western prophets of history. But in the propheet I began to question everything I thought I knew about society and humanity.

This is normal? This is what's going to make me normal? To make my parents love me? To make me a better student? To maybe get my bans lifted? Being herded in a circle with adults unlike any I'd met, pretending to be my father and mother, my psychiatrist, and my second-grade teacher?

As if on cue, one of the older supporters ratcheted up the decibels while going into the time his stepfather called him a junkie. He'd been arrested for possessing cocaine at school back in California before coming to Idaho. Tess whipped our group up, while I processed talking and listening simultaneously. All at once, a little louder, we all started mumbling bad things we had been called. This must have been what we were supposed to be doing, because Tess called us out. She repeated our words, and we kept vocalizing our private content and escalating the mayhem.

"My mother said I was crazy. Who said that, Micah? Say it again, Horatio! ONE MORE TIME, Blaire! LOUDER, Yu-Yu! Melanie say it again, honey, MY MOTHER HATES ME! She BLAMES ME! That's right, GALEN, tell her! I'M NOT STUPID! I'm NOT an IDIOT! Tell it all, Zack!"

Tess went quickly to the tape deck and put in a fresh snot ripper.

Is that Kenny Rogers? "Tell it all. Tell it all brothers and sisters. Don't hold back."

After a few listenings, I'd had enough of that track, too. But, of course we were just getting started.

"Yeah, say *that* again. Just keep saying it. Feel it now. It isn't fair, and it *hurts*, doesn't it? Tell it ALL, Melanie. TELL IT, ZACK! What's that, Yu-Yu? Good work!"

Keith and Tess called out between louder parts of the propheet music, to maintain the frenzy.

My peer group had long ceased shooting furtive looks at one another. Sarcasm had left the room, completely. Many were sobbing, feeling generally miserable as we stood there with our defeated, tear-streaked faces. It was impossible to think clearly. My lungs could only produce air that came out as self put-downs.

We are making public our thoughts that should be concealed.

I was participating, but at times I shifted in and out of an observer role: The event was about everyone; it was only about me. The feelings were my feelings; the feelings mirrored the pain and the emotions projected from eyes, the faces of people – the doogers – in my peer group. I sympathized and started listening to them. I began to see my peer group in a new way. It was never going to be fun anymore. They were all angels – with hurt little babies inside themselves.

However, going deeper into how bad I should feel wasn't on my personal agenda. I wasn't even sure what was expected. How was all this supposed to make me feel? What about these feelings was "right where I needed to be?" Why were we actually bringing up all of these miserable memories? Why was I getting angry and sad? I wanted to leave this room, now! I didn't want to think about my parents and my brother hating me.

The feeling at RMA that I absolutely had to escape, that I was trapped, was actually not new to me. Now a sustained feeling, it resembled the intensity and immediacy of moments when I had run away from my real home, and my real mother and father, back East. Oh! What I would do to leave this place, this room, these people far behind. Where could I go if I left? I pondered the question ceaselessly – keeping these pertinent, secret thoughts in an imaginary red binder in the back of my brain. My deepest regret and fear lived there, and it would be months before I was willing to open it and examine its contents.

Tess suddenly stopped the music and rammed the dimmer switch up on the lights. I could feel their heat radiating on my neck. The white beams gave everyone longer noses. Tess spoke slowly and pedantically after another shot of brainwashing water.

"I want you to walk in the circle now and really feel what it's like to have been hurt, and think about all those lies. Keep working the feelings you have now. Whatever you're feeling is always OK. It's RIGHT! All those things that happened to your core, your shooter marble, the YOU – rock bottom – those messages that that little kid inside of you heard – they had a real impact. Didn't they, Dooger? I know you were hurt. And it wasn't your fault."

She squeezed a tear through her left tear duct, and wrinkled her chin up. I noticed Tess didn't even make any efforts to cover her face, or hide her emotions. With increasing volume everyone started walking in our tightly orchestrated circle. Keith walked around the outside of our little circle and pressed us into a tighter, introspecting, unit. Our toes were right on the next person's heels. I could feel the hips of the person behind me occasionally brush my buttocks. We trudged clockwise while Tess diddled the volume control until we could just hear her over it.

Chet and Kelly and the older boys and girls would be knowledgeable about my peer group's deepest feelings. I wasn't sure I wanted my dorm head knowing what my teachers, shrink, and parents thought about me, or what I thought of myself. I said what I said, because we all had to say something as we circled. To be vulnerable and share what I thought of as deep personal embarrassments was the point. Why? I didn't know.

A paranoid sensation prevailed: *Anything I said could and would be used against me at an ad hoc trial in the future.* What was even more uncomfortable was hearing Kelly and Tess and Keith also sharing. Keith would belt out over us: "MY FATHER USED TO HIT ME. HE HATED ME. CALLED ME RUNT. YOU'RE JUST THE FUCKING RUNT, ain't you, Keith?! He used to SCREAM at ME!"

Tess then yelled, as loudly as she could, "YUP, JUST A FUCKING RUNT, RIGHT, Keith? YOU WON'T BE NOTHING!"

"When did you tell your little kids to grow up? What did you say to them? What did your parents and teachers tell you? Hunh? Fuck You, Spider-Man, I DON'T NEED YOU ANYMORE? FUCK YOU, SPORT, YOU'RE JUST A STUPID RETARD?"

Keith repeated what Ernie's dad had once told him.

Next, Keith went over to Jamie Durant, and walked along, whispering into his ear. Jamie soon burst into tears. Tess turned the music back up. Whether it was inadvertent or not, I'll never know, but one tape deck was still playing "I Won't Grow Up" from Peter Pan, when "Tell it All Brother" came back up after the tambourine's aboriginal opening.

Tess was in Horatio's ear after a moment. "Come on, weren't you HURT when he made you do that, an innocent little DOOGER? This is a safe place for us. Let me hear what Daddy said? Again."

We all were yelling at the backs of the person in front of us. Our old teachers, and our dead fathers, and the mothers that put us up for adoption, our parents, grandparents, uncles, neighbors, former molesters, the man who'd shot our family's dog – anyone who had ever said or done anything to hurt us when we were children was subject to being conjured up by our circle. In my mind, ever present, was my father's act, leaving me to this therapy as punishment.

Discordant and irritating to the mind were the shrill cries of the girls. And the two snot rippers, spliced together, made such ugly noises that my ears felt like they were turning inward. Keith urged us all to be louder, and go a little deeper inside our memories.

"Don't HOLD BACK HERE NOW!"

The room came alive with some of those childhood nightmares I thought I sensed walking toward the Stellar Annex on my first day in Idaho. My memories contained the little demons inside me. The demons had to be exorcized: My mother's friend had once asked me if I wanted to make it to my eighth birthday. My mother later explained it had been because I asked too many questions. I couldn't understand the questioner's intent. Why would this lady ask me that? It confused me that the lady hadn't been smiling. I knew she wasn't a threat to my life, but it was easy to see that this woman had made a comment to an eight year old that was designed to sting. We had been in MY living room. What a bitch.

I had forgotten about it years ago. I could yell at her in the propheet, though. I summoned up the memory and spit it out. It was insignificant, I knew, but it got me started.

Tess picked up on it. "You were just a little kid? How old?"

"Like eight."

"Eight. And what did she say to you exactly."

"She said if you want to make it to your next birthday, shut up."

"She told Spider-Man to shut up? And how do you think that made Spider-Man feel? Can you remember for me?"

"Well, a little angry, you know. Mad, I guess."

"It's OK to be angry. Do you remember her name?"

I shook my head.

"Do you remember why you were angry with the lady?"

Because I didn't remember her name, I thought I should have a reason to have been angry. "I guess because she was a bitch to me and I wanted to be with my mother."

"Yeah, she was a bitch? You don't have to justify yourself right now. What you're feeling is OK. It is OK, yeah. Do you remember another time you wanted to be with your mother?"

I nodded.

"Well, go ahead and tell me about that."

When I spoke I wasn't going to be just talking to Tess. Other people were still talking, so Tess and I had to be louder, which meant I had to be succinct enough over the vocalizing and circle-shuffling group, and the music.

"There was a time that I fell out of a tree in our front yard. I broke my wrist."

"Awww. You broke your wrist? You fell out of the tree in your front yard. You wanted your mother and she wasn't there? Do you remember that feeling? Yeah. Be there. Be there now. That's right. Do you remember if she came out?"

Had she come out or not? I didn't remember, but I shook my head anyway. "No."

"Were you scared? Were you hurt? Yeah. It's OK. You were just a little kid, weren't you? It's OK to feel that."

I mixed my voice into the moving mayhem. I jabbered to Tess about how it had made me mad and hurt that Mommy didn't come to my rescue when I hurt my wrist. I punctuated my passing thoughts just enough not to get myself too completely jumbled up. It was all such an uncomfortable feeling. I had just wanted Mama's attention, so I kinda half yelled that into the nape of Melanie's neck. She was in front of me, verbalizing about when the kids in her high school found out about her abortion. Making these outward displays, and overhearing the ones my peer crew were making, caused hundreds of other things come up. Things I could say to the parents, say to my old girlfriend if I masked properly so as not to disrespect Ivy or other girls in there. I could remember the numerous tutors and teachers, the snobbish soccer coach, and the psychiatrist I blamed for having had a pivotal role in my abandonment in Idaho.

Was this what introspecting was all about? Did I just have a break-through?

It became a tad easier to think of shit to put out there in the moving circle. Bodies only existed to purge emotions, our brains only to verify and translate the sensations for the staff.

The music was triumphantly loud, and its physical presence grew the more we yelled and moaned. A sickening, warped tincture leached down upon us from the wooden speakers bolted to the room's highest corners. Tess and Keith whispered in our ears individually, while we trudged along the tight track. They'd talk to two or four of us at the same time, punctuating what we were saying with our little dooger nicknames. They didn't have to read the labels on our chests. Uncannily, they remembered the names of our little doogers.

If the constant noise ever started to ebb, Tess or Keith would come yelling into the moving circle.

"That's right, Zack, tell us what it was like to run. Getting kicked out of schools – OH! That's right Micah, FUCKING LOSER! YUP. WORTHLESS. RUN AWAY! Run away from camp. Run away from home! It is not fair. LET IT OUT, KIDS! Let it out. Give that little Spidey a voice! Go on, Monkey-Boy! What about you, Kissnose! That little dooger needs a voice. Give her a voice. That's right."

Another freaky feeling came over me as I zombied along behind the person in front of me, doing this ill self-identification. I had the feeling that something was wrong. It was guilt. It was shame. Maybe I'd deserved some of the things I was called, but I didn't think I should say bad things about everyone I knew. My parents' friends weren't immune to my memories, not the extended family on both sides, not my real big brother, now in London. I imagined he was studying beer and tits. As I admitted all the things my mother and father had implied or said over the last few years, I thought of heaps of things I would say in reply. Then these things morphed into material I directed at myself. Even though I was being required to do this, I was unsure if what I felt or thought was the correct behavior. We could say whatever we wanted. My version of my history mushed together with the stories of all the adults in my life. Blame them / blame me.

I knew I was a fuckup, but all this talking about why I was a fuckup produced more pressure, and more introspection. I wanted to explore a few of the things I'd brought up for myself, even to discuss them publicly, if that's what was required and would make me a "better person."

Maybe, just maybe, all this is really good for me.

I wanted to stop doing it though.

How long will we do this before we get better, and feel the joy?

Going limp with exhaustion, Melanie had started wailing for her mother. It was heartbreaking watching her gently pushed around the circle while her hands were plastered over puffy blue eyes. We circled another twenty minutes with the Peter Pan song still blending in and out of the "Tell it All Brother" snot ripper. I steered Melanie by the shoulders, trying not to kick her feet, before she took a box of tissues from Keith. The two totally different songs, simultaneously, provided an extra nightmare quality as the two artists' voices became freakish aural vibrations. Keith ripped tissues out of the box one by one, handing two at a time to people as needed when they passed. I took some to cover my dry eyes and face.

The claustrophobic, loud, tight, hot, spitty, smelly room began to disappear. It was killing me. I was physically uncomfortable on many levels. Though I hadn't lost my voice like some of the others, I was still yelling, and listening to Wally Gold screeching maniacally. He was upset with his father, too. When he toned down, Tess was softly cooing in my ear, though Keith was barking at me from over the circle. I knew that it was my chance to perform again, and I poured myself out of my brain and body. I called myself a loser, a liar, and a fuckup two hundred times. I didn't not believe myself more than once.

Maybe being a loser, a liar, and a fuckup is what got me into this miserable situation, after all.

Tess interrupted the moans of our slow moving circle to assure us that we were doing vital work.

"I'm not making you do something that will hurt you. I'm only here to help. To facilitate in this very important process."

Another quick bathroom break came and went. We returned to a standing circle. Still nobody had touched the cassette player – the two songs melded and overlapped, ending and beginning.

"While we, and our little doogers, may be feeling angry at all the people and things that made us grow up too quickly, it did happen. That shit happens. And it's how we accept that pain and recognize it that's the most important thing. Melanie's seeing that, see. Yeah. And Chet, good work there. I want to share that this is a really important tool, for me personally. ANGER IS HURT. Every time we are angry, we are really feeling hurt, and that is most of why we act as we do. Anger and hurt are the same thing.

"It's verrrry verrrry important, what we're going to do next. Stay in the circle and think about your life before you came to RMA, and this special night. This is the chance for you to come clean, to be real,

139

and start the process of forgiveness. For yourself, and all those people who have, along with you, scuffed up that shooter marble – your true selves. I want you to think about life two, three, five, ten, and for you older guys, twenty, and thirty years ago. We all have done things to scuff up our own shooter marbles, too. Not just the things others have done or said to contribute to that. We had to accept what was said. To believe it, in order for us to be angry or hurt by them, we had to be responsible for what we did to hurt ourselves too."

"Yeah," Keith took up from there. "We all have our own secrets, our skeletons in our personal closets, and we're going to take out these secrets and disclose them to one another tonight. We will expose ourselves. We will expose ourselves to the hurt, but first let's look at our reactions to that hurt, right? This peer group is going to be your peer group for the whole time that you are here and even for the time far in the future, when you're out of our family. These other wonderful kids are going to know each of you inside out, while we take a good look at ourselves in this special room. This is our Truth propheet, and our school, and there's so much here that's going to support that truth in you. Trust this process. This is important work. You are here *for a reason.* That work starts tonight. What you put into this experience is what you will get out of it."

Tess added, "And don't forget, these are the people that are going to share these experiences tonight and for the rest of your entire lives – this is a real here forever moment for all of us."

Tess grabbed a few of us by the shoulders and maneuvered our larger standing circle into two smaller circles of approximately equal size. Tess cued Keith with a wave of her head and he scurried to the music. Finally, the genetically altered music went dead. My ears were ringing. Even though the music was off, I was still hearing echoes. Chet and Kelly unstacked our black chairs and quickly the two groups scrambled to sit and rest our legs. The room was bright, cold, and silent. Everyone in my circle looked at one another vacantly. Tess slammed the door to the outside, and before she took a seat at my circle, she went to the front of the room and opened the other door – the one to the entrance corridor.

Prescott Freshwater, the Warrior family head, stood with one of the other staff from his family. They were steering Ari Korta into our Truth propheet. Another moment of unwanted suddenness and surprise hung in the room.

"Let's welcome a few more passengers on board tonight. Everybody, you know Prescott, and also, we have a sp... well, two special guests tonight. Ari is here because he realized he needed to relive this experience tonight. Is that right? Yeah. You ready to finally come clean? Yeah? You're gonna go for broke here now? OK! We're going to show these young men and women how to do it, right?"

Empty seats had been left in our two circles. Why hadn't I noticed, and considered those extra chairs? Then maybe I wouldn't have been surprised for the thousandth time. I was compelled to be aware of everything happening around me, and yet, just as intensely, I wanted to block it out and close my eyes for the night. As the new passengers took seats, a tired and sullen looking Ari joined my circle. Next to him, Prescott sat down.

Being the Warrior family head, Prescott appeared a lot different from the other staff. For one, he dressed immaculately. Members Only and other designer clothes were all he ever wore. Tonight the pompous prig wore a bowtie with a crisp pink oxford, and baggy corduroy pants held up with suspenders. His mustached face with its shiny demeanor was just another of the adult presences I saw around the campus. I recalled Prescott was a former military man who had served with Nat Farmer, the headmaster of our CEDU school. It was ever unclear what qualified him to be a counselor.

With all this activity, my brain was getting fuzzy. The music's echo still oozed around contours in my brain, more staff had been injected into the event, and now the front door to Walden slammed hard again – heralding the arrival of another surprise entrant.

SIXTEEN

THE TRUTH PROPHEET PART TWO

She arrived in costume. When I shot my eyes and neck in the direction of the entrance, I did a double take. A little wobbly figure appeared in the door. On her head, a huge owl face in native headdress with wide, lash-lacking, gaping open eyes. What I first took in, though, was not the mask, but the casualness of the person wearing it. She had a gray ponytail that trailed below the crowning fixture. She wore brand new white tennis shoes and blue jeans. Her black sweater meant something to me, too. Students were not allowed black clothes.

The fresh, real flesh faces took their seats while the owl slowly approached and stood between the two circles. All of our attention was on her. In her hand, she slowly lifted a small scale with two balanced pans. In one was a meaty caterpillar encased in acrylic. It had been white and furry while alive, and remained so now. In the other pan, weighing in at the exact same mass, was an encased butterfly in an acrylic bubble. Brilliant oranges, and greens, and blues, elaborately patterned, were imprinted on its wings. The encasing had been done flawlessly. The owl-woman stood there holding the scale, motionless.

What next? Were we going to be the mice?

Tess continued as if the owl-woman was nothing unusual. "Ari is joining us tonight because he has decided, just this week, to come clean. Right, Ari?"

Ari grumbled and nodded without lifting his eyes. When I arrived my first day, he was pushing a wheelbarrow. About a month later, in the days leading up to his entrance at the Truth, he had been in trouble again. But it wasn't unusual and I didn't even think about Ari before he was steered in and sat at my circle.

Ari got us going by having to cop out to all of his dirt, and that brought us to the next portion of the freaky evening. I had been expecting that we'd be allowed to sleep, since so much had already happened. The desire for sleep remained, but instead, with the new entrants to the propheet, there was clearly more to do. Everything so far tonight had been leading up to this. I had paid attention plenty in my raps. Over the previous weeks I had heard some of the most amazing things admitted to in raps, by students and staff. Everywhere else in the country these would be "unacceptable" topics.

I didn't understand why staff knew the details about the issues a kid had. How, for example, did Darlayne know so much about Jennifer Oyama, a girl in the upper school, and her eating issue before she came to RMA? How did Darlayne and Tess actually know so much about Tim Chalmers' drug problems? Why had Tim himself felt like he always needed to tell me the details of his shame in our DMT's at the house? How had staff in raps known to talk to kids about their abortions, adoptions, and personal demons? I mean, could power staffers really read minds? Or were kids so obvious and easy to read?

In the raps I'd had with her, Jennifer talked about barfing at her aunt's house after some holiday meals. But Darlayne shared details that Jennifer hadn't yet brought to that therapy session. So I knew more than I needed to about Jennifer, and I became reluctant to let any staff know too much about me. Turned out a kid at RMA would learn to keep many secrets about others, but keep none for themselves. This proved we were trustworthy.

I didn't know it was going to become routine, but I was in my first "disclosure circle." Whatever discomfort I felt in those endless fucking raps, it had nothing on this.

At the start, the process seemed innocuous.

Tess: "Who's ever spray-painted something in the graffiti style? Slashed tires? You set off a fire extinguisher? And who has started fires? Talk about THAT. Have you ever broken bottles? Me and my brother used to do that. Acts of vandalism are an important thing for us to explore."

Keith: "Who here has ever stolen?"

Our hands went up again. When I saw hands go up, I raised mine. Similarly, when I raised my hand, someone else put up theirs. I didn't have as much experience as others in our group in legally gray areas, but I wasn't silent either. Our disclosure circle first copped to everything we had ever stolen or shoplifted. We answered all the questions that could be asked about the object, the place of the crime, our reasons for stealing. This encompassed a lot, naturally. Everybody liked to talk about themselves and their lives, even the bad shit. It was like showing their credentials – stories that would support their membership in the fraternal order of delinquents.

Staff: "Have you ever stolen from a family member or a relative? Who's stolen a car? Nobody will get in trouble for anything they say in this room. We are not here to judge. We are here to not judge, right, everybody?"

Tess: "This isn't about things you've been caught doing. This is about those things that you knew were wrong. Right? OK. This is about coming clean so you can have the option to start all over. My dad's been calling it 'hitting the reset button.'"

We were supposed to be impressed at the reminder that Tess's father had set up this whole damn fraud. We all had little stories to tell. I heard a similar experience going on in the circle Keith was running. All eyes were on Tess as she stood up to address both groupings in the room. "I can really feel the safety here. In this room. Can you feel it?"

Obviously, having two new power staffers, and an oversized raptor among us, we nodded. We were supposed to divulge all of our secrets. We were being asked to pretend it was more safe. In reality, from where we kids were sitting, it became less "safe" the moment it became clear there were now at least six staff in the room. And the woman under the owl mask was Hedwig Farmer, one of Solomon Turnwell's original CEDU groupies. She was in charge of gardening and punishment.

Sure, we were safe.

Staff intermingled their statements, dovetailing on the themes laid out before:

"The work we do in this program confronts our fears. I know that nobody in here makes judgments. That's not what we're doing in here, or anywhere in this special environment that we create. We're going to be talking about mature subjects and I expect you to be truthful, aware of your peers' body language, and really listen to the things we've been through in our lives. I was molested myself for a period of two years. You know, I've spent a lot of time working though that and introspecting on how it affected me in my teen years. I reacted by drinking and putting drugs in my body. I took unnecessary risks. I didn't practice safe sex. I abused alcohol. I hurt me's body...Listen up! That's really important these days. I know you all know what I'm talking about. Every single one of you."

"Most of us probably have sexual stuff in our personal pasts. Right? I see you all nodding your heads. Well, we are going to go into some of that stuff, in this room, tonight. Be adults, be honest. The truth is not to be feared. It is to be embraced. The more you put into this, the more you're going to get out of this."

Having blurted out about her molestation, Tess, one hand rubbing at the fabric over her belly button, let a pause gestate a full minute while she sighed a few times.

"Do you have anything you want to add, Keith?"

What is up with the owl?

Still seated in his circle of moral inventory, Keith solemnly shook his head. The owl moved the scale to her other hand. Evidently, Tess had said it all. She returned from the console after dimming the lights significantly, and starting "Tell It All Brother" on the stereo again.

Now we moved on to the meat of the "disclosures." Much time was dedicated to the sex or drugs my group had done, or had done to them before arriving in Idaho. I'd paid attention in health class, and I thought I was a pretty hip little dude. So did guys and girls back home: they thought I was cool. Alcohol had started all of us – me, my friends at home, my peers here, and the staff – on our paths into escapism. Pining first over all the things we did while drunk lent us the bravery of drunkards. We shared our stories. We weren't sharing about any buzzed fun times.

I didn't know that cocaine could be shot up. Or smoked. I'd never even seen the white powder up close. I'd never known what speed did, or what crack or crank was. Or how much it might cost. Or how long it might work, or what it felt like to ingest. Or where I'd procure these vices, if I wanted to give them a go. I'd never met anyone who did heroin. I was shocked to hear that Keith had been a heroin dealer back in West Virginia, and also then on the West Coast, after leaving the confines of CEDU for the only period of his life. It sounded to me like Keith needed to be here a lot more than almost any of us. *And he'd already graduated the program.*

Over the hours, while learning quite a bit about the staff and everybody else, I contributed to the growing epic of my innocuous experiences. A couple of times, I smoked pot with my cousin. She was the only other relative I'd ever smoked with except my brother. We even shared a joint the day of my cousin's wedding, right before this Idaho nightmare started. With my family, I'd shared wine at the holidays. I'd been drunk a few times. I'd been falling-down, throwing-up drunk, only once. That was no doubt part of the reason I was standing here. It seemed that everybody's story began with drinking or getting high with someone in their family.

145

I was tired. I shivered, although I felt warm, not cold. The temperature differences reminded me a little of being drunk, ironically. Perhaps it was the nausea that made me reflect? I wondered, also, how long the rest of the campus had been sleeping. This night contradicted all time measurements that weren't part of the Twilight Zone.

"Why don't you get us started, Chet?"

I could hear the other group begin talking. Chet Lively was across the circle from me. He was about five feet tall and worked on the farm permanently. Although he was on staff in the Brave family, he'd never been through the propheets. I knew him because he had been in one of my first raps, with Darlayne. Then I had seen his wood chopping demonstration at the wood corral, the week before the propheet.

I couldn't stop thinking about it. Chet Lively came to the wood corral carrying an axe as long as his own stout body. He was going to chop an enormous log in half. The log was between three and four feet wide. The chips he sliced out of the massive log were as big as decks of cards. They flew off while we stood around him, giving him a wide berth. He wildly swung the blade. He switched his body quickly around on top of the giant log, facing the other direction, and chopped a while longer. He had been turning back and forth on the log for ten minutes, when he split the massive stick. The display had been impressive, and the challenge had made him pant and sweat profusely. He was strong, very short, and spoke with a Wyoming accent that was much more tentative than he probably wanted it to sound. The two previous times I'd seen him he was covered in pig shit or mud, with his beard unkempt.

The demand to admit to worse and worse disclosures grew more perverse as the night wore on. The accounts of sex and violence began to escalate. My whole body felt cramped as Tess began to trade members of our groups back and forth between the two circles. We did frequently as it got later and we were almost asleep.

Keith Rios, Prescott Freshwater, or Tess Turnwell would pull you out of your chair and onto your feet if you nodded off. I had to stand behind my chair more than once. We stood until we could sit down and keep our eyes open a few minutes longer.

I was not the only one shivering. The staff tried to keep everyone talking. Normally four or five voices were going simultaneously in each circle. One girl admitted to having sex with two guys at the same time, and an hour later the number of marauders had grown to four!

At first she had made the acts sound voluntary, but her experience didn't sound consensual by the end of the propheet.

Tess's responses were always direct:

"How old were you?"

"Who were you with?"

"How did you get the marijuana?"

"How did the coke taste?"

"Where were you?"

"How did that make you feel?"

"What happened after that?"

"You just wanted to get fucked up, is that right? That's escaping. Want to say that again? That's right! I WANTED TO ESCAPE! FROM ALL YOUR FUCKING PAIN!"

Tess could get loud, when she had to.

"You're not going deep enough. I really want you to get honest. This is growing pains! Don't make us do the work for you! This isn't an interrogation! This is called sharing. When we share of ourselves it's because we trust those around us. And I trust you. And I know you trust me. It's going to go a lot faster if you own what you say.

"Keith, are you here to wipe their asses? No! Me neither.

"Is that why you're staying up all night with us, Prescott? NO! FUCK NO! It's time to get fucking real! To the degree that you feel sorry, to that same degree, you will feel forgiveness.

"When are you going to just let go, Ivy? Or you, Jamie? Let's get honest now!"

The longer we sat there – and it had already been a couple of hours – the uglier it all got. I fidgeted and then would become suddenly exhausted. Every few lengths of the song the staff switched a few of us with someone from the other circle. We repeated a lot of the disclosures more than twice, as twisted facts. The two groups exchanged people at a frenetic pace and it seemed that everyone now was fighting to stay awake. I started waiting for the sun, not in an "unacceptable" way – I mused on the Doors album and song title reference.

After turning the music up a notch and the lights down some more, Tess sat down and turned to Melanie.

147

"Melanie, I want you tell us how old you were when you started having sex. How many abortions did you have? Two, wasn't it? No, look up, honey, it's OK, if you need them there's some tissues. Micah, hand her a few. Yeah... I had an abortion, too. I was a bit older, it was in college. I never did finish, and that's something I will always live with. How old did you say you were?"

"It was last year. It was the same boy, OK? We broke up before I came here." Melanie had not stopped crying since before the bathroom break. Probably that's why Tess began with her.

"And did you tell your parents?"

"No, but they found out." Melanie wailed. "And then my father smacked my face and called me a sluuuhuuuut."

I consciously attempted to let my mind scramble out of the room while Melanie took more tissues from Micah's hands. Melanie smeared her salty fluids around the rest of her contorted face. Try as I might, I was still in the room.

"How many boys have you had oral sex with, Melanie?"

I sensed relief passing through the room, when Tess finally uttered these words.

Melanie gave Tess a skeptical and untrusting look through tears and rolled her eyes toward the ceiling. "uhchhUhchh, I don't know."

Tess's voice was gentle but tugging and insistent. "Well, it's not really a difficult question, is it? Two, five, twenty, fifty?"

"No! Fuck, what the fuck? Maybe, I don't know. Six."

"OK, thank you. And were you younger than any of these guys?"

Melanie answered, and Tess asked more questions. The processing of shame and guilt became more detailed. "Yeah, how old were you the first time? Yeah, only ten years old? Do you remember what you were wearing? Can you tell me where this happened?"

Boys weren't immune to sexual privacy invasions. My brain commanded my ears to try to leave, but I got hemmed in hearing Ernesto in the encounter behind me getting asked the same kinds of questions: How many girls had he fucked? Had sucked his dick? How many girls had he eaten out? When was the last time? Had he also ever tried to suck his own dick, like Ari? Had he ever sucked another boy's dick?

WHAAAAAAT?

Incredibility and shock sent the creepy meter shooting up to eight.

Staff: "Zack, eyes over here.

"And did you ever do that with two guys at the same time? It's OK. You did? How old were they? One was twenty? How old were you? About fifteen? OK. It's OK, Melanie, honey. You remember their names? You do? Go ahead and tell me their names. Where did this take place? In Marvin's car. You didn't really want to do that, did you? No, you just wanted them to like you. You wanted to be loved, right? Yeah. We're going to go into that. It's OK. Yeah. How do you feel right now?"

"Dirty!"

"Dirty. Yeah, it's OK to have that going on. Own it. Say, 'I am Dirty!'"

"I'm Diiiiirtyyyy! Shiiiiit."

"This is good work, Melanie. Yu-Yu, is this kicking anything up for you? You can't identify with anything Melanie is saying?"

"Uuuh. I don't really know."

"You don't, hunh? Well that's not really fair to the other people sitting in this room. Your PG. It's not fair to Melanie, either, to take safety away from the work that we're doing. Now, how many boys have you had oral sex with?"

As Tess waited for Melanie to come clean, she fixed on Chet.

"Chet, this is a safe place. These young men and women need to hear honesty and truth. Let them trust you! You've been with us a long time here at RMA. Since the beginning, right? Yeah. Well let's hear about your experiences growing up."

Chet looked at us. With a defeated sigh he made a facial expression like that of a condemned man. Chet's job depended on the appearance of having come clean. I didn't like most of the things I heard in that disclosure circle. As I moved through the program, I would hear the worst of the worst that staff and students would cop to. The perverse one-upsmanship of these insane midnight disclosure circles fed into the culture of confession.

"Let's get honest! To the degree that you feel sorry, to that same degree, you will feel forgiveness. When are you going to just let go, Ivy? Or you Jamie? Let's hear it all, my little brothers and sisters."

"I carved on my arms."

"I've punched myself in the face."

"I took girls' tampons from the house during work crews and jerked off on them."

"I tried to hang myself once when I was thirteen. I used my dad's necktie."

"Me and my big brother were driving down the street and I leaned out of the car and hit the guy with a bat. He fell down and didn't get up."

"My friend's father beat me and him with a belt one time when I was staying over."

"When I was seven and eight I used to lie down on the floor and let the girls in my grade school stand on my stomach. Then I'd look up their dresses."

"I felt so bad when my father died that I carved his initials on my leg. I did this with the X-Acto blade."

"I used to fuck one of my stuffed animals. I did this at least twenty times."

"I put ice cream on my pussy and let my dog eat me out when I was fourteen. I did this at least three times."

"I was molested by a retard. He was at my bus stop, and then my parents didn't believe me after it happened."

"I got like really high with one of my friends one time and we got some spray paint cans and went down to my school and spray-painted a bunch of shit about my principal on the wall."

"I was made to drown a bag filled with kittens in the Snake River. My stepfather made me do it."

"I used to smash caterpillars with a hammer when I was like nine or ten."

"My mother spanked me once when I was thirteen and I got a hard on."

"I put a zucchini from the farm in my pussy hole."

"I gave my little sister LSD when she was twelve."

"I ate a girl out when she was on her period. One time."

"One time when I was like six, I saw my parents having sex. I thought my dad was killing my mother."

"I blew two guys in the car when I was fifteen. They were both twenty. I let them come in my mouth."

"My babysitter used to get me high. Her boyfriend locked me in a closet for the night and threw lit cigarettes in with me. He threatened me with burning a lot after that."

"I used to steal and wear my stepmother's underwear."

"I got fingered during the movie in class in seventh grade."

"The first time I had sex, it was standing up in the rain next to a Mexican restaurant. I was only thirteen and the girl was fifteen."

"I had two abortions before coming here."

"I had sex with two girls at once. They were older, and one had a lot of tattoos."

"I had sex with two guys at once. I didn't want it to happen."

"I stole beer out of people's refrigerators and booze all the time."

"Me and four of my friends from school rolled a bulldozer tire into traffic and caused an accident. Yes, I know people were hurt. I don't want to talk about that."

"When I was like twelve or eleven, this was right before my father died, I got caught with a porno mag under my mattress. My mother showed my father in his hospital bed."

"I set fire to a shed of my neighbors and lied about it."

"I stole ten or twenty times out of my mother's purse."

"When I was in the Army, I was stationed with some guys, and well – we used to take off all of our clothes and sit in a circle. Each troop would sit on the finger of the guy on the right. I still go out on my wife sometimes."

"Once when I was like fourteen and we were on vacation in Maui and when my mom was getting ready for dinner, I opened her wallet and took all of the money. I ran away with my boyfriend and we bought drugs with it. Heroin."

"Me and my two friends stole a cigarette machine."

"One time I threw a firecracker at a friend from home and he shat his pants. It sounds funny, but I felt really bad. He was my friend."

"I used to run with a gang and we committed numerous assaults."

"We had a bottle rocket launcher and launched it at people walking down the street once. Our neighbor called the cops."

"I saw my brother got beat up real bad by my dad one time and I was so scared because I couldn't do nothing."

"My stepfather had a friend over once and he made me suck his dick."

"My uncle got me drunk one night after my parents went to sleep. He got me so drunk I threw up. I think something, you know, happened. I was so sick the next day."

"I watched my cousin take a shower when she came to visit. She could see me."

"God I hate talking about this. When I was fourteen – God, I was fourteen – I had sex with a horse. I set up a stepladder behind him and fucked him until I came. It happened at least three times."

"Well, about a month ago, before Victor left, God...he...well. I didn't – he sucked my dick. Like three times. I came six times. OK? Then when he refused the program it was because he was covering for me. OK?...No. Yeah, he had to leave because I'm dishonest."

"My brother used to jerk our dog off. I thought it was funny. Once my boyfriend came over and they got drunk and did that shit. Man, I don't fucking know. Don't ask me that, it was just funny at the time. Yes, it was abuse, OK, IT WAS WRONG! I AM SORRY. NO, it isn't funny. I do feel bad NOW! OK?"

"My father's best friend died about a year ago. AIDS, I think, but they said some kinda cancer. Now I think mom and dad getting a divorce had to do with Mr. Jinto dying." The boy was crying. "We were really close, he was like an uncle. Closer even. I grew up with him. But I got a letter from my mom and dad, and dad's coming out, like copping out to me about him and Mr. Jinto. They were gay."

It took some time to get the skinny.

Doing and saying the bare minimum, I was thinking smugly that I didn't even FEEL BAD about many of the things I personally had done. I thought pot was great. I didn't feel bad about the acts of sex that I had had, either. All that was going to change.

"I did cocaine," I said when it was my turn.

It was a bald-faced lie. They looked at me for more.

"Is that all?"

"My brother made me touch his dick when I was like four." I had just remembered that.

I had never been a liar and here I was telling them I did cocaine. That was a lie! And that other thing, which could have been my brother's disclosure – I was just a kid. It was kids playing doctor – not kids playing Deep Throat. This place, the circumstance, and the process all made me tell lies! I wondered who else in the room was alert to this contorted hypocrisy. Truth and lies mixed in the room as we came "clean" in the Truth propheet. That may have been one of the most foreign feeling things in the whole program – saying things, and then hearing the established parts of our stories brought up to us throughout the time we were there. Being reminded of the false image – which role the staff decided we would play.

The staff watched us with what appeared to be poker faces during the water break. I went into the bathroom to take a piss. I was as relieved to be out of the room as to go wee. I looked at my reflection in the mirror. Like everyone in the room that night, except Tess, I now wore an index card over my heart. Mine said LIAR, backwards in the mirror. My eyes were puffy though I hadn't been crying. My T-shirt seemed very red. I remembered something else Tess had said during my first rap. People wore red when they were angry.

I'll never wear a red shirt during a propheet or rap day again.

I patted some water on my face and washed my hands. I wished I had worn a different T-shirt, so I assisted in putting the chairs back into the horseshoe when I saw Keith and Chet doing it. Helping to put the chairs back didn't seem a thing an angry liar would do. I had to accept the card that said LIAR because I had denied the accusation.

But Ari, the kid who'd been on a full-time and joined my group for this propheet, wore the sign VOLATILE. He had been sent to Idaho for fighting with his twin brother. He got on his full-time for his dirt with Victor, but had copped out to some other gnarly things, too. I reflected on moments from earlier in the night. I knew why Ari really wore the word VOLATILE, but I still didn't understand why I should be wearing my word. The only thing I had lied about was knowing that Ernesto had huffed gas, and I stretched a couple of things because I didn't have the experience of others in the room.

We had all felt loss; we had all felt shame. How could I offer up my most shameful, darkest secrets to be placed on the altar this night? I didn't even know these people.

Is this what they do here – think and talk about everything bad you've ever done? Magnify every shame?

Why are they asking me these fucking questions?

Had Tess known already about my dirt with Ernie? Is that why I really wore LIAR? Maybe I was a liar because Tess actually knew I shouldn't be here, either?

Tess put "Somewhere" back on the speakers, and set the lights to a normal level. They told us to repeat all of our disclosures for a final time from our chairs for the whole group.

"COME ON," she barked. "This is your time to really get honest. When I say what you put into this is what you get out, I mean it. Coming out of the Truth propheet having copped out to all of the things you've done, or that you've had done to you, will free you. IT IS WHY we're in THIS ROOM. The truth will set you free. Just do it!"

Enlightenment through bumper stickers. "Just Do It!" This phrase was taken from a recent Nike advertisement sweeping the nation. Knowing that this phase of the Truth event would soon be over, we tried to give the most. Let's show the woman. She said what she wants. If the night would soon be over and we could stay sitting, perhaps even sleep, I'd perform. *Let's do this, people.* I gave my exaggerated, "most honest," worst account I could tell. The cocaine I'd suddenly "done" became a real situation I had to account for.

"Did you smoke it?" Tess wanted to know.

"Ummh yeah."

"And this was where?"

I quickly made up a story from something I had seen at home. These guys were smoking a bowl under the bridge while I was walking home. I just substituted the marijuana they smoked for cocaine and put myself in the picture. For me, it was not easy telling lies, but I felt I needed to keep up with the sexual and drug experiences my peer group had in their prior lives. I didn't even know you could smoke cocaine, but was weirdly relieved when Ernesto admitted to the same thing a few minutes later, thus confirming the "facts" of my own stories.

More than one person had smoked crack. Jasper and Micah both claimed snorting it in their previous lives, too. Staff members admitted to major drug use with disclosures that involved needles. *Maybe that explains why they work here.* Our assisting facilitator had injected heroin on many occasions and also admitted that he had administered cocaine to himself and his wife at least once. The adults always had the dirtiest dirt.

Sometimes the incriminating behaviors I admitted were things that my friends from home had seen or done. I wanted to have things to say! Like the rest of the individuals in the propheet, I added to my litany of disclosures several times over. I don't even know what I said; this propheet seemed infinite. Maybe we really had entered another dimension?

Some of the girls began contortionist acts into their flannels and sweatshirts in order to generate and conserve heat. We instinctively wanted to ball up in our chairs, so staff perpetually had to push our legs down to the floor. The staff wouldn't allow us to warm ourselves, actually, because just crossing our arms could, in this nut hatchery, be construed as being closed off to the sacred experience. While it felt good to be sitting down again, I was too cold and tired to keep awake. The five feet on the ground rule was just another stupid fucking Agreement. The staff couldn't prevent yawning so they used it to advantage. Much like knowing something about us by the clothes we had chosen to wear, Keith said that yawning was an indication that we were opening up to the experiences of the evening. Goddamn if I didn't start to believe these morsels of knowledge, these CEDU seedlings of truth.

As silly as it seems, I was gobbling up this information as gospel. Watching my peer group trade yawns around the horseshoe, I didn't see the next phase coming. Not even a little. It was inconceivable that we had not concluded. Now that we had all attested to all our "truths," I thought we had finished. Also, Hedwig the Owl-Woman, who had been so rigid for so long, let out a few uncontrollable, body-spasming yawns, herself. She was slowly moving toward the exit – which signaled a transition. She slipped out the door.

I couldn't believe my ears when Tess suddenly shut down the music. She blurted authoritatively from her puffy chair at the head of our horseshoe.

"Let's have a rap."

This has to be a joke.

But no. At that moment, a truly torturous experience began. Just when you thought the heat was taken off you, it would come back hotter than ever. In "normal" raps, after the group had shifted focus to another victim, the torment usually – not always, but usually – ended. The facilitator moved on to the next indictment or kid needing to take care of his or her emotions. In this one, though, the staff would go indicting people in no particular order. Because the propheet rap bled in with the earlier dirt and disclosure circles, the staff had more real parts of our stories, ammunition to use against us. And they could always refer to our "lie" cards as sick reference points to sustain our involvement.

Ernesto, fully reamed for his gasoline dirt, had been reduced to a lowly pile of human shame. He copped out to Tess where the gas had been stored and admitted, after she implanted the word, that he just wanted to "escape" for a few minutes.

Micah made a list of all the unacceptable bands he and Yu-Yu could think of. Keith barked, "Why do you think you would put so much energy into something that stupid? Did you and Yu-Yu get off on writing this list out? This is the exact reason why we have a fucking music Agreement."

Now we had to identify the reasons why we had done all the dirt we had copped out to. Why we had hurt our little doogers inside by doing all those things we had just disclosed.

Oh shit! They got us again.

We had copped to our dirt and disclosed our most personal secrets. But now Tess, Keith, and Prescott acted perturbed with us. We hadn't disclosed honestly enough. We didn't know how to be honest.

Prescott from Warrior staff represented: "You know while we were doing disclosures I could really tell a difference with how my Warrior guys are. It sounded like some of you were glorifying the experience. Why, Jamie, did you talk about the four-foot bong? You're a game wizard. Sounds like a glory story to me. You were just trying to show off for Wally and Ernesto, weren't you? Get real and cut the war stories. You got your dog high, what kind of a person does that? You know, tell me."

"A LOSER. I guess." Jamie publicly shamed himself.

A new term entered into our vocabulary. Telling "war stories" was different from disclosing what we felt bad about. It was jailhousing to tell glamorous war stories from before we arrived in Idaho. We were learning what the staff wanted. Our next two years were going to be about learning how to "get real" with our emotions and words. Eventually we'd be demanding this of ourselves, since there was something wrong with you if you didn't. After all, we were here at RMA for this emotional "treatment."

An adult junior staff in our group was grilled about his out-of-wed-lock flings and rampant drug usage before coming to the program. I wondered briefly whether RMA even paid the people who worked for them. It became clear that each propheet passenger had to say something to each person being indicted. I had a great desire to fold my arms over my chest or leave the room. I was again told not to be intellectual; the reason I was a liar was because I thought I was so honest. *They just want to get a rise out of me.*

"You don't get honest about feelings. You're always analyzing and pretending that your shit don't stink. But it does, you're a fucking snake. I hate how you sit like that. Do something to contribute to the safety of this experience, dude."

I knew what they meant, but hadn't I already heard this a dozen times? *How am I supposed to change what others thought of me?* The place didn't feel therapeutic. The room didn't seem safe. Tess and Keith jutted into the group's indictment: I probably felt worse than everyone there. I must be in denial, I was such a liar – I just didn't know what getting honest was, what it even meant to be real.

Our rap went on and on and on.

If Tess Turnwell was paid and raised to make us feel confused beyond description, and angry at having to watch staff pull everyone's chain, then she was doing great. I guess I really was right where I needed to be. I was focused on my peer group's faces. They were watching to see if I would break down as most others in the rap so far had done. To break down was to agree with the indictments or wind up crying. It was because I wouldn't get honest that I was pretending to be less emotional, Tess explained. Would I take the bait?

"You're not above the work we do here, Zack. I know how you think, I know what you are feeling, and one of these days you're going to have to find someone to trust. I'm not talking about me. I'm talking about anyone. But your peer group is here to hear about you. To learn to trust you. You want that, don't you?"

"Can I ask a question? Thanks. Um. How come I have to take care of my emotions? I mean, I don't feel like that, OK."

"You need to try to…"

"Why, though? I see the message, I'm in touch with what's going on, I don't know. Maybe my tear ducts are fucked up?"

"Well try it on. It's going to be like a big suit. Maybe a winter jacket, you'll grow into it, but you have to try. Your peer group is here for you. Fake it till you make it, right, guys?"

My peer group's eyes bounced between me and the staff, and heads nodded agreement. Tess had given me an out. I had a choice now. I could defend myself again, or I could try to gain an award by seizing into hysterics and lament. I did lament being there, and felt rotten enough about being put in the situation, and I knew there was more to it, but why stir up the sleeping dogs in my heart? I'd need more shame and guilt, more disclosures and dirt. I'd need deeper regrets. I'd have to look at how my mother and father's words and thoughts mattered to me so much. Only then I could build my trust for the process laid down in the CEDU propheets.

Or was it that the angry, trapped feelings I had about being in Idaho weren't satisfactory? I wasn't completely satisfied with my whole life before attending RMA, or this goddamn rap at four in the morning. I could admit that. But to admit that I was a liar and a runaway because of family abuse? A user of girls, and a druggie to cover all my pain? I couldn't admit it. It just wasn't really in me at that point. Nor did any of my story seem glorious, either. I was too upset to consider the possibility of ending Tess's indictments by launching a breakdown. Nor would I give her the satisfaction of proving to everyone that I needed to be at RMA. If I had a breakdown and freaked out, if I yelled back at the peer group to "get honest" with them, if I screamed that I DID NOT NEED to be here, and that every single tidbit of knowledge they believed was bullshit, then the evidence would favor Tess' bias. The group would go back to calling me a liar. Just sitting and not falling asleep was my contribution to self-introspection.

Back home, the term "intellectual," as part of a description about a man or woman, would be a compliment.

During the rap George kept insinuating that perhaps there were WORSE things I had done, perhaps things I couldn't even admit in this safe environment. "I'll bet he's like that because there's things he can't even remember. Why don't you reflect on that?"

How could I lie about feelings I didn't have or know I had?

I sat there taking the indictments. Evidently, by not being as emotional as everyone else, I was either covering up horrible things in my life, or at the minimum, being resistant. Though the indictments stung, I wasn't going into hysterics. I hadn't been grilled to the point of explosion yet. I glanced at a girl in my peer group with the label USED and groaned with dissatisfaction into the horseshoe.

I'll try something different. I'll practice what Tess wants, even if the feeling is as uncomfortable as drowning in raw sewage.

Performing for the first time like my mortal life hinged on being convincing, I pretended to be upset. I was upset because of the situation – not because of the things that I was supposed to be upset about. In the Truth prophet rap that night, as much as I tried to cry, I was still detached and conscious of not wanting to look deeply at my issues with my mother and father – at how my dooger had been hurt. As much as I yelled back to Tess the things I had been called when I was younger – the meanest, lowest, harshest things anyone had ever said to me – I was not connected to what I said. But I'd tapped into something deep within. It's just that exposing it that night, at Tess's command, wasn't on my agenda. Or in my syllabus – I'm not sure which.

I didn't have words to express what I was really feeling: I felt like there was something moldering in my stomach – fermenting. It would take time to recognize, reduce, and then produce the expected emotional results. Although I was very stirred up, I was not capable of the emotional degradation that my first prophet demanded. I had "got into my feelings" sufficiently to get me off the hot seat for the final round of the marathon rap. It was clear I felt sufficiently miserable despite the lack of tears.

Keith turned to torpedo Ivy for a third time. "'Easy Ivy,' is that what they said? Why'd they say that, you think?"

I watched Ivy clam back up.

We weren't supposed to be resistant like that anymore.

Keith had used against her one of her own confidential thoughts, something Ivy had allowed herself to divulge, under the guise of safety. It was pure betrayal. They did it to all of us. However, Ivy received a lot of negative attention. That I couldn't do anything for Ivy angered and emasculated me.

George Daughtry jumped in. "Yeah, Ivy, I don't talk to you that often, but I can totally see what Tess and Keith are saying. All this time you were thinking about splitting and you never ONCE CAME AND TALKED TO ME. That's what I'm here for!"

"Ivy, don't you want to talk some more about the things that Melanie and your peers are talking about tonight?"

Keith feigned compassion.

"Do I have to?"

"WHY DON'T YOU LOOK! Look at what you've done! Your boyfriend says 'fuck my friend' and you did it! That's what YOU NEED TO LOOK AT. People walk all over you, and YOU LET

THEM! Do you want to BE A DOORMAT FOR THE REST OF YOUR LIFE? THIS IS IMPORTANT, GODDAMMIT, I CARE ABOUT YOU! Tell me what's the name of that little girl?"

"This doesn't matter..."

"Unfold your arms, don't cover that little girl up. Come on, what's her name again? That beautiful little girl?"

"You won't even say it? It's Lovey-Dovey, right? That's a lovely thing, Ivy. That's special. Why'd you think you did those things for, what was his name...?"

"Brandon. For the fucking last time my boyfriend's name is Brandon and I miss him..."

Ivy started to cry. I hadn't been allowed to talk to Ivy and still I knew she had a boyfriend. I wished the girls from home I thought about would miss me, as Ivy seemed to miss Brandon.

"Yeah, but honey, don't you think it came out of a need for acceptance to do those things? It's pretty fucked up, isn't it? Your need for acceptance. Can you admit that at least? Do you want to end up needing that acceptance from outside yourself for the rest of time?"

"You can't even take a look at that little dooger because of all the shit you put her through. AND SHE'S STILL COMING LAST, ISN'T SHE? WHEN'S IVY GOING TO TAKE CARE OF IVY?"

I refused to say mean things to her.

My whole PG was starting to show signs of exhaustion. All I did at this stage of the propheet was listen to the weeping and yelling, while holding my head in my hands, staring at the carpet, feeling crappy. I felt crappy about so much, I wasn't yet sure what I felt crappiest about.

I didn't know what to do with my feelings or my memories. And I didn't know how to escape. There were bears outside. How would I avoid them? How could I get back to Virginia with no money and no cigarettes?

Disclosures – including a few things that probably hadn't even happened – and all the things we hadn't thought about until this night, were turned into indictments. Things got confused. Shame was the game. Kids were indicted on disclosures that hadn't even been theirs! My peer group was too tired to correct the inaccuracies, and so we owned the false testimony from staff. It was more important for the staff to keep yelling, than to be accurate. I was stupendously embarrassed, bitter, confused, and tired. I was angry at being called a liar endlessly. I was mad at myself for being intellectual, and not knowing how to surrender.

Although the facilitating counselors and older students mostly carried out the rap, every kid also had to be indicted by every other adult and kid in the horseshoe. Confess, immolate, shame, and repeat. And repeat some more. We must have gone through the wash five times.

✝

> To guide students, the academy has selected a committed faculty of men and women with backgrounds rich in educational and life experiences. Each individual brings to the school a diversity of strengths to contribute to our curricula.
>
> The physical and emotionally secure environment created by our faculty is vital to the achievements of RMA. Much of the program's success depends on the foundation of trust which develops between the faculty and students. Honest and open in their responses to student behavior, the faculty offers feedback that is supportive, confrontational or even both.
>
> —RMA brochure

✝

Hungry.

Even the wrinkled parent facilitators and the older students had been severely, verbally beaten on. George Daughtry had been unbelievably harsh to Ari. And Ari's disclosures had grossed me out. I tried not to judge, but I was freaked. Nobody but Tess, Keith, and George had been spared. Some sun oozed into the room when the rap finally ended and Tess again reminded us that what we put into this experience would be what we got out of it. She read about joy and sorrow again from the tattered book by Gibran. My attention waned the more I tried to focus on the words. She closed the book and promised us that we were only feeling joy missing, at that moment, and that the misery we were all feeling was actually joy.

Just not yet.

We'd feel joyous later, for the work we did.

Of course I wanted to feel better. I started questioning myself. This made me feel worse – and that was good. This was the truth: it was good to feel bad, and the worse we felt, the more we hated ourselves, the more joy we'd feel.

When?

That wasn't revealed, or perhaps I hadn't listened carefully enough to the prophet's words during Tess's reading? My parents knew this was the right place – and were even jealous of what my PG was going to learn here. So Nat, Hedwig the Owl's husband, had said in the Monday meeting that week. This propheet was the beginning phase of a metaphorical climb to the CEDU summit. I was, at occasional moments that evening, convinced that I needed the life changes I would experience in Idaho.

Maybe there really is something wrong with me.

There could be truth in some of the insights that had upset me most during the prophetic night called Truth. Especially the ones filed in the red binder where my worst-seeming moments seemed to live. Most of them had to do with Mom and Dad. My PG didn't like me, and made needsy indictments. They agreed with WHATEVER Tess or another counselor put out there.

There is something wrong with me.

I'm not going to look.

"You are right where you need to be."

Tess repeated the platitude twice more, making significant eye contact with each of us to make sure we were awake and staring at her. Tess's voice was a little hoarse. Some puffiness and a glaze of exhaustion were forming around her eyes. She turned and flipped the tape player's volume up, and instructed us to stack our black chairs again. We stored them in the corner as before.

It was probably three hours that we were allowed to sleep, or maybe it was only three minutes. We lay on the floor. No blankets, no pillows, and no silence.

The music played over and over. Tess whispered to me.

Had I been sleeping, maybe? Had Tess woken me?

I hated seeing her face. I'd never felt this upset just for being woken by anyone. Barbra was still wailing.

Just let me sleep, you fucking bitch!

Tess wanted me to wake the group. I shook off the grumpy as we crawled over to where Melanie lay. Tess put one hand on her shoulder, the other hand stroking her gently on the face and head until Melanie opened her eyes. Tess instructed me to gently wake everyone as she had woken Melanie. I didn't want to do that. But I did as instructed.

I started with Ivy. She woke, but clearly was disturbed to still be in Walden. In Idaho. My face was probably having the same effect on her that Tess's had on me. She rubbed her eyes as I went on to Micah, then to Ernesto, and on and on until everyone was awake. The whole time I couldn't be sure I wasn't still dreaming.

I didn't want to touch my peer group, but the touching told me I was in a wakeful state. Every kid in the room had been a shithead to me a few hours before. *Don't forget*, I corrected myself, *you said a few nasty things to Jamie and others.*

I wished I hadn't – it had only transpired because I was compelled to fit in – do what staff, and by inference, my parents wanted, not because I meant any indictment I'd made.

Or maybe I had? I was back to confused.

Tess perched in her chair watching the process. She waited until everyone was awake. She mouthed "Good Morning" to each one as they looked to me, and then to her with looks that said, "Not again, let me go back to sleep, please."

The male staff, snoring loudly, were hardest to wake. I left them for last.

Tess paused the music on the stereo console, whispering for us to go quietly to the mudroom and use the rest rooms. We were all on bans.

In a wild change-up, we were to put our shoes back on afterwards.

We followed the older students on a silent walk. I was finally out of the building, but because it was daylight, being out of Walden didn't have the accompanying level of freedom that I'd been craving. It didn't even feel like my legs were still attached to the rest of me as I trudged through ferns next to the path. All of me was heavy and tired. We ambled around silently in the forest for about thirty minutes.

Returning to the building at Jasper's quiet order, we noticed kitchen ladies coming up the trail with stacks of paper plates. My PG exchanged quick glances. We would eat. The kitchen staff converged on Walden and soon walked out empty-handed from the building. We heard a truck start up. As it growled away slowly, the growling in my stomach took over.

Back inside the propheet building, after we removed our shoes, the sun flooded in from behind the fitted placards. Awakened by the walk and the sun and the prospect of food, we temporarily exchanged exhaustion for hunger. A bowl of mustard accompanied the sandwiches – yuck! The sandwiches were on paper plates, each with a handful of plain potato chips. The sandwiches were crappy, small, and wholly unsatisfying, but we were all ravenous. The food disappeared quickly. I had a finger scoop of mustard after wolfing down my cheese sandwich. I don't like mustard.

"Lunch" was to become my one bright memory of the event. Call me sarcastic.

Walden had been returned to its original state. Fresh tissue boxes. The garbage that had accumulated during the night was gone. The floor had been vacuumed. Because the sun was spilling out from behind the cardboard shades, and because of the miserable rap that had occurred in the room, Walden's sanctuary no longer had its fake appeal and tin majesty. For a moment I forgot that this night and day would actually end. Was this tired and half-fed state of inner turmoil going to be my new "normal"? All I really wanted to do was go back to sleep. Instead, we were back to sitting in the freshly reset horseshoe.

Tess talked for a while about what it meant to be part of this "special place." Though we were still new, we should understand that being in agreement was a necessary part of "agreeing" to be here. It was never agreeing to STAY, I would note in my journal; it was always agreeing to BE here. She continued to harangue about the "work" we had done in Walden together.

Our "Lie" cards were ritualistically replaced with new ones. Of course, mine now proudly read HONEST and everyone told me what a nice guy they thought I was.

The next couple of hours nothing miraculous happened except that Tess and Keith found nice things to say about each of us, exchanging negative comments for positive truths. While my index card – my Truth card –now had HONEST on it, others had LOVING, AC-CEPTING, FORGIVING, and COURAGEOUS on theirs. Everyone said something positive about each individual. We were encouraged to bring these freshly discovered positive qualities on our new Truth cards to our campus life.

Tess and Keith smiled and pretended to be proud of us and suggested that we all get into a big smoosh pile. It felt really creepy to be touched. All these people had just been yelling at each other. At first, I resisted the necessity to join this pile, but I had to acquiesce when I was the only one still sitting in a black chair. I knew that the propheet wouldn't end so long as there was conflict. I chose the most outside place of the body pile and lay my head on someone's thigh. The stench of body odor heightened in the smoosh pile, but so did the feeling of relief that the propheet was finally ending. We remained like that, in a smoosh pile, gently stroking one another's hair, listening to "Somewhere" for the 757th time.

It seemed my body was vibrating and spinning around in space like the few times at home I had gone to sleep drunk. The spinning wore off. I just wanted the music to stop, if I could stand up. I opened my eyes and the world spinning in my head slammed to a halt. I glanced at the rest of the smoosh pile. The music dizzied me anew and a sickening feeling pervaded my chest and stomach.

I felt bonding love and empathy for my peer group.

I felt guilt and hatred, and guilt for my hatred that overshadowed my empathy for these kids.

The sun started to go low in the sky. Eyes were heavy again, and Chet Lively started to snore. Keith used his soft voice to wake Chet and say there was one last thing to do before we could join the house. We were instructed to take the crayons and markers and paper that Chet and Kelly provided in order to make more cards for more of our big brothers and sisters. We all wrote what was expected: mushy, stupid, childish, and appreciative notions on the colorful, folded pieces of card stock. We appreciated their support, and wouldn't they remind us to slow down, and help us regain our truth qualities as needed?

"Dear Paul, I'm supposed to write somebody new, but I'm writing to you instead. Don't tell anybody. Boy, the Truth was really special. I'm so glad it's over. Let's trade stories."

For a final time we were directed into the little mudroom of Walden. The rest of the mysterious building beckoned me. What would happen in the other propheets? What was in the rest of the building called Walden? Why was it called Walden? We put our boots and shoes back on and used the bathroom. We all tucked in our shirts and held hands in a big daisy chain, up along the stone bordered path that we couldn't see the previous night.

The walk back to the known part of the campus was shorter than it seemed in the dark. We filed past the freestanding building, Denali, where the warm-up had been, past the Papoose family room, and up the final wooden stairs to the main house.

Twenty-one hours had elapsed, according to Keith's watch. Though tired, and still hungry, I also felt a heightened awareness. My senses were more awake. The faces in the house wore smiles. The dogs that ran by on our brief walk seemed extra playful and joyful. The kitchen staff, in their hairnets, stopped what they were doing, potholders in mid-air, and proudly watched us make our entrance. Barbra's redundant, mystical song played. I had every second of it memorized.

We could smell dinner. All staff and students at the academy congregated to see our Truth propheet "come out." Barbra's song congealed out of the speakers extra loudly. The song became a character, removed from the propheet room, like a spirit I'd communed with. It still made my brain mushy and clouded. The house seemed a colorful dream with a cloudy periphery. Our school-appointed big brothers and sisters approached us with soft, knowing looks on their faces.

Paul Renssalaer, who gave me my orientation tour and would be graduating soon, approached me. In an awkward routine that he clearly knew better than I, we did a little performance, along with the rest of my PG and their biggest brothers and sisters. Paul exchanged the wildflowers he'd picked for the card in my hand. These Summit grads, who would graduate in a couple of weeks, were like titans or mini-gods. At least that's how I would think of them while I was immersed in the RMA lifestyle. After graduation day, it was mandatory that Summit grads leave the program. If they wanted to come back and work they were supposed to wait a year – and they couldn't even visit for the next six months.

Paul had told me he was considering this, "before college, to help me cope with the outside."

Right now, he was singing at me: "Za-acky, I am so glad to share this legacy of light with you. You learned the first of many steps to the Summit tonight. In fact, in many ways, it's the most important step. And now you know. Not to drink the water! I'm just kidding. No, the truth – ME knows that you're a little brother I really care about. I'm going to be here for you one hundred percent before I graduate. I really care about you, man. Love you, bro."

The compassionate expressions on our oldest older brothers' faces were genuine, and their shares sincere. They knew we'd been sad, tired, angry, confounded, ashamed, and befuddled during the 24-hour experience. We traded the cards we had made for the flowers in their hands – and long, sticky, semi-mandatory hugs – and plopped down on the carpet. Paul seemed a slightly brighter, more animated version of himself since the day of my tour. He still reminded me of an empty glove, but there was an awakened exuberance because he was going into the final weeks of mind melding, and would then be released back to California.

We endured two last plays of background "Somewhere," while each one of us had to say something about what we had learned during the endless preceding night. Some were crying when they shared, especially Tess. I thought it strange, since she and Keith were the only ones who hadn't had anything done to them. What did Tess have to cry for, anyway? Nobody called her a bitch or a whore, nobody was there to call her out on her disclosures or accuse her of manipulating the group!

Tess and Keith had never worn Lie cards. To follow the facilitator would be a tough act. I made sure there was some time after Tess before it was my turn to share. I went after Ernesto shared about his experience in the Truth, and his promise to try to stay within agreement. Some of the house and staff chuckled at Ernesto's attempt at what they apparently thought an empty commitment.

I stood weakly and the wafting smell of ground beef made me start to salivate as the eyes in the house moved to me. "I just want to say that the Truth is not what I was expecting. But I feel a lot more a part of the community here now, and I'm going to try to continue to be as honest as possible about myself. Oh, and I feel really 'slowed down' right now, and I am glad it's over, though it was really magical."

We all said something, and it was finally over. I couldn't believe taco salad could taste so good. That night the rest of the students paid special attention to my peer group and me. Smooshing didn't seem quite so strange.

Most mental-health experts today strongly disagree with the use of brutal confrontation or humiliation as therapy — particularly for vulnerable youths who have troubled pasts. Research suggests that feelings of being out of control characterize the typical patient's response to traumatic life events; consequently, recovery requires the avoidance of coercion. Experts say that pressuring trauma victims to retell their stories against their will tends to increase stress symptoms rather than alleviate them. And brain research associates feelings of shame and humiliation to stress responses that exacerbate depression and anxiety and may contribute to physical illness. In addition, isolation from parents, except in situations where they are abusive, can increase trauma further.

"There is absolutely no role for shame and humiliation in the treatment of youth," says Christopher Bellonci, medical director of the Walker School, a nonprofit serving children with serious mental, behavioral and learning problems. "I know of no clinical rationale for treating youth for any condition in that fashion ... They are engendering new trauma, not repairing it."

—Maia Szalavitz, "An Oregon School for Troubled Teens Is Under Scrutiny," *Time*, 17 April 2009

SEVENTEEN

> Guess what I went through my truth prophet August
> 9 & 10 and I found out that basically I was a dick at
> home. I have been mulling it over in my mind and I
> know the point of raps and prophets. Just to make
> you cry a lot so naturally being the way I am I didn't
> cry.
>
> —Author journal entry, 11 August 1988 (one month
> at RMA)

The lunch menu schedule was my guide for knowing what day it was and how I would be. Pizza, the single best meal at RMA – most delicious and cheesy – significantly signaled two Wednesdays of every month. Besides well-prepared Sunday brunches, and the taco bar every other Friday night, pizza was the only meal with cheese. We were limited to only two slices per kid of the hand-made, rectangular slices of pizza pie, to make sure that every person received their fair share. The day wouldn't be as good as it should – because it was a rap day – but the pizza itself would be awesome.

I despised the contradiction of reward and punishment, and the idea that food was merely fuel. Monday's French Dip sandwiches meant I had to eat a rap that day, too. Perfectly good pizza on Wednesdays and filling deli sandwiches on Friday were also tainted with the poisonous knowledge that it was also a rap day.

I was doing my best to process the place, putting it all together so I understood what I didn't understand. Information gathering was still my secret mission. My exit strategy required assistance from the rest of the world. I needed access to a phone, and somehow, time for its private use to present my case to my dad. My brain rattled because I didn't have an ally. Even the guidance counselor who'd always been sort of trustworthy couldn't help me now. I didn't have my shrink's phone number.

It was up to me to advocate to my dad: I understood that change had been needed. I learned my lesson. Now I had demands.

Days were redundant. I went on autopilot, doing my chores and cutting wood with the Papoose family. In the afternoons I was pulled up in raps a few times for being sullen and keeping to myself. It was said I came off as arrogant and headsy. Staff talked to me like my truth and my lie were the most important concepts ever to be learned. I had a confidence in me that remained intact, and according to the program, this self-confidence was a game.

For a few days after the Truth propheet, the program was easier on my peer group and me. The place was more tolerable, and the conflict about remaining there tore at me less. I acclimated to the yelling in raps a bit more.

Then, RMA look-goods and staff were no longer impressed that I'd gone through my Truth propheet. The dread of attending raps reattached to my PG and me. Staff said horrible things to young people to stoke emotional responses. The program felt unjust enough to remind me that another word besides kidnapped was needed to identify my supposed commitment to remain here.

Sequestered.

I found the word in the dictionary:

Sequester:
VERB (USED WITH OBJECT)
1. to remove or withdraw into solitude or retirement; seclude.
2. to remove or separate; banish; exile.
3. to keep apart from others; segregate or isolate: The jury was sequestered until a verdict was reached.
4. Law. to remove (property) temporarily from the possession of the owner; seize and hold, as the property and income of a debtor, until legal claims are satisfied.
5. International Law. to requisition, hold, and control (enemy property).

✝

This was pertinent to any further case I would present to my dad, I thought, as I took my chair in yet another rap.

I had already seen four guys and two girls run away since my Truth propheet. Half of them, new Papooses who would be part of the peer group that was currently forming, were returned within 24 hours. One of the girls was pretty. She split again two days after being returned, and never came back after that. She had joined the ranks of the even-numbered peer groups. We knew it was unwise to talk about the even-numbered PG members – the people who'd split and not returned. They were gone, and weren't "ready to be there" yet.

People continued to get dirty and run away even when they were in the upper school, but we lower-schoolers were expected to be dirtbags, out of agreement, splitting so frequently that a healthy percentage would join the even-number PG's, never to be seen again. We would wake up, and somebody else would be gone. It was easy to grow accustomed to the very slim idea that perhaps our time there was temporary; we could – and couldn't – always choose to leave. But what about all the absentees that split? I was sure I was going to be one of them. Did all those not-odd kids who didn't make it go insane, or get killed in car accidents or die by suicide? Would I become a ghostly member of PG 30? PG 32? I liked the idea of being odd, but not the idea of staying in Idaho.

At the wood corral I swung the mallet into the iron wedges, splitting four-foot rounds of wood and meditating on the Truth propheet. I recalled the most recent raps I'd been in, and noticed that the older students' behavior in the raps still had me puzzled and a little afraid. Eventually, they implied, I'd be that "in touch" with catharsis and my personal emotions. Watching people get in touch, and "take care of their feelings," I just couldn't become acclimated to the perpetually shifting content.

Taking care of your feelings – the term applied to any emotional behavior in a rap – seemed to be the program's primary focus. For the newer kids who were in Brave and Papoose, emotionally charged material was demanded. The staff needed our tears and rantings the way vampires craved and killed for blood.

The only means to gaining respect in this place was longevity in the program. Lower schoolers risked being accused of manipulating the group if they tried to appear more program-mature than they really were. As a Papoose, I didn't know the tools of the upcoming propheets. It really didn't matter whether I remained mute or went into hysterics of crying, laughing, praying, cursing, or agonizing over the unfairness of raps. As Papooses we were perpetually reminded that we had no ownership yet, no work ethic of which to be proud.

We weren't even able to meet the strict level of expected cleanliness in our dorm spaces and personal attire. New kids weren't allowed to have shirts with collars; whereas older students would look presentable at night, the best we could do was tuck our flannels into one of two pairs of work jeans. And as for the dorm spaces, we weren't allowed to have the totems that made a bunk space home-feeling. The plain wood in Papoose bunk spaces looked like the occupant didn't care. As for the bed's tightness: our comforters were new, and because they hadn't been washed a dozen times, they bunched up. My bed never looked as tight as Crosby's or Jasper's. The excuses seemed stupid but raps made them important.

I didn't have any seniority, so I didn't have a way to make people stop indicting me. There was no correct answer I could give to CE-DU's questions. Outside influences – the far-removed parents, the day of the week, and staff – determined how bad I would feel that day. I didn't yet know how to make rap days tolerable, so that was three out of seven days I almost couldn't live through.

Often indictments toward me would begin with breaking bans, since I was still getting the hang of who was in which family. They were light indictments, compared to what we'd been through in the Truth, but they showed me I was still estranged from a large part of the student body. I didn't know how to fit in here, and I didn't know that I wanted to. I did have "school issues"; I hadn't done well in years. I brought it up in raps if I thought I could cut short a series of indictments. There was only one line to walk. I didn't want to be dirty, or segregated. Nor did I really want dish duties, bans, and WD's.

I'm still here; how long do my parents expect me to actually stay here?

I was never going to be a rat or a look-good, I was sure of that. Even a few upper schoolers weren't able to pull that off. We'd see them in Friday raps because dirtbags and surfers like them were never going to make it to the pinnacle of Summit and graduate. Kids who continued to get out of agreement, or who attempted to surf their way through the program without living by its unwritten bylaws of self-deprecation and verbal assault on others, didn't make it past Warrior family, the third tier.

There was no way I could succeed here.

I lived in angst. How did people perceive me? My new paranoia and superstition didn't classify as fear to me. But I didn't know shit about shit, as Keith had reminded me in the Truth.

Peering at an atlas in the library during a Saturday morning work crew gave me a better idea of where in the USA I was. I marveled at how far we traveled for my father to dump me here. Now that I learned what a panhandle was, and how far Idaho itself was removed from civilization, it was an additional shock. According to the 1977 atlas, RMA was in the vacant and removed part of the vacant and removed part of the USA. I'd soon learn that there were many people living in the area who didn't even want to be considered Americans.

It was not going to be possible to tolerate RMA. I'd been biding my time until I could see my parents, or at least talk on the phone without some brainwashed freak in the electronically monitored Bridge. Any passing thought that I could see this thirty-month program through, or remain sane in Idaho, had dissipated.

I had heard my parents might be visiting Idaho soon, for an RMA parent event at a resort. Maybe if I saw them in person, we could resolve things and I could go home.

✝

Is there a parent support program?

A series of Parent seminars are offered to parents and step-parents 3 times per year, which provide the opportunity for greater understanding and communi- cation between faculty and parents as well as specific information about adolescence, the Rocky Mountain Academy program and your child's progress. A visit with your child is part of each weekend workshop.

—RMA New Parent Handbook

✝

We are pleased that you plan to attend the Sep- tember 1-4th, 1988 Rocky Mountain Academy Parent Seminar in Coeur d'Alene. We're sure you'll find that you participation in the seminar will give you a better understanding of the CEDU education process.

...There is time set aside on the weekend for visiting your child. Please understand that these visits must follow the guidelines recommended by the school and can be re-adjusted or cancelled at the advice of your child's counselor and/or School Director.

As this will be your first visit since your child's enroll- ment it will be an "on campus" visit. ....Remember the purpose of the visit with your child is to re-establish your relationship. This is not a vacation but a time to develop a positive parent/child understanding, show your love and support and to assist them in their growth.

—RMA "Dear Parents" letter, 8 August 1988

✝

Not knowing for sure if my parents would visit Idaho soon, I left RMA without making another phone call, or seeing my parents.

My stewing turned toward planning my escape. I was just waiting to find someone to split with – someone who could hold their own, or was from the West. Finding a person from back East who could afford the gas, owned a car, and would drive three or four days straight seemed unlikely. I couldn't think of anyone besides my brother who met the criteria – and he was in England for his own boarding school experience, not that he'd ever consider such a wild proposal.

I was damn near Canada though! Where could I split to? I might have to be a vagrant until I turned eighteen: three and a half years of fugitive living. I was considering it, though little understanding the details of what it would mean to be truly homeless – not in my home-town – not just running away from camp or Mom and Dad to party with older drunken rednecks.

I ran a drill, waking up in the middle of the night and dressing quickly. I went to where the dirt RMA road met Route 1. My palms were wet, my heart pounding for fear of discovery. If they found out that I wasn't at La Mancha in my bunk, I might end up getting ripped a new asshole. That's what happened to Ari, for the same reason, in Darlayne's rap some weeks ago.

Now I know what he was really doing out that night.

I had to go back, yet I knew I had to plan – without knowing what exactly I was planning for. After sitting in the woods just off campus for an hour in total despair, I went back. How could I store some food without Jasper finding out? Where could I get a flashlight? Could I get into Skinner without the night watchmen seeing me? What about the house? Was it worth it to sneak into the one accessible room with a phone, in the Bridge, right in the middle of the main lodge at night? I resolved to answer that question soon.

Back in La Mancha, as I lay in my bunk, I reflected that there'd been several incidents at home for which my wick could be blamed, or at least half blamed. I thought about the first girl I had sex with. We'd done it about ten times. I tried to not feel guilty for my desire, and fell asleep in the August heat. I dreamed about home. One dream involved the first girl I French kissed. It was one of the most pleasurable moments I'd ever experienced, with better moments soon following. Two dreams like this reminded me that girls really could be the reason I wound up here.

I had run away from Camp Minnehaha for a girl, and even before that, I'd hitched 45 miles from my parents' house one night. My brother was baby-sitting my sister, and, truth be told, he'd promised to buckle the baby up and drive me to the next county. But when his own girlfriend came over after he put our sister in the crib, he didn't seem to notice or care that I'd left them alone in the house. I wasn't the little brother he thought I was, and if I could have found Mom or Dad's keys, as I spent fifteen valuable minutes attempting, I'd have driven myself the 45 minutes to my girlfriend in the style and luxury of Swedish Saab engineering. The next morning, Dad was really pissed. So I walked out, jumped on a bike, and got the fuck out of there. Running away from Dad, I felt a different quality of anger, compared to running away from Mom.

At times I felt staff indictments were unforgivable and completely out of touch. I resented the adults for using the sequestration against us, daring us either to stand up for ourselves or defy their persecution. I reflected on the strange goings on I had already seen.

Was I witnessing catharsis? What the fuck was catharsis?

In raps, sex was one of the most openly talked about subjects at RMA. The rest of the time it was taboo. In fact, talking about sex in a rap was both dreaded and perversely desired. Perhaps because of this, the guilt, shame, and anger that students were expected to feel at RMA, often manifested as sexual content, especially for female students, in raps. The consequences for having been born in a female body seemed unlucky for girls sent to Idaho.

Guys who were new, like me, weren't allowed to touch the girls. It seemed that touching privilege was reserved for the older students and staff. Conversely, it was practically mandatory to be touchy with people of the same sex. Yep. Some uncomfortable things would be in store for any kids who decided to permit sequestration and become an oddball graduate. Suppressing a light shudder, I thought about the smell of our smoosh circle on the second day of the Truth propheet. Soggy socked feet, body odors, expired adrenaline, and bad breath lingered in memory, to the ghostly soundtrack of that wretched Barbra Streisand snot ripper.

It was a sure guess that people foreign to the inner workings of CEDU were not invited on campus at night. I never witnessed a stranger in our midst at night, unless they were returning alumni or staff. The touching-smooshing business, in piles or smoosh circles, was too strange for visitors to understand. Public displays of emotions, loud crying – I could scarcely decipher the unspoken rules myself. To interpret the laws of smooshing I guess I needed fuller indoctrination, or un-sexing, perhaps. Or maybe they wanted us gay. Or turned into animals, or Peeping Toms, so staff would have more dirt to use to make us feel ashamed.

At the end of a day at the wood corral, I strapped on my new shoes. After wearing only work boots for a month, the new kicks felt foreign, like pillows on my feet. Someone had handed me a shoebox the day before, telling me it was from my parents. I figured they waited to give us regular shoes until we'd gotten our ups and downs – only then could we be trusted not to run away. Anyway, it turned out that when I left I wasn't wearing those new shoes my Mom sent.

†

When should I send winter or summer clothing?

As needs for additional clothing arise, parents will be informed. Specific descriptions and sizes will be provided to help you choose appropriate clothing items. We ask that you send no more than requested at that time.

—RMA New Parent Handbook

†

"And it wasn't dirty what I did. I just told him he didn't have the words right. You know I actually have a question. I'm NOT making cracks in music. But is ZZ Top acceptable?" I called into the dorm from the deck of La Mancha as I pulled on a green-checkered flannel. My dorm head Jasper shot me a dirty look.

"Unacceptable."

Jasper's sour look told me that I should never again mention the rock band ZZ Top, name or hum their songs, or make cracks in the Agreement by imitating the Texas brothers' famous beards and spinning guitars. This was one of the weirdest Agreements in the place. Conversations about music were restricted, to protect members of Papoose and Brave families, and to prevent fraternizing. The music Agreements kept us from collating information. The staff were looking for split contracts; breaking the music Agreement was gateway dirt.

In staff logic, if you were willing to cut up unacceptable music, you were just as likely to fuck a girl in the woods and huff gas from the lawnmower before you split. The music that they did play at RMA served to unify us, and it wasn't long before we sang along to any tune with lyrics. All the Cat Stevens, James Taylor, and Barbra Streisand you can't stand, was aimed to erase our pre-Idaho self-images.

Though I had earned my up and down privileges a couple of weeks before, I still waited at La Mancha for Crosby Rohrback, my dorm support, to walk up to the house. This showed that I was social and open. He was one of the rich kids – his dad was the founder and CEO of Atomic Industrial Concepts – but he still seemed as fucked up as the rest of us. We had an appointment with Tim to watch Paul's PG reappear on the campus when their Summit workshop got out. They had just finished the last milestone in the CEDU program, and we hadn't seen them in over a week. All Papooses had been ordered to dine and spend time until the Summit arrival with our most special older brothers and sisters.

Jasper followed Crosby onto La Mancha's deck. "Crosby, tell this little dirtbag to stop with his music cracks. He's as bad as you were, you know!"

I hadn't considered that they had both once been dirtbag Papooses themselves.

"Jasper, you are a fucking pain in the ass to have for an older brother, and I can't stand smelling your farts in the morning, but I love you." Crosby closed in on Jasper for a tight, though platonic, hug. Jasper ruffled our dorm support's hair. They each linked their arms in mine and we loped down the steps and headed up to dinner.

The lodge was awash with excitement and chatter. Two weeks after my Truth propheet, the Summit Grads had left for their Summit Workshop. These were the kids in the most senior peer group in the school, the one that included my oldest big brother Paul Renssalaer. The campus looked and sounded more vacant when an expedition was out, or a group of students was missing from the campus like the Summit Grads had been for ten days. I don't think many people missed my PG over the night of our Truth, though.

I was still hungry after dinner. Taco night was always the same: communal bowls full of corn chips with a sprinkle of cheese atop some mysterious red chili. We could dress it with shredded iceberg lettuce and tomatoes that were diced but still half frozen, and then carry our wooden bowls and plates to the picnic tables in the dining area.

"You will fucking love tonight!" Tim mirrored everything everybody had been saying all day. "And my peer group is next." He lifted his eyebrows indicating he also had no idea what Paul's peer group had been occupied with for so many days.

Crosby was busy scooping up the last of his chips and taco salad. I made inadvertent eye contact with Ivy in the background as she crossed the dining area for dish duties.

"Bans," Ivy silently mouthed at me from across the buzzing room.

Crosby, Tim, and I dropped our dirty plates with the dish duty crew and moved into the carpeted part of the house. This evening the furniture had been stacked in front of the Bridge and around the corners of the cavernous room. No kids huddled around the chess table with their eyes glued to the checkered wooden board, and nobody was playing cards. The music was the theme from "Chariots of Fire," now playing for the fourth time. The three of us plopped down in the middle of the floor. The buzz of the room masked the hypnotic musical banter at the beginning of the song. For the first time since my arrival, a fire was going in the fireplace in the pit. Four foot logs crackled in the oversized fireplace and sounded impatient to be ablaze.

Dish crews finished and the whole house was taken up with smooshing piles of staff and students. All staff, the two night watchmen, the kitchen staff, and power staffers were in attendance, along with everyone who ranked in between. I knew all of them by name and reputation. It was much like every Saturday night, so many people had dressed up. As the sun dropped past the mountains, I noted some thirty faces that were new to me, funneling into the lodge. Each guest was dressed in a nice suit or dress.

The new people, who I thought were invaders of the campus, all wore an old-style key. Most displayed them from flashy golden chains around their necks, but some had them pinned on their jackets or sweaters. Seeing people I didn't know in the house did give me a sense that our sanctity had been violated. I thought I had already met everyone in this spooky dystopia.

Every power staff who had been through the Summit also wore this golden lapel pin in the shape of a key. Most had it pinned over their heart. Tess wore her shimmering key on a gold chain around her neck. She was wearing a ridiculous flower-patterned dress. Evidently the outsiders weren't outsiders at all. I watched the unknown faces nuzzle the known in the packed house.

As the last glow of late-summer day lingered and glowed around the giant windows, the room went dark and quiet. We sat there, now silent, for a long pause. One minute passed. Then two. The room coughed politely. VERY LOUDLY, a voice over a microphone intoned, "Please welcome the passengers of Peer Group 21! All the way in FROM STEAMY HOT BOILING BURNING SIMMERING HOT..."

A raucous change in the house drowned out the rest of the announcement.

Everyone who had a key pin stood up, making hissing sounds of rapidly evaporating water or sizzling bacon. Tsss! TSSSSSS! ZSSSZZZZSSSSSS! They put their rigid hands out wide and jumped up and down. Needless to say, all of us still seated were gaping at the jumping, hissing people with their hands splayed.

While the lapel-pin people continued their tribal jumping and sizzling, the lights kicked on as brightly as the multiple dimmers allowed. Primitive, drum-heavy thumping music piped through the wood-boxed speakers hanging from each corner. The room seemed to be incensed with apprehension, like recoil energy from a shotgun blast. We stayed like that for five more minutes before PG 21 streaked into the house from multiple points of entrance. Some of them scared the shit out of our grouping as they burst through the doors from the smoking porch. Others flooded in from the dining area, jumping onto the picnic tables, doing cartwheels, and yelling and shrieking like banshees. My head snapped back toward the jumping freaks, who starting pulling everyone up by the arms, one by one, and soon the entire house was up jumping in unison to the thumping tribal music.

"What the fuck is going on?" I hollered over the music to Tim, but my voice was lost in the mob.

We bounced in place like confused pogo sticks. Paul and his peer group flowed all around us like spirits possessed by kamikaze pilots.

They weaved in and out of the jumping mass, shrieking and making more prolonged contact with those people wearing keys. The Summit people slithered on the ground or, using our jumping shoulders as leverage, tried to fly through the air. Though worried about injuries I might cause or sustain, I was exhilarated by the atmosphere. I wanted to see what happened next. As the thumping drums finally gave way to other instruments, the din from the speakers morphed into sustained music. I didn't know the tune, but, like everyone else around me, started to dance.

I noted the quietest and most awkward of kids bugging out, too. The entire lodge seemed to bounce along with us. There were eighteen people boxing me in, in whatever direction I bounce-turned to go. I wondered if this was what it was like to be in a stampede. No choice. No choice. Dust billowed from the carpet and Peer Group 21 began sweating profusely. Used water dripped from hair and wrists and noses as we made room for the Summit PG plowing their way under and over us, through and with the massive pounding cluster of program people.

Words began to drip out of the speakers over the bass-rich music. A male voice droned behind the music, at times coming into focus, at other times fading behind the drums and bass. A piano sadly droned, but the spirit of the song was not sad, it was eerie. Phrases like: "God's name is me." "Better recognize your brothers." "A work is man is never done." "Don't think me be me" "We are Wooooooonderfuuuuuuuul Giants." While this under-humming went on, more focused higher voices echoed redundantly: "We all shine on, like the moon the stars and the sun. We all shine on!"

Reverberating, nonsensical phrases poked out from the fringe of the music and its colossal pounding of drums, fading in and out. I'm sure Shakespeare was quoted – Macbeth, I thought suddenly. Then I thought I heard "I don't believe in Hitler"! My thoughts whipped around while I bounced. God!

This place never stops getting freaky and scary.

Interaction with the freak show, required every day. New and changing circumstances compulsory.

I saw the horridly antagonistic and much feared Darlayne Hammer across the room. How could someone so voluminous and voluptuous be so un-nurturing and cruel? Tears formed on her meaty cheeks, splashing past the corners of her vicious mouth. Although she looked soft and even happy now, I remembered to treat her like she was an active landmine to be defused, a sick dog, or a broken bottle to be handled with great care.

I tore my eyes from her and turned in another direction, bobbing to the thumps. Keith Rios, near the edge of the carpeting, clutched and bounced with a bearded man I didn't know. I doubted they had been in the same peer group since the other guy was older. He wore tennis shoes with a shlumpy suit. Both men were weeping. Their eyes were locked on each other and they bobbed in a boxy embrace, part of the thumping sea of bouncing bodies.

I turned in the air to check out what was going on behind me. A woman I'd never seen was closing in on my cluster. She grabbed at Tim who was dancing a little less conservatively than I was.

"Hi Zarra!" Tim gave her a normal bouncing hug and bounded backwards a step. I was right there with them.

"Little Chipmunk!" Zarra smiled at me from behind Tim's left ear.

I watched their sweat mush together on his neck. Her face was awash with tears and perspiration.

"You're next, hunh? I can't wait to be here in three months when yours lands!"

The sinister music droned on. Sweaty people panted. Papooses, with bans seemingly unpoliced and unimportant for the moment, looked to one another in astonishment. Faces smiled unabashed. I even spied Ivy dancing near Tess and Ernesto, happily grinning in my direction.

It was a bit of a disappointment when the lights began to dim along with the music. Peer Group 21 scrambled to assemble in the pit, the focal point of the crowded house. As when any propheet or expedition returned, there was bound to be public sharing. For the first time in my five weeks in Idaho, I was damn curious to hear what these people, who'd been locked away for ten days in the longest and holiest ritual in the CEDU system – the Summit workshop – had to say.

"When I came to this place two years ago I was a terrified wreck. A scared little girl. But now Me's a powerful FUCKING GIANT WOMAN!" She stood with her arms akimbo and her legs spread. She lifted her face toward the roof, and while it didn't seem she was growing at an infernal rate, she did, for a second, look as if she might get sucked up by aliens. Most of Paul's peer group struck this awkward, alien abductee pose when they shared.

"Barry, one day you're going to be up here, too. And you'll know how good it FUCKING FEELS AT THE TOP! WHOO-HOOO!"

Whenever a passenger from PG 21's Summit workshop shared from down in the pit, they would be answered with hails and steaming hisses, and whistles from the rest of the key-wearing people. The fire was smoldering when Nat Farmer, the headmaster, got up in front of the house. Like every time I'd seen him, he held a cup of coffee in his hand. Nat, like his wife Hedwig, was a total believer. He lived to go around fucking with kids, under the guise of therapy – a fifth-grade bully, only bigger and better dressed.

"We did some terrific work in there the last few days. These guys have been busting their asses the last several months to get this view. How do you like the view from the summit, guys!"

Peer Group 21 members turned and jumped up to view the house as if from a ship's high mast or a far mountaintop. Some burst into bird noises. Nat picked up the cue and delivered his next words shading his eyes, like he, too, was looking over a great distance. The Summit grads continued making whistles, caws, and tweets over him.

"Yeah. It's a hell of a view up here. And we're all just waiting for those of you that can get past your blocks to success. Make it to the summit, and earn a ticket to fly with eagles! First, it's to be the fight of your life. And THAT's the work! Right? Then we can release you out of here! We've got important messages to spread out in the world. In our world...the work will make us free. Participation within agreement is mandatory, right, crew? Let's hear more of what you have to say."

With bloodshot eyes and a frozen smile, the girl in Paul's PG struck the arms akimbo, palms out, alien abductee pose. She stood on the flat cornerstone of the pit and waited for the ornithological noises and steamed applause to dwindle: "You know for me, I watched Summits get out for almost three years, and I always wondered what it is that they knew. Now I have a conversation with myself that works for me! And I never thought I could make it up here. Me is feeling thankful that it's over and proud. I'm so fucking proud RIGHT HERE, RIGHT NOW!"

The house whistled and clapped as she stepped away. More steam and sizzling noise came from the people wearing the keys. By now, the rest of us were doing it, too, just to be a part of things.

"First off, from now on, I need for Me to be known as Daniel. From now on, no more Danny or Dan – call me Daniel. I'm a new man and we learned all the tools that this program has to offer. I still can't believe how powerful ME IS! I can't wait to get out in the wild wild world and share what I have to give. I'm learning to..."

A breakdown here. People clapped and hissed even louder for Daniel while Paul Renssalaer jumped up on furniture to deliver his. Nobody seemed to care that Daniel was sobbing or that Paul had shoes on the furniture, which was clearly out of agreement. "Me knows. Me knows. I can't wait to expand my family. I am free! And I am fucking HOTTER THAN A FIRECRACKER! I wish my father could see me up here. Me is crying but Me knows he'd be proud. We've learned to get all we can from every moment. Please be slow around our house, I'm really fucking vulnerable right now. I'll fly for you, Daddy!"

"Wow. What an experience. Here Forever Forever." A hand over the heart from the next Summit passenger.

"I thought the key was going to be unattainable to me, but I've seen the jailer, and I'm going to fight until there is no thinking left. The conversation can be one-sided. Thank you Nat, for giving so much. You've made all the difference in me, for the rest of my life. I love you. Me doesn't want to leave RMA but knows it's time. I've done the growing I'm going to do here."

Nat raised his coffee mug in a show of friendly solidarity.

"I want to thank each of you for being here tonight to see me. I know most of you know me as Christopher, but from now on, I'm going to change my Me, I'm taking my grandfather's name: Reed. Call me Reed from now on. Now that we've got that business out of the way, let me share. I'm going to explode from all that I need to share. I can't wait to move on from this incredible place! I'm scared, too, but for the last several weeks I've been running. It's time for me to let go of the fear and SHINE!"

People come back here, and dance like crazy, and then they change their names too? What the fuck is going on here?

I was curious. Curious as to the new language my older brother's peer group used, and why they all seemed so changed. But I wasn't still going to be here in two years, was I?

Actually, I wasn't going to be here in four days.

I'm getting a yoyo when my parents come up. I'm stoked.

—Author journal entry, 20 August 1988

EIGHTEEN

    I missed Paul Renssalaer's graduation because I split. Of course it was a rap day.

    An older girl named Jennifer Oyama, the chubby one that didn't like to see people skip stones, was raising her voice to me on my right. We'd been seated in the rap room about twenty minutes. I'd had a rap or two with her already; Jennifer Oyama didn't like me. The only thing she did like was barfing up turkey and gravy with white rolls into the toilet at Auntie's house – and sucking up to the staff at RMA.

"Let me go now! Zack! I saw you after lunch just today blowing smoke rings and, you know, that really kicks up shit for me..."

"He's not listening! Look at him! What do you want to really say!"

"I had a fucking boyfriend who used to blow smoke rings. It's a streetsy image, and it's NOT OK! That's not OK WITH ME! I don't want to be reminded of that life because of your baggage. I'm trying to work my fucking program!"

"Stand up to him! You care about this place, don't you, Jennifer? Tell Zack – let's do some work together – look at Zack and tell him, Jen."

"I had a fucking boyfriend.

"Tell HIM!"

"You used to blow smoke rings – you had a streetsy image – you made me do shit. You did this!"

"What? What did he make you do, Jennifer?"

"Like strip in front of him, and you know. He...and say shit to me, call me his 'little cocksucker' 'n shit like that. FUCK! I keep trying TO FUCKING FORGET! YOU CAN'T MAKE ME FEEL LIKE THAT! YOU TOLD ME I WAS FAT. I AM UGLY. I'm fat."

"WHO's sitting RIGHT THERE NOW?"

"MY FUCKING DAD! My fucking DAD AND BROTHER!"

"They told you what? WHAT DID THEY SAY to JUNEBUG?"

"That it's never going to be good enough, it's NEVER GOING TO BE GOOD ENOUGH. FUCK! FUCK! I'm NEVER GOING TO BE GOOD ENOUGH!"

Nobody consoled Jennifer as she melted down like Chernobyl. Jen had brought it on herself. She was maturing, by demonstrating an immediate desire to internalize her magnified grudge against me. The group called Jen's behavior – conjuring up a third party to the rap – projection or triangulation; I hadn't figured that one out yet. I'd seen the technique during my weeks at RMA, so I knew that directing attacks toward me, and ducking into tears had been Jen's calculated effort for her breakdown.

That got the rap going.

The staff next to me tugged at my pants cuff, and my heavy, mud-caked boot dropped my leg to the floor.

"Quit being so closed off!"

"I'm not closed off, I was just sitting like that, sorry."

"SORRY? Sorry. I'll tell you what's SORRY! You just sitting there, not even knowing that you're out of agreement."

"I'm not. I've got five on the floor."

"Jen's doing serious work here, you know? Get with the program, dude."

Here it comes.

It was obvious I was "closed off" because my leg had been crossed. I was a cocaine swinging street pimp, for blowing smoke rings.

That clunking of my boot, being dropped onto the ground when I wasn't prepared, changed me, too. I felt a shift inside me. Memory intersected with instinct. It was something I hadn't felt since my mother cut off my rat-tail.

Rage.

I didn't do anything but simmer. Inside me though, I felt like a guy eating a spoonful of acid as the group built a fire under my ass.

I fucking hate it here.

Darlayne was smiling and watching the action unfold as she stared into my eyes. Her eyes were about the same ordinary brown hue as mine, but her face, smooth and large, appeared pale white like the moon. She bent her lips into a subtle, heinous grin that brought out white teeth and dented dimples. She looked at me like a human-hyena hybrid, as if I were already dead and she only wanted bones. I finally broke the primal eye contact. The stench of my anger, fear, and fading patience attracted the scavengers like carrion. I hadn't even interacted with several members of the rap who were pointing fingers at me and rallying together to put on a show for Darlayne. If their performance was up to standards, they might not even get reamed that day.

They piled on:

"You know what, I was supporting in the wood corral while you were on WD's last week and I saw you rocking out, like singing unacceptables, playing air guitar."

"Do you get pulled up for that a lot?"

"Does he ever!"

"That's what I thought. People only sing to themselves because they are demanding attention, you know."

"So true! You're a walking attention game, man!"

"And I know you got feedback on this exact thing last week."

One of these was a dude in the Warrior family. I had seen their group come back from a wilderness challenge the previous Saturday – he was angling for Warrior Leadership. That meant he'd be able to have better tasting coffee, and smell like a gigolo every morning, after his visits to Bonners Ferry were permitted.

"Yeah, that's true. I've seen you sneaking a second cup of coffee too."

Another lying rat from the peer group above mine: "I gotta tell you that's not why I'm indicting you now, though. I see you've gotten really dirty like with your clothes and stuff. Look at you! You've got some stain on your shirt, and fucking nasty B.O. stains by your pits. Man, I'm sorry but that kind of grosses me out. It shows you certainly don't give a fuck about yourself."

With every indictment, every piece of needsy, shame-inducing commentary that passed for constructive criticism in this pseudo-psychological regime, it became more apparent that no reasonable person could construe this group encounter as therapeutic. More infuriating was that I knew better than to defend myself. I could counter what was thrown at me – I only had one day to do laundry and I only owned a few changes of clothes – but I wouldn't say anything if I could help it. When there's chum in the water, the sharks aren't there to play backgammon.

Darlayne watched the indictments closely, but said nothing, storing her ammo up for when it might inflict the most damage.

People flung bullshit about me into the rap circle with no reason. It wasn't about me, it was about what they thought of me: I was too intellectual, I appeared to judge everyone, they said. One male Brave student said something about how he knew he could ask me to split, and I'd go. Comments were thrown at me from most of the chairs on the other side of the room, one after the other without pause. Right when one assailant took a breath, another was flinging an indictment at me about my floppy straw hat from over a month ago, calling me a "stoner." Someone shot in a line about my wearing sunglasses in order to impress people.

My mind flitted back to my first day in fucking Idaho.

Spit sprayed me from their "safe" distance of six or seven feet. People were really acting VERY pissed at me as they waited patiently to switch chairs with those who were done attacking me. They had plum-red faces, those who were screaming. I didn't even know who many of them were, so I said so. It came out more exploratory than I intended.

"Who are you? I don't even know you. You know nothing about me. You don't have to yell at me."

I wasn't the picture they seemed bent on painting of me.

"We do when you're resistant and not being accountable for your feelings!"

"Listen, please wait, just, I'm trying to explain – I don't like being yelled at. I'm in agreement, I've been on bans, I follow them. I get WD's, I do them. Agreeing to stay in agreements is dumb, so why don't we just call them rules? Because then you'd have no way to MAKE ME FUCKING FOLLOW THEM!"

"This is MY HOME, MOTHERFUCKER. You either agree to follow the program and the Agreements here, RESPECT THIS PLACE, or you have the CHOICE!" The older student stopped abruptly without realizing he hadn't finished his nonsensical sentence. I must have forgotten where I was because I allowed logic to guide my response.

"They can only be Agreements if I agree to them is what I'm saying, and I AM! But if you tell me one more time that I agree to get skinned alive three times a week, because I live by the fucking Agreements by 'staying here,' I'll fucking scream. I don't want to be here – I've done it that way! I've tried getting in touch with my issues, I have tried passive resistance and you won't let me be. I'm in a bad mood. I'm not trying to manipulate or be resistant, I swear. Nobody will just leave us alone – leave me alone!"

I tried to seem deflating and proud as all of those words rushed out. It was like my feelings were still in a cage. In my house, at home, we didn't talk about feelings like this. I wasn't sure how long I could take the knotting up in my guts. It felt like eels were battling it out, wrapping around one another in my stomach. I was clenching up.

I won't do it. I won't explode.

I closed my arms across my chest. "I choose passive resistance."

I leaked this air through my gnashing teeth at the end of a drawn-out breath.

That was a miscalculation. I had tried hard for over a month not to appear "resistant." But now I was looking and acting how I felt: Resistant. And this was the catchall phrase. Being resistant and a manipulative kid, I had just fallen into a juggernaut. Catch-22. According to the program, I was resistant, and was manipulating the rap – questioning the validity of program logic. In some ways, it was the last time I would question program doctrine.

How could I now "look good," look like I wanted to "work the program," make the emotionally themed culture something that I depended on and loved? That wouldn't happen. I was only a Papoose. There was no way I could succeed here. I knew this.

I could feel it happen when the pitch, frequency, and tone of the rap shifted. My pieces were being taken. I'd seen enough. The end of the puzzle – like the end of a game of chess, a pastime I was becoming fascinated by – was always the same. Only one solution remained: Retreat! To leave this place, and hide from RMA – and the police – was the gambit I had to wager, or lose my own internal king. It was impossible to live where this rap situation was the norm.

Now that most people had exhausted what they needed to say, Darlayne saw her opportunity. The numerous insults she began hurling at me registered near 250 decibels. They were humiliating and designed to draw blood – or an emotional response. She wanted anger or tears, both preferably. I thought she would get tired. Bits of her staff saliva flew through the air. Some of it landed on me. A consistent tingling rang in my ears between her phrases. She was loud but she wasn't saying anything substantive. My being passive meant being aggressively resistant – and a "brainy little fuckup."

Darlayne resolved to break me apart – I resolved to breathe and stand strong, and survive.

"Listen! Passive resistance is ACTIVE resistance, isn't it! You think you're so smart! You little dickless bastard, I don't like the way you walk around here. You...I put you on bans with girls and you break them all the fucking time! PATHETIC little shit! Pathetic – You! No one likes you. You DO KNOW that's true, right? Maybe you've got contracts, but no real friends, just girls you cop feels with. Nope! Not gonna let you do it! That's why you're always alone."

She didn't stop there.

"No, you act like your shit doesn't stink! You're no island. I'm starting to wonder if this is the right place for you. Don't look at me like that! You manipulative dickless brat! Your crying to your parents isn't going to help because they don't want you. If they WANTED you, you wouldn't be HERE! Yeah, I heard about your little phone call! You're NOT GOING HOME! SORRY, ha-ha. What are you going to do? You don't have any balls. You don't have the balls to leave. Well, aren't you gonna get headsy and talk? This is so the work can start, right everyone? You're no different! Say something dickless… we're waiting."

She shouldn't be talking to me like this.

I felt worthy. I had been pulled up and indicted in raps. I had survived the Truth propheet. I had been trying to live within agreement. Darlayne shouldn't talk to anyone that way. I hadn't DONE anything bad. I just hated being there – maybe I just couldn't stomach a rap that day. I thought that Darlayne was all bluff. I figured she thought that if she escalated enough, she could push me into breaking the violence Agreement. She wanted me gone. She had obvious favorites, and I was not one.

In a monotone I explained, still trying to be as personality-free as baking soda: "Are you done? Can I retort now? STOP! Let me, I didn't break bans. I don't know what you are yelling at me for, I've done nothing wrong…wait. WAIT!"

Being interrupted by another round of screaming, I didn't get a chance to finish about the existence and functionality of my penis. I was leading up to that. Kelly Grainger, the rap's co-facilitator, and the older students paid no heed to the look of consternation growing on my face. I didn't know all of the codes of conduct in raps and I didn't want to know any more. I was trying to remain calm and not cry, to not yell back.

I had seen enough of these encounters to know that resistance was futile but some part of me knew I should stand up for myself. I certainly wasn't going to be a whipping boy for thirty fucking months! It was an unattainable goal. I couldn't remain basic and unmoved. I couldn't be baking soda.

"OK OK, do you want to tell us what's going on in that brainy little head of yours?" Darlayne feigned concern for causing my sputtering.

"I'm getting really pissed off right now."

"What are you getting pissed off at?"

"Pffft. Just. Don't even try it."

"Try what? I'm trying to get you to look at the truth: WHAT YOU ARE FEELING. Right FUCKING NOW! Tell me what that feeling is? I can see it on your face!"

Self-preservation erupted as a primal emotion. Words never would express what I felt in my bones. I was not going to cry for this bitch, even if she did scare the shit out of me. Now I was in an even worse mood by a magnitude of ten, than when I entered Darlayne's fucking rap.

"Fuck you, Darlayne!"

"Give IT A VOICE! Let it out then. Tap into –"

"I FUCKING HATE YOU! DARLAYNE, you fucking BITCH!"

"Yeah. You're never pissed for the reason that you think you are! This is good, and this isn't about ME, is it? This is OK. We're getting somewhere. Can you remember another time that you felt like this, Zack?"

"Don't even fucking try it!"

"AGAIN? TRY WHAT?"

"Your fucking feeble fucking MIND GAMES!"

The other side of the circle, the look-good suck-ups that surrounded Darlayne exploded in unison:

"You're the one PLAYING..."

"Who was it that hurt you so fucking bad?"

"You better TAKE A LOOK!"

"WRONG! You're the MIND GAME..."

"BULLSHIT on THAT! You're the one playing MIND GAMES!"

I went off, exploding like a rocket before launch. "This is not about my MOTHER AND FATHER! THIS IS 'BOUT YOU BEING A FUCKING BITCH, SO DON'T EVEN TRY TO MAKE IT SOMETHING IT FUCKING ISN'T! This is so fucking unfair."

"HE DOESN'T WANT TO LOOK!"

I stood up, which interrupted Darlayne's ranting at me. The room went quiet for the first time in an hour. My legs were shaking. It felt like the shaking was spreading through my whole body. Blatantly breaking an Agreement, fury quaking within, my voice was barely a whisper and felt very far away from me. For an instant I was stoned again; I was out of my senses. It was astral. I was detaching from myself; my consciousness lucid, my mind and soul in cold terror, my vital organs chattering and knocking against my ribs.

"I need to get out of here. Do I have permission to leave the rap?"

"Sit down you little shit."

I complied, though the feeling I was in a vacuum became more pronounced. Sounds muffled. Looking up, I saw Darlayne perching her fat ass on the edge of her black chair. Her body extended more than halfway inside the rap circle, her finger invading my meek portion of the radius which supposedly divided us for "safety."

"You don't have anywhere to run, asshead, you fucking dickless faggot, you don't even have the balls to leave. And you're out of touch! It's your HURT! OWN IT! This anger will kill you! You can't even take a look at your anger. THAT IS WHY YOU ARE HERE, KIDDO! TAP INTO IT!

"You don't HAVE THE BALLS TO TAKE A LOOK!"

"I'm going to freak out in a second." Disappear!

It was now or never. But I knew there was no escaping reality.

"You don't have the COJONES, THE FUCKING BALLS! I know you want to leave my rap, dickless. Sucks, doesn't it? Respecting me! We have a choice to be here, right girls?"

"OK – MY CHOICE!" I exploded, meek no longer.

I closed my eyes wondering if I could disappear. For a second I thought I heard wind howling outside or a whooshing noise as my muffled hearing cleared. I heard myself breathing and the thump of my heart.

Taking another beat, I very timidly asked again, in a voice that sounded like it came from under deep, still, water:

"Do I have permission to leave the rap, or not, because I have got TO GETTHEFUCK OUT?"

My agony was leaking.

There was a long, meaty pause as everyone looked at Darlayne, who had abruptly gone silent. She probably was wondering what would happen if she ordered the others in the room to tackle me. It was as if a steel mill had suddenly shut down, the silence was so profound. The little hairs in my ears remained inert, ready to cushion another sensory attack.

If she yells at me again, I'm going to pick this chair up and whack her one. She'd look funny missing a tooth, bleeding.

I reopened my eyes and saw Darlayne perched on the very tip of her chair across the little room, her big ass swathed in totally imagey and unacceptable acid-washed jeans. Her rump poised, a centimeter of coccyx and plastic was all that kept gravity from bringing her down to the floor. When she leveled her glance at me, she didn't raise her voice in a sharp yell. Her hidden, flabby white abdomen wasn't taut, but her voice betrayed stress. The tensest moment I had ever experienced in my fourteen years of life did not pass rapidly.

I ached.

I wanted to leave so bad.

She was so confident.

"If you want to be out of agreement and on a booth so fast your balls'll fall. Double-dare, dickless."

I stood and walked out. I prayed nobody would stop me. If a bigger student stopped me, I would be physical. One way or the other, I was getting out of this room. My resolve must have appeared fierce, because I was stiffly standing at my most vulnerable, with my back to the rap circle, unlatching the door, praying out loud that I would get out of the room called Papoose, without committing violence.

It was my forty-second day in Idaho and my sister's third birthday. If I was supposed to stay until past her fifth birthday, I knew I would be a raving lunatic.

Fuck. This. Place.

I'm splitting.

I did not want to ever again feel that anger.

It was in the enclosure of the RMA campus, though, where I'd be guided in to the anger, an anger so deep that I'd never escape.

SPLITTING

NINETEEN

I stormed La Mancha. Bounding up the steps and into my vacant dorm, I grabbed the day's food supply I'd previously stowed behind shirts hanging in the big clothes bay. Each hanger was separated precisely by the two-finger measurement every dorm on this evil campus required. I took my rucksack containing a stale bagel, a few pieces of fruit from the RMA kitchen, and some stolen nuts. Nabbing my new journal from the stuffing in my mattress, I quickly changed into some fresh jeans and threw on a sweatshirt. I could well be spending tonight in the elements, and I eyed a sleeping bag. It belonged to Crosby Rohrback, my dorm support. I should steal it. But stealing the sleeping bag would detract from the righteousness I felt.

If I split it's going to be the real thing. I won't be coming back to this freaking loony bin.

Certainly I wouldn't return just to be punished like so many other RMA kids. I'd rather be an absentee – a kid that left for good – and join the ranks of those even-keeled and even-numbered PGs that had permanently disappeared. I didn't care if I ever saw my big brothers and peer group again.

I had made my decision.

It's over. List me with the even PGs.

No person I knew from home, from the life I used to live before being dumped in Idaho – including the people that called themselves my loving parents – would ever stay in an impossible situation like this. Nobody could tolerate the conditions here. Shit at RMA was insane. Tempted to spit or piss on or burn the carpet of La Mancha, I stormed out, slamming the door. Behind me the latch broke.

I would not let myself be spotted on the road by someone who'd report me to the police in Bonners Ferry and return me to RMA. I had learned how to elude curfew cops back in Charlottesville. In fact, it's a good thing I wasn't born with wheels attached to my legs: I would have met my parents only one time – at birth. I'd been running away from my parents' house since I was four years old.

†

When I was four, I packed a purple suitcase. I called it my "brief-case." I filled it with paper, some crayons, and other accouterments that I surely needed at the office. I was going to the law school where my father was a professor. "A professor is like a teacher," I informed my mother, as I walked out our front door.

Carefully checking that the way is clear, I sprint the breadth of the street, into the firm grasp of a little old lady. She does not let me pass. She pulls the purple briefcase out of my hands with a wrinkly finger. Instead of helping me commute, the lady turns me in the opposite direction and holds the colorful attaché out of reach.

I have to get to the office, to my father. Her hand still grips mine. She isn't letting me get away. We have to visit the King. Doesn't she understand that my palace is somewhere else? I am going to be late for work. Finally a car that I recognize comes to a stop. The lady tugs on my arm to keep me close. The face looking out of the car in our neighbor's driveway is my colleague: Daddy.

She was nice. I was never mad at Mrs. Seargent for misunderstanding the situation and returning me to my parents. Under house arrest by her own son, because of the number of years she had lived, Mrs. Seargent had escaped her own sequestered detainment in order to save me from certain death by vehicular homicide. She saw a lost child struggling with a purple suitcase to cross a busy street. I'm sure if I'd had access to different words with which to negotiate, we could have come to an arrangement that would have benefited us both.

†

Between the ages of four and fourteen, I had improved my technique. Instinct took over as I left RMA, moved alongside the road, and hid from passing vehicles.

Get to an area where there are different roads.

There was only one road from RMA to Bonners Ferry, eight miles from the entrance gate. Now, if I could find a ride from someone who didn't recognize me as a runaway delinquent – a driver who had nothing to do with Rocky Mountain Academy – I could ultimately get to another area of the state. From there, perhaps this paranoia I felt – the sense that I would be recaptured – would cease.

Get lost, don't get spotted. Stay off the main road. Don't let them nab you.

Prepared to hike for as long as it took, I had made my escape.

Please let me just get off of the campus without being stopped!

For the first time in six weeks, I was alone. Alone in a good way. Something forgotten clicked into place when I walked out of Darlayne Hammer's rap: Confidence. I was in control of my destiny, of what I wanted to feel – not what RMA wanted me to feel. Choice was mine again, and it felt good. As my boots hit the blacktop, my anger from the rap with Darlayne began to burn off.

What I was doing was not novel. The police regularly answered calls about kids ditching the academy. So instead of taking the road out of RMA to Bonners Ferry, I went the opposite way. I didn't know where it would lead me, but getting lost was my only choice. Everyone who split seemed to attempt to get to Bonners Ferry, either walking or running the eight miles along Route 1. We almost always saw the kids again twelve hours later. Unless they were in jail, refusing to come back to the program, the police or a staff member would return them to the school. I don't know how other Papooses felt when they split, but I was committed to escape from the moment I left Darlayne's rap.

Splitting is the right thing to do. I don't regret.

Where the Kootenai River wound toward Bonners Ferry, a logging road led the opposite way, upriver. I started foot pounding that-a-way. Ankles, calves, and shins, go! Spring in my stride, knowing I'd be thirsty any minute, it was imperative to make the distance grow. I focused.

Forget anything but distance. It is priority one.

I had walked a few hundred yards when the first car passed. I didn't bother to get off the road only because I was still pissed off. The car was going in the direction of RMA, not away from the school like a possible search vehicle. It was a blue Nova, and there were two small, dirty, children staring out the back as it passed.

I'm cool. They were unrelated to RMA.

I was approaching the farthest stretches of my nocturnal reconnaissance missions. To become lost might be my only salvation. I felt worried and angry, not rational and linear. I recognized it was a disadvantage that I hadn't been able to leave the campus before. Which way was the nearest gas station? Or a pay phone? On the lookout for water, I saw nothing but trees. Finding a faucet or a sprinkler became priority number two. This was different; when I split from summer camp and school, there was always a store nearby.

Soon raps would be getting out and staff would start the man-hunt. I'd already witnessed it a dozen times. Tess and Darlayne would gather the rest of the family heads in the Bridge, alerting them to the situation. They'd lost another one. Then a staff member would carry the news down to Skinner, where they kept the parent communicators and the keys to the search vehicles. The chase would begin. They wouldn't call the cops until later, I knew, but time was running out for my free getaway. They were already looking for me, I was sure of that. Once the pursuers drove up and down Route 1 to Bonners Ferry a few times without retrieving me, they'd be thinking about the remaining sunlight like I was.

My eyes were glued to a house up ahead, when I heard the gurgling of a van. The rumbling sound carried from the dirt road behind the previous curve. Ducking ten yards into the woods, I squatted down. The vehicle moved at walking speed.

My hiding place was sufficient as long as I kept my belly to the duff. It was taking so long for the van to reach me. Why did it go so slowly? Because of the terrain blocking my view, I wouldn't get a look at the van until it was right in front of me. I could have covered a few hundred yards by now. And I had to piss. I hunkered all the way down, rump up, eyes up, peering through decomposing lumps of dead plant material. There was a stump nearby and I really should have been there. I sighed and inhaled the musky earth.

The side of the red van identified it: Rocky Mountain Academy.

I knew it.

I could see the driver smoking. It was Andrew Oswald, the fucking pervert from orientation my first day. The gas burned as he trolled, the red van sliding past like a giant mechanical snail.

A little bit of piss almost leaked out with the relief of knowing I'd not been observed. The rear of the van disappeared around the next curve. When I was safe, I yanked my jeans down and let urine fly. Zipping up, listening for the engine noise to become inaudible, I moved back onto the road.

The asshole drives too slow.

The RMA van was still struggling for the correct fuel-to-air ratio, but had moved out of sight. I hustled until I was near the old, one-story house. Avocado green with cracked white shutters, it was abandoned – running water unlikely. This dilapidated place had no help to offer.

Whenever cars passed, I ducked into the wilderness on the side of the road. The sun set. I was lost, and felt fulfilled. Just as I planned. In Bonners Ferry, the police had to know the academy was searching for a runaway. I must avoid the police at all costs. It would have been obvious that I was the runaway RMA student, especially at night, with this haircut and these boots. I sprinted to another house as its lights became visible. The back yard had a kiddy tub filled with water. I soaked my shirt in it. I felt creepy taking off my shirt while there was a family inside getting ready for dinner, but knew I was blessed to discover their garden.

I snacked on an unripe tomato, as I followed the hose that filled the tub to a work shed behind the house. There I uncoupled the hose and drank a camel's hump of water. I nibbled on liberated bean sprouts from their garden. They tasted terrible and weren't ripe, but it gave me something to do other than smoke. I hated running out of cigarettes. I only had a half-pack of Marlboros remaining from my weekly rations. I poked around my unknowing hosts' shed in search of a bike. There was no bicycle; neither was there a way for me to carry water.

I turned back to the road and started pounding feet again. I set a pace for myself as dusk ended and night covered over the mountains and me like a crisp, blue linen sheet.

TWENTY

The intersecting road ahead descended down a steep hill from the right. Cruising down to the crossroads was a light colored truck with writing along the side, and a ladder rack. I could intercept it at the bottom of the hill, if I hurried. I covered the distance to close the gap, standing in his lane before he could continue on his way.

An indicator light signaled right. Away from RMA.

I'm in business. I need a ride from this person.

I trotted up to make eye contact with the driver. A scraggly beard and a John Deere baseball hat framed the driver's rugged face. I'd already made up my mind to ride with the driver even if the word FELON had been tattooed on his forehead. Flinging my arm like I was throwing a football, I signaled I was going his direction. The window unrolled as I approached.

"Need a ride?" asked the stranger in the cap.

"Yessir, if you please, I sure do."

While it was true he had no facial tattoos, his arms were permanently adorned with naked women. He had a dark, scraggly beard, bad teeth, and the truck smelled as bad as his breath. Distance was more important than proper hygiene, I decided, and I hopped in. His name was Herb.

While excited to be adding miles to my adventure, I was still nervous that RMA might catch up to me. I didn't want to sleep in the woods tonight. I had done that enough at summer camp for the last seven years. I was never afraid of the dark or being alone, and I was thankful it wasn't yet winter. During the preceding weeks, kids at RMA had clued me in to the specialized cold-weather gear I would have to wear, things like snowshoes and balaclavas, for weather more brutal than any winter I'd ever experienced. In late August, I knew I could camp out, even without a sleeping bag.

Wherever this truck leaves me, I hope to God there are some woods where I can hide.

I wanted a real dinner, like the one my Papoose family was chowing down on right now. I felt a smidgen of jealousy. French dip sandwiches would be on the menu tonight, and a wooden plateful with macaroni salad would have been satisfactory.

"I could give you a ride to the Circle K in Sandpoint, if you've got a couple of bucks?"

"The what?"

"It's like a 7-11. Wher'ya from anyway?"

"Sandpoint? Is that near Spokane, Washington? I want to get to an airport. I'm so sorry, mister, but I don't have a penny to my name."

"'Bout two hours mo', I guess. But it's on the way to the airport in Spokane, like you said. I don't know if I can getcha all the way 'ere, but you 'lax, li'l boy, an' I'll getcha t' the Circle K."

"That'd be great. Thank you, sir, I sure appreciate it. I have smokes, you want a cigarette?"

Unaware of how far or how long we would drive, I considered my options, now that it seemed I'd successfully escaped RMA. I'd have to find a way to make a phone call to my parents, but I wanted to let them sweat for a while. When would the academy tell my parents that I ran away? They had to inform them, right? I had mixed feelings about any conversation I would have with Mom and Dad. I needed to think about what I would say, now that I had some leverage.

"Well, I's young once. Sometimes a man's just gotta get away, right? Go find some action. I understand."

He really didn't understand, but he was right about my needing to get away.

Herb kept bumping me with his right hand while he smoked and drove lefty. At times I thought he jabbered at me only to have an excuse to bump me with his hand. With every question he asked, comment that he made, and brush of the hand, his hand would linger on my leg or thigh a little longer. I'd never been on the receiving end of a pass like this before. As we drove toward Sandpoint, I started to feel like one of those girls I had made passes at back in Virginia at the movies and on field trips.

"Ya got any smoke? You know herb for Herb?"

He evidently liked the sound of his own name.

"I wish."

"Yer from over th'cademy, ain't ya?"

"I don't know whether to answer that, Mister."

"I told ya call me Herb, like weed, Herb? An' I ain't gonna rat on ya, neither. I used to run 'way as a young'un too. Shit. Kids run 'way from th'cademy there all th' time. We used to listen on th' scanner. Th' sheriff's sure got a hard on fer y'all kids. Ya got real rich parents, don't ya, boy? Where'd'ya say you's from again? Ya gotta li'l girlfriend back 'ere at th'cademy? There's some prime twat there, in't that right?"

This time his hand turned on my leg. His palm clamped down on me. "I used to have a cousin worked o'er 'ere, says you was all a bunch of gay, Jewish kids. Is 'at true, sonny?"

"What!"

Before retracting it, his hand gave an extra firm squeeze to my left thigh. I was threatened.

"Ever heard th' 'spression 'it's gas, ass, or grass, the' ain't no such thing as a free ride'?"

I shook my head "no." I had seen it, though. When I split from Camp Minnehaha at the beginning of this fucking summer, before Idaho, that truck had that exact same phrase stamped to its fender.

"D'ya wan' me t'get some beer, kid? Ya like beer, right?"

"How much further is Sandpoint, Herb?"

"About twenny."

He let a few minutes go by with just the rumbling of the engine.

Then: "Shit! No gas dinero, no weed, and ya don't even have some o' that sweet prime pussy fer me! Tsk tsk tsk... Well, maybe we can get a little action on th' way t'gether? What'ya say, li'l partner? Me 'n you. You'd like that, wouldn't ya?"

"Uh. Yeah. I'm not from the academy, OK? And I don't know anybody 'round here."

I was disgusted at the way he talked about girls at RMA, and my veins filled with an icy knowledge – *it was a mistake getting into this truck.*

"Well, ya know me," he said.

I felt his hand again move and squeeze even tighter, deep around my thigh like a vice clamp. Cold blood drained out of my face and I realized the "action" he meant was with ME. RMA taught me in raps and in the Truth prophet that it was impossible to will one's body to disappear, but I was attempting it just the same.

"Please. Please don't."

I could already feel his hand moving up my jeans near my zipper. I grabbed his wrist with both hands to stop the climb over the crotch of my pants.

"Come on, we're almost there, 'n I could pull over? Get yer little jeans off and suck yer dick. Don't be tellin' me you don't wan' that?"

His leer broadened, showing rotted molars.

"Come on, whattaya say?"

Forcing his wrist into my crotch again, he gave my balls a little squeeze before returning his right hand to the steering wheel.

"No! Please Herb, I wouldn't like that. I just need to get a ride to the airport. But, you can just let me out. Now. Here is good. Here?"

Instead of pulling over to the side of the road, Herb pointed to a sign: Sandpoint – 11 miles. Just behind the sign, Herb made a deep turn to the right and slammed on the brakes. We lurched, bouncing to a halt in front of some tall weeds. With the sudden stop, a handful of loose beer bottles shot at the cab window behind our heads. One of the bottles banged hard enough to crack it.

"Goddammit! No good deed, hunh? Now I'm gonna take ya to the Circle K, and I'm even gonna give ya twenny dolla's when we get 'ere, but for the next ten minutes I'm going to play with my dick – and yer gonna help me."

"Please don't do this."

I opened the door, relieved that Herb didn't grab at me. Perhaps I wasn't being taken captive again in Idaho.

Herb pulled his little penis out of the fly of his jeans and looked over at me.

"I don't believe this is happening right now."

I kept the door open.

"You know it. Stay in the fuckin' truck! Now don't make it worse, I'll kick or stick yer little ass and kill you if ya make me chase or beg ya. Ya 'ear me, boy?"

Stroking. Staring. Staring at me.

"I know yer a horny little bastard, ain't ya? Fine. Stay. You just stay in this motherfuckin' truck is all. Just sit there 'n watch. Yeah, don't make me get my knife. Just you fucking sit there. You. Justfuckingsitthere. Yeah. Yeah, little motherfucker."

Herb relaxed his head and slumped down in his seat. His eyes got weird because he was furiously whacking off.

"Yer a little cocksucker, ain't ya, ain't ya?"

Herb grabbed his hard on and whacked it with his other hand a few times, which added to the ludicrousness. After banging his dick against his left hand a few more times, his hand disappeared into the driver door and emerged holding a camouflage T-shirt.

"I said yer a little cocksucker, ain't ya? Look at that one, hunh? Ya like that? I said look at my dick, goddammit! That's it. Yeah motherfuckerlookatmycock. Uuuhhh huunh. I should make you suck it. Ohmigod suckitplease, please, fuck you, please. Make me cum! I'm gonna...YER LITTLE MOUTH...MOOOOHOOOHooomygod YESsss!"

After ejaculating into the T-shirt and putting away his slimy little dick, Herb demanded a cigarette. My hands were shaking as I retrieved one and dropped it in his lap.

"Get out of my truck, faggot. Now."

I was not reluctant to exit the vehicle. Before I even slammed the cab's door shut, Herb gassed his truck, flailing gravel in a wild doughnut, and showering my shirt with flinging debris. A hand protruded from the window, and for a moment I thought I saw Herb holding a twenty dollar bill, but it was just his middle finger.

Fuck you too.

The truck tore back onto the road and streaked toward the direction from which we had come. I then vomited three times. After that, I was sure I was alone. I bawled like an injured child.

TWENTY-ONE

I ate the rest of my fruit. I needed to get the taste of bile out. When I ran away from home or camp back East, no crazy shit like this Herb thing had happened. Dejection, abjection, and disgust combined as I walked away from the row of weeds and Herb's toxic cloud. I didn't know what to do.

Up until now, wanting to be home meant wanting to be back in my life – the life I'd had before being brought here. Now I realized *that life* was gone forever. I hadn't wanted to acknowledge what brought my parents to their decision. Who else was I going to call? Who else could help me?

I really did want to be with my parents. Did they not want me? Didn't they want me to feel safe? Would they never again want to provide me with shelter and love? They didn't love me, I surmised. Why else was I going through all of this?

Maybe they would love me if I were young again – a dooger, the littler kid inside of each RMA kid – but then my sister wouldn't exist, I thought, as if the possibility of time travel were real. At RMA, they taught that we all had these little innocent babies inside, but kept scratching up each other's shooter marbles. So having a clean little kid was a bit like a personal time machine, according to the propheet at the CEDU school. Maybe that was what I needed, to deliver me backwards, to the love I got from Mom and Dad when I was small.

Dejected, alone, and scared – I hated my parents as much as I urgently *needed, wanted, and loved* them in the present moment. But they were to blame for Herb, for Darlayne Hammer, and the cruelty of raps. They never understood me. Why had they made this extreme decision? Had I given them cause?

Would they lock me up the way they threatened? WHY? WHY GOD? Was it even possible that there were worse programs than RMA or CEDU? How could the place get away with calling itself a school or an academy? Were raps what grown-ups learned or did after college? What worse feeling existed than all the compounded feelings I now had?

I wept and slept, shivering inside the sweatshirt and damp T-shirt.

In the morning I hit the road. I wiped my ass with a page from my new journal, briefly wondering if the other one had been found, and my spirits rekindled in the early fall morning.

Time and sleep had travelled me.

There's hope in life.

I warmed as I walked in the direction of Sandpoint. It should be about ten miles. Forget Herb. Forgetting was not my forte, and it was a challenge blocking out the recent consequences of Darlayne being such a bitch, and the program being so unfair. It was possible that evil lay out here in the "real world" – outside the gates of RMA. How was I going to wind up, now I had left their safe place?

I plied my mind to finding a solution to the most important problem. How could I avoid going back to RMA or to a "lock-up" facility? The reality – I might be incarcerated among physically dangerous individuals – could no longer be ignored. I didn't know much about the "other places" I'd heard about as a Papoose: Tranquility Acres, a place called Teton Ridge Boys School, and places with Spanish names I couldn't remember. They sounded like horrible slave camps of tough kids. There were Native American-based schools in Montana where the kids were rumored to sleep in tipis all year around, and had to grow the food they ate. There were tons of rumors about where the kids in the even PGs wound up.

There were wilderness programs that sounded terrifying. One called itself "Survival." Kids from RMA who were rumored to have gone on Survival's program had rarely been heard from again. I would be only one of a handful to return to Bonners Ferry. After me, I noticed that every kid from RMA who went on Survival and did come back, stayed and graduated RMA.

The place the RMA kids called "Sandpit" was, in actuality, Sandpoint, Idaho, I figured. Sandpoint was where the Brave students got to spend the night in a hotel when their parents visited. Just within the city limits was the Circle K, and it was the same as a 7-11. Broke, there was no reason for me to enter the store, but I felt it was an accomplishment to have reached it.

As I dug in my pockets, looking forlorn, a beat-up, silver pickup truck pulled over. It reminded me of Dad's old Datsun with a steering wheel made of wood. I could see as it roared by me at 1 MPH, emitting a raucous noise reminiscent of a stalling lawn mower. A driver stepped out. This man was not too dirty, but exceedingly skinny. I tried not to look creepy, but couldn't think of anything to do to act busy and validate my existence in the parking lot.

We eyeballed each other on his return from the Circle K. After a minute he still hadn't started the car, but he poked his head and arm out and wiggled a curled finger. He was bearded like Herb. I could see through the hair on his face to all the scarred patches in his cheeks. Unlike Herb, an honest look in the man's eyes showed through. I saw integrity in the prim way both his hands clung to the wooden steering wheel. But I wasn't getting in unless I was sure. There was a young woman in the car, and that made me feel safer.

I got in even though I knew it could get me murdered.

We were getting further and further away from Bonners Ferry now, hours. The man, Dennis, got to talking about Jesus, US politics, and then the economy. I was just glad he didn't ask for gas, grass, or ass. I watched trees whiz by. By the time I realized that the little woman, who seemed very young, was his wife, I noticed that she wouldn't, couldn't, or didn't speak.

"Hey there, boy? Where you need to go, anyway?"

"Spokane, Washington."

"That's a long way, we need to go check on the kid. Unless you gotta get somewhere right now, you can come home and check on him with us."

I weighed my options. "That'd be alright, thanks."

He determined in the ten minutes to his home, while I remained silent, that my arrival was a sign from the good Lord Jesus himself. Dennis said I could help work in his garden and stay for lunch. He would get me further down the highway after lunch, and I could thumb a ride closer to Spokane.

The truck stalled and knocked after we parked on a long, overgrown driveway. The home, a one-room shack, had no floor or furniture. The area was tidy, and reminded me of a shelter on the Appalachian Trail, or the bays in the wood corral.

I imagined I'd be weeding a garden of luxurious flowers and organized rows, but the "garden" was just a small slanted area with a few meager looking stalks of corn and some forlorn carrot tops poking out of the dirt. I milled around, plucking the occasional weed and playing with the little boy. I was impressed with my work on him; when we were finished I presented him to his parents and we all laughed. The infant now had smears and thick globs of mud pasted on his torso and neck. He'd plunged into a mud puddle or two while I was weeding.

Dennis' wife had no teeth at all. She was about my age, with long red hair parted down the middle of her head. She was giggling as I handed her squirming youngster back. She didn't mind the child's dirtiness. She never once spoke, but seemed like a happy person. The house smelled like a cross between a gas station and a freshly snuffed candle. Dennis set a blanket on the dirt floor, and we said prayers that ended with Dennis wishing me safe travels. We all concluded with a heartfelt "Amen."

After we finished a succotash of potatoes, corn, and onions, the meal was over. I decided to explain how and why I had been at the Circle K. I appreciated their kindness to me, and my tale was all I had in return. And I needed a little more time to feel relaxed, for perhaps the only time in Idaho. Telling them the name of the school that I'd run away from and its function, as I understood it, proved trying. I automatically had to qualify my thoughts.

"I was there because I'd been thrown out of other schools, and I ran away. I mean running away from home and staying with friends. I got drunk some and I think they found out I smoked pot. I quit now. I'm not, wasn't like, a delinquent or anything. I'm trying to be accountable."

"So they sent you to Rocky Mountain? For running away? Drinking and smoking a little shit? When I was a younger man I used to hit the vodka pretty hard. It's been five years since I's reborn...and I ain't taken a drink o' that stuff. Have kids, thass what did it for me, buddy-boyo."

I only used the term "delinquent" because that's what RMA always said we were when we ran away: delinquent to our "contract with the program." In a flood of words I explained more about rules – but they're Agreements – and bans, and the propheet that I'd been through. I left out details from the Truth propheet but mentioned the disclosure circle, as when I got to that part, my brain was racing and I couldn't shut my mouth.

I'd promised never to take things out of the propheet, since that was an important Agreement at RMA, so although I relayed that there were confessions, I left out anything freaky. I heaped my trials upon them, trying to make them understand how weird RMA was. They didn't get it. The expressions on their faces portrayed bafflement. I wanted to relay a true sense of the place. Words that had no significance for them poured out of me: raps, splitting, contracts, unacceptable music, WD's, disclosure circles? Trying to describe a rap turned out to be impossible. They politely stopped me when they'd had enough.

"What happens if you go back?" Dennis asked.

"I won't, but it would be a full-time."

"What's a full-time? Do they pay you?"

To my surprise and paranoia, even though we were fifty miles away, they knew a lot about my "Academy." A scandal had occurred. Kids had been kidnapped from the campus. The FBI was said to still be lurking around the area, hunting down gun-dealing Nazis. There had been some kind of armed confrontation a few days prior to my splitting. Since we didn't have newspapers, radio, or TV at RMA, we wouldn't have known if separatists had taken over the entire region, as they were in fact attempting to do.

There were, it turned out, also a lot of rumors about RMA.

"So, are they all like delinquents or whatever you said, there at Rocky Mountain? I heard they got a lot of gay stuff going on there? Is it true that there's some governor's kids there? Some of them staff I heard are a weird bunch, got into it with a lady at the IGA one day. Yeah, can't remember the name, was a few years ago. They said the 'cademy guy was yelling at her for not smiling enough! And he was going off the deep end. Next I heard he was there at the mall, and with them kids asking for money? I never got that story."

He paused and put a dip in between his lower tooth and bottom lip.

"They say that campus is haunted. At least the Bonners kids do. They said they heard yelling and screaming one night when they were cruising near the campus? What do you suppose that was? You think that could have been one of them propheticies? Or whatever?"

I ducked his questions that I didn't have answers to. My heart was beating normal, and I didn't want it racing again, thinking about the propheet. Dennis' wife packed me a muffin and some jam and butter. Over a glass of orange juice, Dennis urged me to take the name Jason since Zack was a Jewish name.

"This is a little area called Hayden Lake that we're in. The Aryan Nation's been moving here. If I were you, I'd get straight to Spokane and get the fuck out of Idaho. This place is doomed. To be honest, there's a lot of people that would hate you if they knew you were even in town, Zack."

I didn't really know if I was Jewish, since my mother used to take me to church, and we had Christmas growing up, but I did know instinctively that I should take his advice.

Be John, or Jason – No, Alex! I'll be Alex and leave Idaho by any means possible. Doom lives here.

I briefly wondered if I'd been turned in when Dennis mentioned that everyone knew that bounties were paid for kids returned to RMA. Store owners and members of the outlying community did this a lot, he informed me. That was why the sheriffs in the area were so gung-ho about returning us.

I really wanted to brush my teeth. In my haste to split the campus, I had forgotten my toothbrush in La Mancha. Dennis charitably decided he was going to give me a ride all the way to Spokane.

He also gave me a little money when we got near the airport. I knew that the currency was precious to him, and I resolved that making a prayer out loud would be one of the last things I did before exiting the vehicle.

"God, uh, thank you for delivering me here. For making Dennis pick me up, and for his family, especially. I pray that you hear me, even though I usually don't pray. I know you've delivered me out of bondage, as Dennis read at lunch, though I'm not sure that 'everything happens for a reason.' But I'm swearing right now I'll be a better kid at home. And that's it, the truth. Please hear me now and forever? Amen."

I opened my eyes and Dennis took my left hand in his rough one, but not in a creepy way. He hadn't opened his eyes. "We thank you in our Lord Jesus' name, now and forever. Hear our prayer:

"Our father, who are in heaven...."

I was glad he'd chosen the only prayer I knew. Dennis released my hand. As he pulled off from the entrance to the airport, cars streamed by, reminding me how large the world can be. I waved goodbye to Dennis forever.

What should I do?

Could I walk toward Virginia? *Silly.* That had worked when I ran away from summer camp in June, but I had only been two hundred miles from home and had forty dollars. I had sixteen dollars and fifty cents from Dennis. I jammed the money in my pocket. Now I could use the pay phone to plead with my parents.

Get inside!

I was visible, standing by the highway. There were vehicles with siren racks everywhere. The state police were probably on the lookout.

TWENTY-TWO

Minnehaha was less than three months ago!

I had been at summer camp just a handful of weeks before the trip with my dad to RMA. Then the pickup trucks in Northern Idaho, and now the airport in Spokane, Washington. All the most recent turbulence began at Camp Minnehaha, I thought. But the troubles were really years older, and more complex. A newly born part of me was starting to look a little deeper.

If only I could wake up back there, in West Virginia, 200 miles from home, with familiar terrain and customs. Away from Doom. Even summer camp would be better than this.

I always had older friends. At camp, fourteen years old, I was the youngest assistant camp counselor to hang out every night with the seventeen and eighteen year olds in the counselor bunkhouse. Flag raising began every day at 7 AM. Reveille's bugle call blared over the loudspeaker, complete with the scratching and popping of a dull needle over 78-speed vinyl. I had been a flag raiser at Camp Minnehaha many times. It was my sixth season there, the continuity broken only by a summer in France with my best friend Chuck the year before.

Even if it sounded like fun when I was eleven years old, flag raising and babysitting younger campers wasn't a good use of my time now. I had outgrown my friends at camp, too. They would be heading back to successful education at boarding schools like the Hill School.

Truth is, when I got kicked out of eighth grade at Hill, after France, I spent the rest of the school year frequently at home with my parents, and less frequently in places they never knew about. But that summer, I didn't want to be at camp in West Virginia, either. My favorite cousin Gail was getting married in Baltimore in July, and I didn't want to miss it. Gail's wedding was a perfect excuse, I felt, for me to skip the rest of camp this year.

As I pleaded with my folks from a payphone near my camp cabin, I explained it was my decision to make. "I have outgrown summer camp, Dad…. Well, you can't do anything to stop me."

After my parents informed me that I would finish my commitment to be a counselor at my familiar Camp Mini-laugh, I decided to run away. I threatened to leave, and Dad went ballistic, so I hung up. This was typical among my family members, so I didn't feel my decision to split summer camp, and hang up on my father, happened without warning. We were at an impasse. It was the final straw for them, though. They didn't like my easy ability for independent interstate travel.

I had other motivations for leaving summer camp that I didn't disclose. I had sex, and weed, and swimming holes to attend to at home. I had parties to go to; I had friends with cars! I wasn't going to spend the entire summer scratching mosquito bites and serving camp food to youngsters. I had a new girlfriend and was not going wait the entire summer to see her again. I didn't care that the last grade I successfully completed was seventh grade. I had my whole life to learn geometry and Latin, the two subjects – and teachers – I'd struggled with the most.

Splitting from camp in the town of Minnehaha Springs, West Virginia – population thirty – had devastating repercussions. I would be taken to Idaho two weeks later.

Yeah, I fucking wish I had never run away now. I wish I had never gotten caught smoking by Mr. Sutherland at the Hill School, either. But it fucking happened.

When I left camp, I hitchhiked back to my friend Donald "Done" Roff's house in Charlottesville, with a day's worth of stories about how I got back home from West Virginia. Drunk on beer and rebelliousness, I was cool. I had friends. I was greeted with a masterfully twisted joint, and a girl who was crazy about me.

But doom prepared for my arrival in Idaho, and I'd never again see these friends, or think of them as meaningful associations.

†

I stared at a command tower as I walked past the parking lot and into the Spokane airport.

Did anybody from home even know what happened to me? Should I call one of them? How much would it cost to call Virginia from the Spokane airport, anyway?

I loitered outside and had a cigarette.

The airport of Spokane was humble. You could call it small. It certainly had nothing on Dulles Airport in the real Washington. I went to the bathroom and splashed some water on my face. When I looked at myself I was back to being proud and content to be alone, and away from RMA. I was not going back.

This was what I had to get through to my parents, whenever I did finally talk to them. I had already decided I wouldn't mention the thing with Herb. In fact, forgetting the entire incident became a directive unto its own. For the first time since splitting summer camp to see my girlfriend weeks before, I felt that I was in control of things. I wasn't going back to Idaho. I was going to go home and find my girlfriend. If she didn't want me, I'd find another!

That's the old Zack. I was going to be normal! Or I'd move in with older friends and get a job slinging fast food. I was 2,500 miles from my parents and normally sized mountains, but I wasn't going back to RMA, goddammit.

My mind whizzed and whirled. I had options to offer on the phone. I prepared rebuttals to my dad's points of contradiction. The negotiations would have to be delicately worded, or my dad would fly into a rage. After he reached that point, there was no talking to him. My mom was already convinced that RMA was perfect and that I was scum. I changed my mind about one thing: a collect call was in order. They could afford the phone call more than I. I should save the $16.50 until I knew what was what.

The phone conversation was short and all business.

"How could you have just ditched me, Dad?" As soon as he said hello. "Did they not tell you that everybody is NUKKIN FUTZ! They're all junkies and completely crazy, Dad. Mommy, are you there? Are you even listening to me?"

So much for delicate negotiations.

"Yes." My mom's voice betrayed irritation in that one beat.

"Please, Zack, just tell us where you are."

Should I tell them?

"I'm at the airport that we flew into on July 11th, Dad. Can I come home yet? I promise to go to school! I'm being honest. I'll go wherever you want back in town. I'll learn math now and I'll take the Ritalin, too. Just come and fucking get me out of here, PLEASE!"

An elderly couple stopped by me with their bags and watched the drama as I teared up.

"Zack! Wait in the airport. Don't leave the airport. Do Not Leave.

We will arrange for a ticket for you. Just wait."

They understood. They saw the wickedness and Constitutional violations! Had they even realized that RMA wasn't what it pretended to be? Was it so?

Had I won? Had they heard me this time?

They instructed me to call back for flight information since these things take time to arrange.

An hour later I called them collect again. If I hadn't been writing with such concentration in my journal, maybe it would have occurred to me to talk to a flight agent on my own. But I didn't have identification and was afraid of the uniforms. I wasn't even sure how to answer if someone asked my name.

"OK, it's been an hour. Is there a plane I can get on yet?"

My father hadn't even said hello, but I knew him by his typical, deep disappointed sigh.

"This takes planning, Zack, it's not as easy as you jumping on a plane and coming home. I can't snap my fingers and make a flight manifest appear, honey. OK? Now, listen. You are still being impulsive. If you interrupt me again, I'm going to end this call and NOT take the charges next time! Now. A man named, uh, Darren Snipes is on the way to the airport to escort you home. It's this way or no way, OK son?"

"As long as you promise he won't take me back to RMA."

"I'm still deciding what's going to happen with you, but you will have to be with an adult. Do you understand?"

"Yeah, whatever."

Sitting in a wheelchair, I scooted down into the main lobby of the airport. There wasn't even a video game to play, so this was how I amused myself as I waited for the guy. The floor was freshly waxed parquet. I used resistance air to fan myself. I rolled down a ramp, and the wheelchair shot me down along stairs leading to the terminals. Braking a little with my left hand to compensate for the level left turn, I could just avoid the seating area in the lobby, and get a little g-force on the turn. Little waves of travelers passed through the empty room with their bags every so often. Wind breezed through my hair as I shot by the small locker area. The wheelchair was dangerous and fun, zinging down the ramp around the steps.

I would comply with my parent's request to meet and talk with

Mr. Snipes when he came to the airport. I had no recourse. If he had a ticket to Virginia I'd do anything my parents said.

Just give me the magic ticket home to regularity and people I know!

I just wanted home. I could learn to love my parents again. I assumed that they still loved me, since that was their excuse for all the disagreeable things in the last few years. But what they had put me through lately was too far. I couldn't handle more abandonment from them.

My parents didn't tell me that Darren Snipes was a Sheriff with the Bonners Ferry Police Department. They knew me better. I only found out when he turned up.

TWENTY-THREE

When Darren Snipes entered the airport I knew him immediately. He clamored into the room with his head swiveling in every direction. I rolled myself behind a wall that led to the men's restroom. With a good view of the main entrance, I watched Mr. Snipes and tried to guess his intentions. He looked around the airport lobby authoritatively.

He had light colored hair and fair skin, about fifty pounds overweight but pretty solid, in a tan suit. He wore sunglasses. I slowly rolled behind him as he scanned the area scratching his head. He looked for me while I looked at the tire marks from my luge run. He turned and started when he saw me.

It gave me a flutter, too, because he turned so abruptly that his jacket took a second to catch up. I saw a pistol. *Whoa*. I said nothing. Whatever guilty thought's I'd had from causing marks on the parquet floor, disappeared from my mind.

He asked, "Are you Zack?"

I left a healthy pause. "Who are you?"

"I'm Sheriff Darren Snipes."

"Do you have some sort of identification?" I asked.

He laughed and pulled out a fat wallet with a badge and his photo inside. A thick, smelly leather flap, anchored to the wallet with brass pressure clamps, bore a weighty Sheriff's Star.

"That's pretty cool. Thanks."

"Are you, um, injured?" the sheriff asked.

I sprang out of the wheelchair. He let out an uncomfortable laugh of relief.

"I saw your gun," I said.

He looked around us. "Um, are you hungry?"

"Very hungry." I replied.

While I ate, he had three coffees and explained that my parents wanted to talk to me in person. And again, it takes time to send flight tickets to a third party.

The hamburger was dry, the fries limp, but I ate all of it, gulping down the coke to its final slurp of the straw

Sheriff Snipes continued. "I'm not going to Virginia, son. In a few days, maybe you'll get this straightened out with your parents and the folks at the Academy, but you have to go back to Bonners Ferry with me so that everyone knows you're safe."

When were my parents coming? How long did it take to send a ticket to a third party? Why did I need an adult overseer? I didn't like the sound of any plan that involved RMA in any way. I hated that the particulars were left indeterminate.

"Do you think you could give me your word that RMA won't know I'm in Bonners Ferry?"

"They aren't going to kidnap you, son, if that's what you're afraid of. You Academy kids are a funny lot, I'll tell you. I'm not making any promises to you, except that you'll be safe where I'm taking you. After that, it's up to your parents."

"You have to promise me that you won't take me back to the school, or I'm not going."

"The state has places that you can stay without having to go back to the Academy. I promise."

Sheriff Snipes gave his word that I would be going to a foster home. I didn't know why I needed to go to a foster home since I already had parents and a real home with my own room in Virginia, but if it had nothing to do with RMA – and I didn't have to attend a rap – I'd give it a whirl.

We got in the car and left Spokane for Bonners Ferry.

TWENTY-FOUR

I learned how to box. This wasn't a foster home with a swarm of Spartan-like youths, all wound up with testosterone and pitted against one another. My guardians were an old man and his wife. They said kids from RMA were their favorites to take in. I spent my several days there cleaning in the kitchen and around the yard. We were good to one another.

The boxing lessons happened at night. The kindly old gentleman rose from his chair, and directing my elbows inward, told me to jab, jab, and jab. He wove his sagging frame in front of me saying "peek-a-boo," as he launched slow-motion rights toward my face. He told me to mirror the boxer in black shorts who danced around the ring on TV. "That's it, but do it in slow motion. Ya see how he lurches left and swings the right. That's it. We've got a contender in here, Mama! Mama, bring us some lemonade, dear?"

We practiced in the living room, encircling his wife, who offered words of encouragement from the La-Z-Boy. "Oh, look at those muscles." "I hope you never have to use those sandbags against anyone."

They were cool.

A few days later, when Sheriff Snipes came without warning, I thought we were going to the airport again. Instead, my few belongings were loaded into a garbage bag. I was being moved to another house, on the other side of the little town of Bonners Ferry. In a squad car. We hadn't taken a squad car from the airport.

The sheriff drove us across Bonners Ferry. On the dashboard, I could see a manila envelope with my name on the information tab. Also, a xerox copy of my most recent photo was paper-clipped to the front of it. With horror, I saw a copy of the Polaroid shot that Darlayne Hammer had snapped of me on my first day. It was proof that Sheriff Snipes had contact with the fucking Academy.

The face in the picture had an expression, the mouth slightly agape. It was the look of silent shock.

The house at my next stop was more ramshackle than the one with the gentleman who wanted me to box. I surmised that an equitable arrangement had been made: Income from my parents back East had to be distributed evenly in the teen prison town of Bonners Ferry. Nobody tried to hide the conversations about the money they got for hosting me.

The new place housed an old lady. Her face wasn't the catcher's-mitt wrinkled face of my own grandmother or Chuck's grandmother in France, but this Idahoan was still old. More remarkable was her mother, also living in the little drafty house. She was so old: half blind, three-quarters deaf, and all hands. From her wheelchair, she inspected me, and her prunelike hands felt around my chin and springy hair. When she was done, she went back to staring off into the ether, listening to religious tapes.

There was no sign of a man, only photographs of a few young kids and of Jesus on the wall. It wasn't easy to imagine that both these women had to have been conceived at some point. I didn't dwell on that.

These women were old and boring! There wasn't anything to do. As soon as I walked in the door, they threatened to call the Sheriff if I ever acted up, or wandered from the property.

Why were they both afraid to leave the house? A burly escort from down the street took us all to gather groceries at the IGA when the ladies needed something. The IGA was just blocks away. Religious tapes played all day in the cramped room they called the parlor.

I knew that God was not what the people on the tapes were talking about. I didn't feel that something evil was living in me. *This was like the tools of the Truth prophet.* They had channeled convoluted interpretations of human diversity and essence of spirit into uniform, catchy language. According to the people on the tapes, whatever caused me to run away from Rocky Mountain Academy or Camp Minnehaha was a negative thing. But I didn't consider it evil to assert more control over my own life. Older kids at RMA always talked about "the struggle" and "thinking." *So demons and CEDU people must have a lot in common.*

The tapes played messages from former cocaine addicts and winos, saved by God, who told them that they didn't need addiction or false loves any longer. One tape was about a young promiscuous high school student who at the end joined a European cloister. I listened with interest to the first half of the cassette, a little let down by the ending. The subjects who told their stories in the tapes were always powerless. I didn't feel like that yet either.

I wasn't powerless, was I?

I stayed in line, didn't act up, and didn't take off. Everyone was so worried about my running away again. I reveled in having that leverage. I wanted home and that was what I was waiting for. If playing the Perfect Christian Boy was going to get me that ticket home, so be it. The ancient duo did like me because I offered to help them constantly. For the remainder of my time there I carried boxes, did volunteer work for their church, and even swore off smoking for a day. I read the few books they had, mostly Reader's Digests and paperbacks about born-again Christians.

Sheriff Darren called me after I'd been reading on the cot in my room.

I needed to know. "What's the latest with the ticket?"

"Your parents are in Boise, son, so we'll fly down there together this afternoon. It shouldn't take but an hour or two once we get to the airport, alright? ...Good. I'll be there in an hour, pack it up."

Suspicious at first that I was being duped, I let the effect simmer. The sheriff hung up. I stood there a long minute with my eyes pointed at the cracked ceiling. *My parents are in Boise. MY PARENTS ARE IN*

BOISE? My eyes teared up with appreciation and my mouth ripped into a long smile. I even jumped with joy, before rushing to my cot to pack.

Packing for the last time!

I shoved everything back into the Glad bag. During the week I had been provided with some socks, underwear, and pants from inside my storage cube at La Mancha. I gave my most gallant goodbye to my virtuous and ancient hosts. They hugged me, both of them shaking from the exertion of rising, and reminded me that Christ died for me.

"How can I ever forget," I solemnly replied.

To catch our flight to Boise, Sheriff Snipes drove us back to the Spokane airport where we had first met. The two-hour ride passed by in relative silence. It occurred to me to mention the encounter with Herb, but I wasn't sure how to broach the subject.

I swore I'd be on my best behavior when we got to Boise. *My parents did love me, and were letting me come home. Thank God!*

As we cruised along the highway toward Spokane, I thought back to where I was one year ago.

How the hell had this happened to me anyway?

TWENTY-FIVE

[continued] P.P.S. I'm going to keep writing to you
even if you don't write for a while. Eventually, I know,
you will. I think one of the happiest days of my life is
when I got your letter from France saying you'd gotten "the bug – the reading bug." I've saved that letter
and will save your other letters when they come.
—Letter from author's mother, 11 July 1988

To go back in time to Garlan would make it all different. Before
my first boarding school, before Camp Minnehaha, before RMA,
before Idaho.

*I am in Garlan. In Brittany – in France. Chuck's grandmother, Baba,
had an estate there. I had never been so free. Beauty surrounded us. The
ocean, the terrain. And the girls were topless, just as Chuck had promised.*

Gypsies used the field near the castle. For over a hundred years, a
caravan had stayed nights on Baba's sprawling property. I was fascinated with the Gypsies. I wanted to follow them when they left.

By the end of this thirteenth summer of my life, I would be a
young man. A Croatian girl whetted my appetite for the lessons I
would be shown in the same cornfield by an older French girl.

I'm deposited into a memory of Paris. *Chuck Driems and I are running through the Louvre, the museum that museums should be taken to.*

Being unleashed in the enormous world inside the Louvre, my best
friend and I acted out, in pantomime, the interesting sculptures and
paintings. We tried to be mimes, but we were loud mimes. Acting as
ringleader for these fun charades was my duty. It was why I had been
invited to France with Chuck and his mom.

Mr. Driems, Chuck's dad, had died just a few months before.
How could there be a god that would steal my friend's father from the

Earth? I felt so shitty for Chuck. Mr. Driems had always been a friend to me, too. In the few moments when I managed to make Chuck forget about his father's sudden departure from the pain and cancer that killed him, what a fun time we had!

That was when I'd been bitten by "the reading bug," as my mother put it – while I was in France with Chuck Driems. I finally learned the joy to be gained from books. My mother, a writer and teacher, had turned me off to reading. But books, unlike most of the people I encountered that summer, spoke my language. My reading bug combined with the cultural exploration that Chuck's mom provided. She took us to burial sites, the catacombs, Versailles, Roman ruins, and countless museums. I learned to appreciate art, and understood there were cultural nuances that made the United States and France different. I learned the magnificence of the world.

My letters from France to Mom reflected my freshly acquired awareness of art and literature, and intellect. In letters I explained that I wasn't content to follow in my brother's footsteps. I didn't want to go to the Hill School up in Pennsylvania. But the decision was made for me.

When I came back to the United States, headed to that first year of boarding school, I had a Mediterranean sheen. The Puritanical, square-headed Northeast was a distinct contradiction. I had a bad feeling about going away for school. I was a different person than before I went to Europe, more independent and focused on my future, my own developing sense of myself. My vision for the future was becoming the opposite of Mom and Dad's. What they wanted for me – schedules, obligations – was what I didn't want. Feeling great apprehension about going to the Hill School, and going north to Pennsylvania, I marched into the gauntlet of life. I was a full-fledged teenager. I wanted to be free.

†

Spokane: 45 miles. Sheriff Darren Snipes let out a cough from the driver's seat; I lit another cigarette.

"God, you smoke a lot."

"Well, I can't smoke in front of my parents so I won't get to until I see my friends tomorrow."

"So you got kicked out of this Hill place for smoking, then? Just smoking cigarettes, hunh?"

I was expelled from the Hill School the first week of October, less than a year ago.

"Unfortunately, yes. It's probably the main reason my folks sent me to RMA, sir," I replied, the movement of the cop car lulling me to sleep. Remembering.

✝

As I had correctly predicted, the new school was even more uppity than St. Anne's, the middle school in Charlottesville I'd been "not invited back to." The Hill School was a boarding school – a full-time affair – and reminded me of a cross between Camp Minnehaha and St. Anne's. We lined our trays up in the dining hall and used belt-fed toasters. It was like summer camp, except we all had to dress up like lawyers.

The admission interview had freaked me out. The Hill School was the opposite of what I was hoping for. Dress codes and serious stuffiness. Didn't they know I would fail? I did. From the minute the Saab dipped onto the driveway lined with sculpted holly. From the moment during the interview process where I was told about the "rigorous curriculum."

This is not a good match, I am going to fail here.

I tried telegraphing the message to my father as we sat in wooden chairs. Across an expansive desk of oak, the man in front of us had a face like a seal. He looked like he shaved both his eyebrows off, and plucked his lashes, leaving a face that remained seal-like, but stern. I impressed myself for understanding some of the Latin slogans embossed on plastic picture frames on the walls and doorways. The man declared how proud the school was to have me, and promised my father I would be looked after while I transformed into somebody, perhaps more seal-like – somebody mature, somebody more like the two of them.

The imposing campus continued, through patches of oak trees, steadily manicured lawns and shrubbery, to a path that brought us to my new dorm. My dad did have the courtesy to help me unpack.

I peered over the open trunk lid of Dad's new Saab. "This is a bad idea." Was he listening? "Please don't leave me here."

He just smiled at me, in that way only Dad could – as if he was a benign foreigner who didn't speak the native language. He wasn't ill-intended, but his mind was made up.

I could sense Dad's impatience. The looks toward my trunk and my other stuff in his car; the sighs, the glances toward me alternating with those to his wristwatch. I met my roommate, Jason. He politely left the room while Dad and I lugged the trunk in and made the bed. I was not going to last at the Hill School until Thanksgiving break. I knew while I was explaining it to him – while he feigned acknowledgment – that this was a rotten match. Dad was even quieter than usual, so I couldn't tell if he heard me.

Daddy gave me a short hug with a triple beat of thumps on my back to indicate the hug was over. "You're going to study hard, and get that math under your belt. Geometry and Algebra are important for a person to learn, and they've got the resources to line you up to have a great year!"

"But I just don't understand why I can't stay at home and go to public school for ano..."

"Your mother and I have been through this. We don't need the grumpy teenagers clumping around. It's important that your baby sister grow up without the fighting and yelling. Don't you agree?"

"I guess."

"Now remember how unhappy your brother was at Hitchkins in Connecticut? He was miserable for months, and then when he got into that school in London he didn't even want to leave!" My father at his most dramatic. "Now get those books organized for your classes Monday, I am sure you're going to have a great fall. Don't worry, your mother and I will see you at Thanksgiving, I think. Or Christmas in New Jersey. I love you."

The trunk I was supposed to live out of from now on wasn't really black any more. This trunk I'd had all the years at summer camp was covered in stickers and dirt streaks from where the stickers had rubbed off but the adhesive had attracted schmutz. I unhitched the trunk, pulling up on the latch.

Wait! This is important!

I grabbed the silk neck tourniquet and ran out of the dorm, down the steps. I shot toward my dad's Saab as it passed over a speed bump. The highway would take my dad right back to Virginia. The window unrolled and I thrust the necktie I was clutching into the open window, into Dad's hand, explaining that I still couldn't tie it. I was to wear one at all times and had never tied one on my own! This was positive proof, and proof beyond a reasonable doubt, that I shouldn't, in fact, be here at all.

225

"I don't know how to use this thing!"

"Jason and Mr. Sutherland will help you with the ropes. I'm going now, Zack, and I know that if you try, you will succeed at this. I'll see you in November and you can call us anytime from the Mail Center. This isn't a punishment; it's a step away from childhood and into adulthood. It's important that you do well this year to show us you are serious about your education."

"This is a mistake," I managed to slip out, before the window rolled up with a whir. The Saab carried him away with its characteristic hum while I stood glumly.

I explored the surroundings. I saw that the Hill School was immaculate. The loneliness dissipated as I unpacked my trunk and reported to the dorm master, Mr. Sutherland, for orientation. It was new and uncomfortable and I didn't know anyone, but I recognized that none of the other kids knew anybody either. There were a couple of kids whose fathers had been students here. Their ties were tied correctly, with pristine knots. These eighth-graders in my dorm already had ties with Hill School emblems on them. Like me, they were only thirteen.

Although it was located in Pottstown, PA, I realized how close I was to the New Jersey Turnpike. I remembered the Turnpike. When I was a child, before my sister was born and my grandfather JJ died, my whole family would pile in the Datsun and race up the Turnpike to see Mom's parents. People up there talked in a boxy, curt tone that always sounded too city and too preachy. The teachers at the Hill sounded like my mother's parents in New Jersey, not the Southerners at home.

On an unconscious level, I must've understood the importance attached to a fresh beginning at a new school. I hastily told everyone that though my name was Zack, I went by the name Berz. The past summer, just before leaving for France, I discovered on my passport that I had another name. I had never seen this document before and thought it marvelous that there was an unknown "Z" in my name. Berz's life didn't last too long.

Jason, my new friend and roommate, kicked a soccer ball around with me. Impressed enough with my skills and rat-tail, he offered to show me something. He launched the ball from our area, then nailed it past the tennis court nearby. We gave chase. It rolled down a hill. Beyond Senior House – for the twelfth graders – Jason dribbled the ball to a small maintenance building.

The shed housed a lot of mops, sprays, and cleaning supplies. There was a smell of fertilizer. Behind a sliding panel, two armchairs filled a smaller room. A big "steal your face" flag appeared on the sliding door when Jason closed it behind us. The room smelled of freshly smoked ganja. Jason reached into his pocket and pulled a little reefer out of a cigarette box.

"Reach behind the couch," he said with a twinkle in his eye. "Berz, my friend, it's time to get high."

I giggled at Jason's stupidity and did as asked. This would be my third time smoking marijuana, and I had zero qualms about it. While we toked out of the long bong, our eyes turned red and teary. Jason revealed the significance of the room to me. During most work hours, this shed was the Custodian Department, but at night it doubled as the meeting room for the most popular Hill boys.

A week went by and my confidence grew at my first boarding school. We were the youngest boarders on the Hill campus, and there was some jibing and hazing done to us by upperclassmen that would have been unacceptable at RMA. My hazing began immediately, which is why I was late to my first several classes, but taking it in stride, I began to acclimate well to campus life. It didn't last. I was only at Hill a little over a month.

Berz tried to remain good, or at least not get caught for anything, but the struggle was short-lived. I missed girls. There were none to be found here. My ties were sloppy, and it was close to torture for me to sit at a desk for four hours. I simply could not purge the class-clown routine either. Mr. Sutherland consistently reprimanded me for getting up during the silent study halls.

Jason was my only friend at Hill. He wanted to study at night; I wanted to do anything else. There was no escaping the growing anxiety I felt. I was going to let my father down. I was going to let myself down. I just plain stood out at the Hill School, too, with my rat-tail, and Southern drawl.

It was 2 AM when I got caught coming back into the dorm from an evening stroll and smoke. Mr. Sutherland was shirtless, in boxer shorts. He had me follow him to his chambers. I stood by his front door, a little annex off the dorm house we all lived in, and waited for him to change clothes. Mr. Sutherland reappeared in jeans and a sweatshirt, ushering me inside his wing.

He called the headmaster's house. I dozed off while he and the headmaster each made a phone call to my parents in Virginia.

Berz was expelled from the Hill School, and Zack didn't care. It was pretty simple in my mind: I couldn't do anything right. I couldn't follow rules, and I didn't really want to, either. I felt ashamed.

Disaster was approaching. I'm sure that's how my parents saw it, too.

Back to Virginia my father and I drove in a cloud of regret and mutual disappointment. I should have known that this marked the beginning of a difficult year. I spent the next days and nights sleeping and doing ANYthing to avoid conversation with them. I was supposed to be in eighth grade. The school year had started and I was without a school.

After I came home, Mom and Dad sent me to the local public school, but I got in fights all the time with the bullies who were picking on girls and little kids. The teachers didn't like my attitude in class, either. Later in the school year, I received a medical depression-related diagnosis that recommended home schooling or placement – or at least NOT being in school for a while. I had hoped the diagnosis would be a ticket to freedom. It wasn't. My antics at public school had caught up with me.

So I spent the rest of my eighth grade year not in school. I knew I had failed out. This definitely contributed to my parents' search for the "educational consultants" who found the Idaho shitpits. It wouldn't surprise me if an educational consultant told my parents how to contact the Bonners Ferry Sheriff, too, when I split from RMA.

†

Dear Zachary:

I have reviewed your academic history....Needless to say, I found your academic performance during this past year distressing if not alarming.

[...]Your instructors will be demanding, they will expect much from you, but they will be fair in their judgment and ready to help you at your request. You will not, however, be able to indulge in the luxury of academic indifference or procrastination. Such attitudes and behavior direct the way to certain educational destruction.

Your scores on aptitude test indicate that you have a bright mind and fine reasoning ability. You have an opportunity now to nurture and enhance these intellectual raw materials through the inspiration and discipline afforded by a superior educational system.

I hope you are both excited and a little apprehensive about the wonderful circumstances with which you will be surrounded come September. But most of all, I hope you are even now strengthening your resolve to derive from this opportunity all that it has to offer and to impart to your studies all the personal effort and sacrifice which they will demand.

   —Letter from Director of Studies, The Hill School, to author, 27 July 1987

TWENTY-SIX

Speed bumps at the entrance to the Spokane airport jolted me back into the sheriff's cruiser.

Soon, the sheriff and I boarded a minuscule aircraft. He hunched his big frame in the cramped seat next to mine, careful to keep his firearm concealed. The steward calmly offered peanuts. We ascended into blue sky. The mountains seemed like behemoths. I imagined being a housefly, buzzing over the fierce mountain range that lay to the west of RMA's campus. The plane shuddered and banked south toward Boise.

Boise is the capital of Idaho, and I'll see my parents there soon.

Flying in canyons, between mountains that were thousands of feet high, gave me a feeling I'd never felt before: Redemption. Soon I'd be with my parents, and this entire miserable experience would fall forever into the nightmare category, which is in the red binder in the very back of my conscious brain: the image of Herb staring at me from the truck, girls shrieking to their aborted babies, people pulling at their ears and hair in the melodrama of raps, Melanie sobbing uncontrollably during the Truth propheet, Darlayne's pretty but menacing face. When redemption came, I prayed I would forget fast.

That I'd ever imagined walking home from Idaho was laughable and idiotic. The difference between these Rockies and my round mountains back East was vast. These were some sharp, high-peaked, mean-looking mountains. The terrain was so expansive.

Thank God, Idaho will be a memory soon. I'll be reunited with my parents, and they'll get me the fuck out of here!

The mountains began to melt into normal elevations, and finally lowered toward flatter terrain to the south. I reflected on my few friends like Ernesto and Tim back at RMA. I had talked about splitting in short whispers with Jamie or Ernesto and wondered if they had gotten in trouble because I split. Just a conversation about the possibility of leaving would have been called a "contract," in RMA's backward jargon. My carrying it out would, necessarily, have caused the Papoose family to be interrogated. The staff would find out that Ernesto knew I still hated it there, and wanted to ask girls in to the woods for a romp – of that I had no doubt. Hopefully they wouldn't go too rough on him just for having been my pal. Wondering if I would ever see Ernie or my "older brother" Tim again, I guessed I did care a little about my five or six friends at RMA.

Delicate negotiations for my return to Charlottesville were a must – they were bound to demand something of me for splitting the shitpit. I'd already decided to be on my very best behavior when we got home. I would even quit smoking.

I'll have to mention that.

Sheriff Snipes knew not to tell me that I wouldn't be meeting my parents in Boise's airport when our plane landed.

While fall had already arrived up North near Bonners Ferry, it was still hot summer down in Boise. The airport was about the same size as Spokane's. A dry scorching heat greeted us on the tarmac. In the fuel-drenched, jet-engine-screaming shrill air, my police escort dropped the evil newsflash on me. Just outside the entrance to the Boise airport, the sheriff tugged my arm and yelled over the earsplitting engine noise.

"Your parents aren't inside, buddy. I'm sorry about that. I hate lying. Maybe in three weeks you will get to see your parents. They ain't coming to the airport, son. I had to lie to you."

The screaming jets in the background signified my feelings. *Foiled again.*

"You're going with a group called SUWS. Wilderness Survival. Urban something. I'm sorry, Zack. Your parents were clear about it."

"WHAT!"

"I said they were clear! They're sure! I don't know. Maybe Survival will straighten you out?"

I'm going on Survival. Holy shit! I had heard of that!

I felt fear barf in the pit of my stomach. Danger. The jet noise, for a moment, sounded like a million cheering and whistling rock fans at some massive outdoor concert.

This whole trip from Spokane to Boise had been a set-up, a ruse. Was I that gullible?

Yes.

Sheriff Snipes' sunglasses gave me a bug-eyed reflection of my face squinting at him. I stowed my anger and resisted the urge to kick him in the balls. There was nothing to do except ask to use a phone. He reminded me that he had handcuffs and would use them on me if he thought I would run away. I was young, probably stupid, but I knew that trying to ditch an armed officer at an airport – and trying to flee by foot – was futile.

"SUWS' people are inside, so smoke a cigarette, or whatever you're going to do."

They pronounced it "Sue's." I'd soon learn what those initials stood for.

While the sheriff stood there, I tried to call my best friend from home, Chuck Driems, at his mother's house. No one picked up. I was running out of people who would take a collect call. Almost everybody back home still lived with parents. I called Donald Roff, also in Charlottesville, so that I could talk to someone familiar. I had his number memorized. He was eighteen and had his own place, which he never left. I prayed that he'd steal a car and come get me.

He picked up. "Oh my god, WHAT THE FUCK, MAN! I'm going to talk to someone and find out if this is even legal! You could petition for emancipation from your parents like I did. But I think you need to be in the state and have parents' signatures for that. Well, I got it! We'll start a 'Get Zack Out of Jail' fund. We'll get donation containers at the 7-11! Hang in there, buddy!"

I never spoke to "Done Rough" again.

TWENTY-SEVEN

SEPTEMBER

SUWS, the School of Urban and Wilderness Survival – nicknamed "Survival" by all – was enough of the proverbial kick in the ass I ever needed. I had believed that my parents would be in the Boise Airport with my little sister – that the expressions on their faces would tell me they, too, regretted ever having heard of Idaho, and CEDU's RMA campus. It began to dawn on me that my parents felt I needed a good metaphorical ass-whooping after running away from home, then camp, and now Rocky Mountain Academy.

I was beyond disturbed that I wasn't going home, that I had been betrayed again.

Adults are evil. Adults are perverts. And they're all liars, to boot.

All people are full of shit, I decided, finally.

I took Sheriff Snipes on his honor because of his badge and his words to me. I regretted that. I stayed in the foster homes that whole fucking week, on a promise, and now I thought that a grown person's word wasn't worth salt. Nobody was seeing the situation from my rational perspective.

I had learned. I was scared. I would be good from now on. I swear it. No more lies and deceit, PLEASE.

I reluctantly trudged into the terminal of the Boise Airport behind my armed escort. Instead of being reunited with my parents, as I'd expected all day, I was introduced to two young, scraggly, and sturdy adults named Leslie Starr and Will Bender. I was pretty sure that Leslie was female.

These two were the faces of Survival. They gave me a brochure that explained I'd be on an expedition for the next several weeks. An "expedition" didn't sound the same as camping. Unceremoniously, Sheriff Snipes handed over the file with my picture on it to Will Bender, who signed for my custody.

I had only been the sheriff's cargo.

I inspected the Survival brochure as if preparing for the bar exam:

†

The 21 day wilderness experience will impact nearly every youth who participates. The youth will have the opportunity to experience significant success, perhaps for the first time, as they learn life-sustaining skills. Teens will experience more attitude and behavior influencing hours in our 21 day program than in over six years of typical weekly therapy. The school specializes in working with youth with attitude and behavioral problems.

Students travel up to 120 miles in the wilderness on a safe 21 day wilderness expedition. They live in primitive conditions, learning ancient Indian living skills by first-hand experience. They use their wits and newly acquired skills to live off the land in a raw, demanding confrontation with nature and with one's self. In the process of conquering real adversity, their better self emerges.

In the course of up to 120 miles, students confront many seemingly insurmountable obstacles, changing inwardly and building self-esteem with each real victory. Our people know the experiences required to change and build young people. These experiences are carefully integrated into the expedition, relying on the natural obstacles of the terrain and climate for soul-testing challenges. Despite these struggles, the expeditions are safe for youth.

The wilderness expeditions are organized to stretch the participant mentally, physically and emotionally. If you have not been on an expedition, you can't comprehend how emotionally demanding it is.

Hunger, thirst and quest for simple comfort drive them on. Mother Nature is a perfect motivator. Where else could people be placed in such a stressful but positive environment where old habits must be discarded for positive new ones?

No other program can duplicate the high stress and positive reinforcement of our wilderness expeditions. The combination of high physical and emotional

stress results from the concentrated full-time activity
of wilderness living. Life is simplified to its basics of
constantly struggling for food, water, shelter and a
little comfort. Other programs use artificial means to
create stress or push youth to greater endurance.

We know of no program that can equal our extraordinary results, particularly in such a short period of
time. Our program is therefore cost-effective. (Cost
$4,000 in 1988)

—SUWS brochure

✝

Will was dressed in tight blue jeans and a full-sleeved, red stretchy
shirt. Leslie Starr, evidently Will's assistant field guide, looked rugged
in her beige cargo pants and a camouflage sweater. Seeing the camouflage pattern on Leslie, though I tried to resist it, reminded me of Herb
jerking off, his skinny, half-exposed butt lifting off of the truck seat
next to me.

Leslie and Will both wore bandannas on their heads in a way
that was unacceptable at RMA. Without shame, they both seemed
to flaunt the aroma of body odor. Will already had a little swath of
blond facial hair forming, reminding me that I still didn't shave. They
seemed to have stepped off an unbeaten trail, and through a magical
portal into the airport terminal. Our grouping looked out of place,
even suspicious, in this corner of the polished airport. Business-suited
travelers gawked in our direction as they moved to their assigned gates.

Sheriff Snipes stood around the airport's exit with Leslie, Will, and
me while more kids arrived. Butch, the next one, emerged, handcuffed, from the parking area, with an escort. This man stood almost
seven feet tall. Gray haired, he moved stiffly like a tin man, keeping
his elongated hand on the chain between Butch's bracelets.

The sheriff gave me a squeeze on the shoulder. When I looked at
Sheriff Snipes' face, he wore an expression of mild awe.

He took me aside before leaving. "Again, I'm sure you'll be fine,
son. Sorry. Try and get the most out of it. Try to remember that you
have your life ahead of you, too. This is just a hurdle. You're a tough
kid, you'll be fine."

Sheriff Snipes gave me an apologetic shrug and turned away. His
duty fulfilled, he left me with my new legal guardians. Now what?

This all scared me a lot. It's one thing to hear kids talk about being handcuffed – kids say a lot of shit – but another thing entirely to sit with the likes of giant, stinky, stained Butch, his handcuffs still rattling on his wrists. His escort freed him of his shackles and departed. The burly kid in the cuffs was clearly several years older than I, and I wondered if others, closer my age, would arrive. Butch's expression, holding to the sacred tenets of the Truth propheet, was the opposite of joy. I tried to reconcile his facial expression with that metaphorical one from the propheet, but I could not find a trace of sorrow in him.

The opposite of joy may not be sorrow after all.

The opposite of joy was the feeling Butch and I shared in these miserable moments.

The rest of the kids came. They were all older. The one closest to my size said something about having wanted to come here. He went by the name of Todd. Todd's clothes were better. We assembled to be shuffled out of the airport's air conditioning and into to the blistering parking lot, Leslie in the rear and Will in front. A procession like this would be common in the weeks to come.

The dented, unmarked white van waiting for us had a man and a dog inside. Leslie's dog, Reba, was coming with us on our trip. Butch, still bitching about what an asshole his "escort" was, shoved me over in the van when we piled in. I wasn't sure if it was a playful shove.

When Leslie took the passenger seat, her doggie bounded over, punching us all in the nuts with her sharp paws. It was a decent icebreaker, a term I understood after the bubble gum "exercise" in the Truth propheet.

We weren't on bans – we were just freaked out. We could hear Will and Leslie talking about our "insertion point" with the driver as our two-hour drive to nowhere ticked down. The driver yanked the wheel hard, and the truck bounded off the main road at 45 MPH. Ahead, I could see that the place called Bray Lake wasn't a lake at all. Maybe it had been a lake when there were dinosaurs, but the only water to be seen was a trough for watering range cows.

We piled out of the dinged-up van. The area by the dried lakebed was about as boring as a square of matzo. We were not allowed the luxury of pissing until we emptied the van of boxes of supplies and rolls of wool that turned out to be for us. We danced around waiting for Will and Leslie to tell us it was OK to urinate. Finally, the van emptied of provisions, we were given permission to empty our bladders. After we guys peed, Will had us all strip. Leslie stayed several paces off.

There was no vegetation at our spot near Bray Lake, except for little bonsai-looking bushes. I was going to learn a lot about this plant called sage. Rolled up wheels of sage, having been dried almost to dust by the desert sun, whipped by.

Tumbleweeds, really?

The first play I ever had a lead role in was called "Tumbleweeds." It was in sixth grade. I played Snakeye McFoul.

I wasn't going to be bringing my cigarettes along, after all. Will gave me a disgusted look as he snatched the Marlboros from me. He went through all of our belongings before bagging them and writing our names on the paper bags, which went back in the van.

Will said we were being outfitted with everything that we would need. The snakeskin-hat-wearing man who'd been driving the van surprised us by speaking to us kids for the first time. I'd never seen a snakeskin fedora, and I liked his leather jacket. Since the man was at least twenty years older than even our field counselors, his voice and demeanor demanded respect.

He looked over our sullen group. "I'll be seeing you young men, soon. I'm Mr. Jade. Good luck. Do as Will and Leslie say, and do it exactly."

He shook hands with Will. Keys were exchanged, radios tested, and the man with the snakeskin hat pulled the unmarked van away into the tumbleweeds.

We received clothes and what Will called a rig: one pair of liner socks, one pair of wool socks, one pair of long underwear (cotton), one pair of blue jeans. Two T-shirts made of cotton and a wool button up shirt, the scratchiest material I would ever depend on. We each had one pair of men's briefs, a toothbrush, and one red bandanna like Will and Leslie were wearing. Our footwear was whatever we were wearing when we landed at the airport – for me, my work boots. Most importantly, we were each given a wool blanket, which would become our "rig." Lengths of thin white string accompanied the blankets, and Will instructed us to fashion a "bedroll" out of them. The wool blanket folded into a scratchy, uncomfortable apparatus that carried our belongings rolled within. We were given a small length of flat black strapping so we could carry the bedroll like a backpack. This harness was necessary with the sun and the distances we would be hiking, Will assured us.

"You can't just use the cord like a suitcase, but you can try if you want. But don't you slow everyone down because you can't carry it any longer. A bedroll on your back is the right way."

Just rolling the damn thing up with all my shit inside and getting the knots right, some of which Will called hitches, was difficult. We each had the same clothes, same colored toothbrush, and identical sizes of socks. The only thing differentiating us was our shoes and our hair.

After the bedroll making session, Will gave us the lowdown. "Don't think you're the only kids that we've had that think they can run away. You're not. Going AWOL is going to be bad on anyone who tries. We're experts. That's why we're here with you. We've had dozens of delinquents to deal with before you, so you're nothing special to us. OK? Trying to go AWOL will probably end in death for the student if Mr. Jade doesn't relocate you. You will be captured or you will be dead!"

I paid special attention.

"We have at our disposal all terrain vehicles, and, since the accident last year, we also have a Forest Service helicopter – if needed. Now, I don't want to have to be a cop out here. If we're going to do something, we're going to do it as a group. I don't tolerate attitude, either. Keep that in mind – I can be your friend or your worst fucking nightmare out here, OK?"

Will lost me for a second when he sad "cop out here" because I flashed back to the disclosure circle in the Truth propheet, and became concerned at the prospect of doing it again. Then I realized he was still talking about my expedition members' potential escape plans. Cop, like police.

"What happened last year?" Todd asked for us.

"A kid fell off of a bluff and got...fucked up...real bad. His location couldn't be ascertained because he went AWOL. And, he died before he could be relocated."

Leslie continued the story. "He was stupid to begin with. He made several mistakes. He went the wrong way, for starters. You kids need to know how far in the outback we are. There is no 7-11 out here, no Circle K, no IGA, definitely no McDonald's. There's not a store for eighty miles. You're not going to use a phone, and unless you have ESP, you're not going to talk to anyone else except Will and me, and these other kids, until Trail's End! So, let's suit up! You might want to re-tie your shoes over there, kid. What's your name again?"

Lastly, we were given our food rations, with a warning that this food was to last us until resupply. At some unspecified time in the future some other unknown person would bring us another unknown amount of food. For now though, I had: two cups of rice, two cups of lentils, a little baggie of bouillon cubes, a little baggie of flour, and a little baggie of another white substance that made some of the kids chuckle. It was powdered milk. That it was reminiscent of cocaine was no coincidence. It was pure luxury. It didn't go with anything except the oatmeal, of which we also had two cups. We were provided with two water canteens each, and informed that we were lucky to have two of them, already filled.

We were handed two thin pieces of crosshatched wood and a hunk of metal with a hole in it. These came with a tiny baggie of minuscule screws. *That was a knife?* Then we were shown how to put the beveled edge and its handle together. My group spent much of the next days scraping metal against little sharpening stones. Also in our inventory were a few lengths of leather to make sheaths, and artificial sinew that we'd use for everything from dental floss to tourniquets in an emergency.

Then we got bums' knives, the black-handled kind, that were a three-piece combo of can opener/screwdriver, long blade, and awl. At least these knives were already sharp.

Are you sure you want to give a knife to the guy who was just in handcuffs? Really?

Finally, after we re-rolled our bedrolls – they were quite full now – an unopened can of peaches was tossed to each kid. Mine was hot to the touch, having been stored in the van. Off we hiked, an imprecise group following Will Bender and Leslie, each one of us tossing or carrying our can of sun-heated peaches.

That evening, tired from the day's events, although the group hiked only a few hours in silence to our nondescript, desolate destination, we attempted to open the cans of peaches. I had no experience with the can opening tool before. I sensed the wetness of blood on my hand before I knew it wasn't peach juice. I said nothing, but had a difficult time finishing the task now that the top of the can was gooey and slick with blood.

The peach-can tops were supposed to be bent in half after being removed. If I'd known this before I'd wrenched the top off, I'd have been more careful. Bits of cotton from our brand new T-shirts were inserted into the jagged fold of the metal. Will and Leslie showed us how to place them in the coals of the campfire.

A few minutes later, char cloth had been made. My peach-can top had more jagged edges than any of the other dudes because of my wound and inexperience. I carried it carefully and was cautious every time I used it. I tried to be private about it. I was embarrassed that my char cloth maker was prickly.

The woman in our group, field counselor Leslie Starr, gave us all a demonstration of the flint and steel fire. She flicked her knife against a piece of quartz. Sparks generated by the collision flew off in a magical arc. After the second strike we could see that her char cloth, which she clutched with her fingers holding the quartz, begin to glow. She had landed one of the flying sparks on that tiny piece of char cloth. Leslie then carefully set the glowing speck of burnt cotton into a twist of sage bark that she deftly retrieved from her pocket. She breathed this little tinder bundle in to flames and used it to light a second campfire.

After a round of lighthearted applause, and in the growing firelight, Leslie next demonstrated a primitive fire-making technique called the bow drill. Using a length of shoestring, a pencil-pointed stick she called a spindle, a fireboard – a flat piece of wood with a few notches in it – and the handle of her knife, she began to move the pieces of the primitive machine.

The pieces squeaked at first, as Will commented: "That's it, wind the spindle into the bow. See how straight she kneels, her posture. She's got her weight distributed and the fireboard isn't moving. See how straight her arm is moving. LOOK! Already got a little pulp building there, see it? In a minute that's going to accumulate and begin to...there it goes."

Leslie's face wore that empty look of deep focus that can be seen on ballet dancers. She swung the shoestring and bow, spinning the spindle back and forth rhythmically in the fireboard. The parts all loosened up together, we heard a little purr or *whirr-whirr-urrr*, and then the smoke started.

"See it smoking? Now she's gotta keep going, that's it..."

The fireboard – the little chunk of wood under her bare foot – began to emit a growing cone of gray smoke. Smoldering pulp from her fireboard created a tiny coal just as Will was explaining that it would, and Leslie pulled the fireboard away from the little pile of pulp. Then she very gently nudged it into a second tinder bundle. This she also successfully blew into flames.

We were all impressed with the terminology, and even a little excited at the prospect of being able, in time, to do the same thing.

Our applause was heartfelt; however it wasn't going to be as easy as she made it look. Reality dawned: I was expected to do all of this at some point soon. I made sure that nobody saw the wound on my hand or the disbelieving expression on my face as I sat back from the fire-pit listening to my stomach squish up warm peaches.

As we settled under our wool blankets, I used my boots as a pillow. Will Bender reiterated that no kid had ever successfully run away from Survival. Then he moved over to his nicely organized sleeping arrangement on the ground, thirty feet away.

TWENTY-EIGHT

We did not keep journal entries on the first night. It was a given that our entries would be monitored. In fact, I was under the impression that my entries were to become the property of RMA. Unable to separate myself from the idea that this punishment was somehow connected to splitting from RMA, it took a while for me to realize that the SUWS program had nothing to do with the CEDU system. It was a separate program, and these kids were probably going home after our three-week expedition.

Will and Leslie sang, and let us sing "unacceptable" music almost all the time we hiked. I recognized a lot of the songs, but there were just as many that I didn't. While it was fun for the first six hours, the fact of a song's unacceptability, according to a stupid rule that only existed at RMA, soon ceased to generate any outlaw feelings. Besides, whenever I sang, I wound up even thirstier. It was a few days before I realized I would rather have saliva in my mouth than prove that I knew every rhyme on Eazy-duz-it, or License to Ill.

From the few words exchanged between Sheriff Snipes and my expedition counselors, I could tell that Will knew one thing about me: my options were minimized, shrunk down to doing whatever he and Leslie told me. I later discovered that the SUWS people had been in communication with my parents, and that Will and Leslie knew early on that Mom and Dad preferred my re-matriculation at RMA.

To have wasted my successful splitting would be a shame, a total waste.

I intended to stick to my guns because I didn't ever want to see Darlayne Hammer, or sit in another rap, ever again. Return to RMA after this "expedition" part of my banishment? I was incensed with my parents; outraged that RMA gave them the idea to punish me without seeing me.

That was the whole point of leaving RMA, so I could talk to them without some older student or staff sitting there taking notes and calling me on "manipulation games" every time I opened my mouth. I would not be able to contact them for at least three weeks, which just added to the uncertainty.

What would happen to me next, after Survival? Going someplace worse than a CEDU school, whatever that might mean? The thought of a third, unknown place gave me the trapped feeling I recognized from when I realized that RMA wasn't just an unentertaining, concocted performance. My entire life was at stake in a more immediate sense than at RMA, causing stress, sadness, and desperation. I acted on all three.

Morning came.

I pulled dirt out of my hair, yanked on my boots, and stood up. The vista stretched in all directions, reminding me of what I'd read about the "red planet." The terrain was brown though, not actually red like Mars is rumored to be.

Especially after a long day of hiking, I tried to let my mind wander. I wanted to escape from the insecurities and failures of my day, but was not able to achieve this level of distraction. I learned, though. By my last week in the desert, I was in a trance state almost all of the time. Uncertainty was now an ever-present condition. There was little or no food on my back that didn't have to be cooked, and I didn't have matches, a lighter, or a pot to cook in. I was worried about shitting without toilet paper, or what I was supposed to use the toothbrush with, since I had no toothpaste. Every detail of life was in doubt.

Will Bender was more silent than quiet and spoke only when he thought it necessary. He delivered his commands with no niceties. His leadership style spilled over to the whole group. A pecking order had to be established and there was no way I was going to be anything but Omega. I was the youngest and smallest. After three days of posturing, it was set: Will was Alpha, Leslie and Butch the Beta's. We were hiking all over the place, several different directions during the day, though Will acted as if he knew where the hell we were going. As usual I had no goddamn choice except to wake up when told, hike when told, dig a pit, cook, set traps, etc.

My first discourse with Will Bender occurred during the third evening in what he sometimes referred to as the Great Basin Desert. Everyone else was wrapped up in their blankets, flattening out after a long day. Will came across my leftovers from dinner next to me.

"What the fuck is this food doing here? Are you trying to get us eaten by coyotes and bears?"

"I'll eat the rest of it later. Or in the morning. That's all it is, I promise!"

In my inexperience, I had prepared too much food, and it was lumpy and crunchy – I couldn't possibly have eaten all of it at once. I figured I'd save the leftovers for the next day.

How had I done wrong?

Irrationally, and with strength, Will Bender picked up the peach can that was presently filled with lentil gruel, and threw my can full of food into the sagebrush. He jutted his neck at me with a rough grimace that said, "I oughtta pound you in the face," and stalked back toward his fire pit.

He had just thrown away half of my entire food ration. Being hungry brought a deep desperation that churned into irritation. Now I would be really hungry. It was going to be a sorry state of affairs. What in the world was there to live for anymore? You can't derive nutrition from anger. I searched and retrieved my peach can before the sun set. It had two or three days of food in it, since I hadn't figured out how to cook rice or lentils yet.

Outwardly, I was unabashedly pissed and indignant.

How am I going to keep living on this fucking earth? I hated the planet and everyone on it. I fumed until my lungs hurt from not crying out. I wanted a cigarette. I tried to pinpoint the direction that civilization would be, but couldn't navigate by stars.

Which way's East?

I stared into the heavens, entranced with despair.

It wasn't a prayer, what I muttered aloud, but it was close: *Give me strength. Please let me live through this so I can paint the earth black with the anger I feel right now. Don't ever let me forget the injustice and misery that I feel. But please tell me why is this happening? Am I bad? Shouldn't I die?*

Eventually, my heart slowed and the lump in my chest melted. Unresting, I slept.

Our tracks covered the boring, shrub-encrusted landscape. The ground on one side of a bluff, butte, or valley was the same gray and red, sage-infested earth as on another. There were usually two or three stops a day. It felt odd to stop. I could feel my brain continuing to send "hiking" messages to my muscles. Will lectured that it was better for our bodies to remain standing than to sit down during these pauses. He explained that warm muscles constrict as we rest, and to avoid painful cramps, we were supposed to resist collapsing on the ground. I wasn't listening, so I threw myself down, using my rig for a pillow.

I didn't care if my legs would cramp. I intended to slow down the pace because this was preposterous! The canteen's refreshing water melted over my tongue deliciously. My other canteen was full and I was reflecting on that one shred of goodness, my possession of that other container of coolish, luscious, wonderful water. I slurped another gulp out of the army green colored plastic and looked to what I knew to be the west.

Since the first day in the desert, our group could easily sense the evidence of the forest fires that plagued the western United States. This wilderness program had us so close to that war between man and nature that I could smell the burn, and occasional incinerated particles floated by me, out of the dark soot cloud to the west. It was always there – that's how I knew which way was West. Back East we didn't have forest fires; at least I'd never been threatened by one. One of the counselors at RMA, George Daughtry, claimed to have been a smoke jumper before he came back to work at the emotional growth program.

While looking toward the clouds of smoke to our west, Will reminded us that smoke jumpers were there now, risking their lives. First, by parachuting out of airplanes into forest fires, and second, by having to battle the flames to escape alive. I thought these specialized soldiers were valiant.

Finally I relaxed enough that my mind wandered away from the group. An image: the burning of RMA's campus. That would be so cool to do. I panted and pondered while collapsed in the sun, so hungry I could eat mud.

I sprang up with as much energy as I could muster when it was time to hoof again. I wanted to show Will that I wasn't muscle fatigued. In the minute waiting for the others to slip bedrolls back on and stop picking at the blisters on their feet, I took another long haul from my canteen. Will shook his head at me.

"OK, crew, we'll be dry camping tonight. I know it's hot, but try to conserve your water. You hear me, Zack?"

"OK."

Will looked pointedly at me and approached me as I enjoyed the feeling of a final sip of water on my dry tongue. As soon as he reached me, Will slapped the open canteen from my hands and it tumbled to the ground! He had just gotten through telling us to conserve our water.

What the fuck is wrong with this guy?

"Why did you do that?" I accused, sharper that I ought to have.

"Because you're going to run out anyway, Bonnie."

I furiously grabbed the canteen before it bled its precious contents onto the ninety-degree, dusty ground.

†

Zack conserved his water on the hike today and did not go thirsty. I think the lesson learned earlier sank in (or should I say "absorbed"?).
—Official Journal of group leader, Day 6 of SUWS expedition, referring to previous day's interaction with author.

†

Survival wasn't the same as the six weeks I'd so far spent at RMA. For one thing, what Will did would arguably have been against the violence Agreement. It left me in a bit of shock, along with my anger, and shame at being too small to retaliate.

Out here we had finite goals on a list. Requirements in Survival included making fires, keeping a journal, filling out workbooks at night, gutting an animal that you caught, making and setting traps to catch a critter, catching a fish with no pole, and going five days without swearing. The swearing requirement, a five-day period absent of all obscenities, seemed a simple enough task, even though at RMA we were allowed to cuss about anything. On Survival, when the adversity of being out there caught up to us, and guys in our group cursed, I could see the look of disdain in Will's face. There were twenty days left to complete the five-day requirement. Nobody took it seriously.

In some gloomy landscape called Ferguson Flats my group began to meet our primitive fire-making requirements. So far, every fire we'd had was "Prometheused" from one of the counselors' fires. As predicted, to create a flint and steel fire wasn't as easy as Leslie had made it seem at Bray Lake the first night. I chipped away at a piece of quartz with my knife the way Leslie had demonstrated. I could reliably produce a wimpy four or five sparks with each strike. It seemed impossible to aim the sparks so they'd land on a square inch of char cloth. The cut on my hand from opening the can of peaches still foiled my attempts. After a few more strikes, I saw the char cloth glowing and shoved it into a tinder bundle. Blowing the little nest into flames was easy, this time. I would sleep warm, and could scratch one night of

246

that requirement off my list.

Except for the times I had to start a flint-and-steel fire on command for Will, I had no problem starting a fire that way. It was always more difficult with him watching me, because I responded to his constant, silent frustration with insecurity. There was something about the way he hovered around me that reminded me of my father trying to watch me learn long division. Will didn't have to be out there, he was a field counselor, not a kid.

If he hates us so much, why doesn't he just go home, or work at Pepsi, or go die fighting fires? I worried he'd lash out and kick or punch me if I failed making my fire or other requirements.

The asshole Will did know his shit though. Early in the morning one day, we killed a rattlesnake. Well, Will killed a rattlesnake. Impressing our small group, Will slayed the poisonous snake within seconds of its being discovered.

"What the fuck! Ohmigod! Snake! Yo snake, yo. SNAKE, YO!" Butch exclaimed, "It's huge!"

Sure enough, a rattlesnake shook its long bung of rattles in a menacing manner. I naively assumed we'd avoid it, and go around the threat, but Will had a different idea. Our other field counselor, Leslie, handed him a gnarled stick. He promptly broke a piece off, and in a moment the snake was meat. With movements full of decision and a complete lack of hesitation, he pinned the snake's head to the earth with the Y-ended stick. The snake, immobilized where it mattered most, spun around itself in an endless psychedelic loop, trying to free its head. One more deft move with his Bowie knife and Will removed the head from the gray argyle, rattling tube of nerves. The snake kept moving while Leslie and Will warned us that the venom inside the snake's fangs and head was still lethal. The severed snake's head was more dangerous, in some ways, that when it was alive and attached, Will claimed. Pondering this, Butch and I dug a deep little pit, where we deposited the serpent's head.

After a quick referendum we arrived at a unified decision: the snake was, indeed, food. The spasmodic reptile corpse was stowed into Butch's bedroll and didn't stop being the subject of conversation until it became food that night. Everyone got a tiny tasty bite, at what after that became rare – a communal fire. I sucked on my bite of rattlesnake meat like it was butterscotch candy – it tasted so good. I hadn't had meat in a week. While I savored the buttery morsel, I tried to forgive myself for not immediately recognizing the snake as food.

✝

Nicki Bush, a child psychologist and professor at the University of California, San Francisco, says, "What we see is that these places are almost always in remote areas or near small towns, and they create a situation where everyone in the region is a big proponent of the facility. They provide a lot of jobs and stimulate the local economy, and that creates a sense of pride that they're helping the youth of America. So there's social capital to having one of these in your area. Moreover, because the youth that are put there are predominantly at risk for something—either they have some peer problems or behavior problems or social problems, etcetera—when something happens to them, people tend to dismiss it as, 'Well, they're bad teens.'"

Bush is concerned that the lack of regulation is creating an environment where untrained staff is often given free rein with an extremely vulnerable population.

"[These programs] call themselves wilderness therapy or come up with their own categories so that they can avoid the criteria that would apply to, for example, a mental health treatment facility," she says. "Then because they're not regulated, no one is really ensuring that their staff has adequate training, and in many cases we've seen, the staff are by no means qualified to provide the type of care that is being advertised and certainly not the type of care that these facilities require."

— Sulome Oswald, "When Wilderness Boot Camps Take Tough Love Too Far," *The Atlantic*, August 12, 2014

TWENTY-NINE

I was halfway through my weekly rations, and unable to comprehend either if there was an outside schedule attached to the expedition,
or how long the rations I now hoarded were designed to last. We were
skirting another prehistoric dried up lakebed, when up ahead, we
saw two figures. The adult had a snakeskin hat and could only be the
man who'd driven the van away at the start of the expedition. A visit
from Mr. Jade meant that over one week had passed. A girl was with
him, dressed in a blue Survival T-shirt like our own. I recognized her
instantly. Vera Cruces was a student at RMA with me!

The first thing Vera said was: "I think I split the day after you. They
were looking all over the fucking place for you, though. Congratula-
tions! Zack, hello! That's your name, right?"

"Hey, I'm sorry I blew you away in Darlayne's rap that day, but I
take a lot of ownership in that rock wall I was working on. You look
skinny, dude!"

I was shocked to see a familiar face. Vera was the girl whose boot,
the very one on her left foot now, had been the victim of a bouncin'
two man saw up at RMA. Also, I'd had at least one rap with her in
that shitpit, and she'd been all over me about how I flossed my teeth. I
had never even spoken to her outside of raps because of our bans from
each other.

A strange new feeling, of having shared the RMA experience, con-
fronted me. Our predicaments were similar. I felt close to her. I knew
we each had uncertain futures; I had no way to relate to the rest of the
group on that level. A sense of familiarity and brotherly love for Vera
filled me when she spoke my name. Vera reacted with the same happy
familiarity. She saw my face and, smiling widely, closed in for a big
hug. Any question I had as to whether we were still on bans faded.

"Yeah, I split with Rob Warner. He got busted shoplifting beer
in Sandpit. Dumbass. I ran, but the police found me behind a gas
station. I think he may just get to go home, manipulative fucker. But
I'm sure the school would tell everybody he's in a lock-up, right? Fuck
RMA!"

If Vera had run away with a guy, that automatically made it a split/
sex contract in RMA jargon. CEDU Education had kicked her out,

but she seemed all the happier for it. Vera would be taken the next morning to begin her sentence, so we had all night to "cut up" RMA.

When I was done making my camp and setting my traps, which Will austerely checked, Vera and I sat down together. She understood my predicament. She had split three times from RMA, and swore she'd never return.

"Yeah, I couldn't help but get dirty the whole time there. They hate you if you stand up for yourself, or if you're a blob. That's the worst thing – they're fucking playing games, right! You know Geor…I'm not even going to GO THERE! I fucking hate it there, let's just leave it at that. I'm not going to let them brainwash me."

The uncertainty of our situations bonded us. We both believed RMA was trying to mind-control us into being robot-thinkers like the teachers, guidance counselors, and parents. Or worse. She reminded me of the totalitarianism, the absolute choice-sucking, ratting, culty, weirdness of that place near Bonners Ferry. The rest of the kids in my Survival group came over and sat with us to hear about the older, look-good students and the whacky, hippie, touchy counselors at RMA. They were interested in CEDU, which Butch had heard of; they were interested in Vera, for more obvious reasons. Trying to assert my familiarity with Vera, I clasped her hand.

We compared our own notes on WHY our parents had sent us to RMA and SUWS. Todd told us that he had been doing some drugs and went to his parents with a few brochures and the idea to come clean. His father did drugs. I'd never thought about what that might be like. Todd wanted intervention in this unconventional form of Survival. Would they pay for it?

Vera and I were shocked, and called bullshit. I wasn't sure his story was absolutely true. His actions would soon set us right: they spoke volumes about his personality. Todd Jerde was a gallant and humble young man. Just a real winner, like my brother, one of those kids my mom wanted me to be. He listened and talked with us that night about RMA, about how weird CEDU stuff sounded, how it must suck to be so many miles from home, to be threatened with lock-ups for four more years after the Survival expedition. Two and a half years at RMA was a long time, we all agreed, but it would be more than that if I got locked up somewhere until age eighteen. Nobody in the group thought that being sent to RMA should have been allowed without a crime attached to it. Vera and I weren't juvenile delinquents, Todd noted aloud, after Butch asked if either of us had ever stood in front of a judge.

Vera was too distracted with starting her Survival expedition the next day, and our conversation about RMA, to notice Todd's fairgame attempts at flirtation. I approved, but I knew her first.

Maybe she was wondering what was in store for her over the next three weeks. Would her expedition group be grumpy? Would any participants come to the outfitting in handcuffs? Would there be another girl?

After the rest of the group went to their rigs to eat, Vera described some of the next propheet – the Brother's propheet – to me. My peer group would go through it next at RMA.

"I will say since you're out here, you're probably not going back to RMA, dude. If you already went through the Truth, it's pretty much the same, only the shooter marble is your little kid. Your "little kid" or "dooger" does everything inside you and you'd better be good to it. You hurt your little kid when you don't rat on your friends, blah blah blah..." Vera stared off for a moment or two. "I know you were there when the last Summit got out. That was fun, but it's always different, each time. Then there are these physical exercises, you know the story. The Brother's Keeper propheet...if I thought you'd believe me...And you know who ran mine?"

I shook my head.

"George Daughtry, that pervert. During the nap session in the morning, I caught him trying to go up my shirt! Fucking pervert. He made me promise not to tell anyone, but I'm telling you, because they're, like, into some weird shit up there. That guy Chet Lively fucked a horse? Ohmigod. And Darlayne Hammer, holy SHIT, WHAT A BITCH!"

Talking with Vera made it clearer for me: On Survival, growth was reduced to mental and physical survival. At RMA, though, where our physical needs were met, we were supposed to learn social survival, according to their methods. Put simply, SUWS encouraged a lack of social dynamic; physical and mental survival were stressed. At RMA, social survival was the objective. It was everything.

Vera had to sleep near Leslie for the obvious reason that we all wanted to keep her warm.

THIRTY

The next morning I sensed that I had burned three inches of my right boot and part of my blue jeans in the small fire. I had kept it stoked all night so I'd have warmth in the morning. The stink of burning rubber drifted over our campsite to be replaced by the steely smell of a frozen morning. I wasn't the slightest bit embarrassed by my combustion. Appearances mattered very little, and besides Vera must already be on her way. I had heard an engine earlier.

She was no longer among us. Mr. Jade, with his special hat, had retrieved her. I looked at Todd while he slept, Todd who actually

WANTED to come on Survival. He was the only one in our group, or any group that we heard of, that went willingly into the Mojave Desert, or what they told us was part of the Mojave Desert. They also called it Owyhee, whatever that was.

My blue jeans deteriorated rapidly in the elements after the incident with the fire. Constant walking wore holes into the knees. I cut off my back pocket that morning to use for toilet paper. I didn't need pockets – everything was in the bedroll. Now my ass had air conditioning.

We hiked into a thawing sunrise to tackle another long dry day in the heat without water. Daytime passed with the miles. That night we settled a camp that was exposed to ferocious cold wind. Now we'd freeze. Awesome.

I had had a tough day reflecting on the previous night's conversation with Vera and the group. Was this purgatory? Where would I wind up next, a hell? I knew now that my parents hated me and never wanted to see me again. Mom and Dad had to be gambling I'd die by starvation, fall off of a cliff, or get eaten by coyotes.

When our group did talk during the endless days of hiking, the subjects ranged from things we encountered that can be eaten, to the final days of the expedition. At some point during Trail's End, our group would jog the last few miles with our bedrolls strapped to our backs. We'd run to a restaurant that would appear out of this bland sage-scape, as mysteriously as a mirage, and magically out of a desolate brown landscape, pass into waves of air conditioning and cans of Pepsi, and the heavenly smell of fried chicken.

"So, we could eat these crickets, Will?"

"Go ahead. If we collect some, they pop up a little like popcorn over fire. Or a hot stone. Add some salt, a little cayenne pepper. We'll do that if you guys want. Just collect them."

We walked more. Nobody had the energy to capture the hopping creatures, or a place to store them. But I wanted to cash in on Will's seemingly bright mood.

"Tell us again about the menu at the, um...

"It's just a truck stop, you guys." Leslie didn't seem to like it when we talked. She said all we talked about was food.

"Yeah, but there's ice cream, right?"

"Yes I said there is ice cream. There's a little section of the restaurant with a couple of tubs. And if you order from the waitress, they'll bring you a shake. That's what I usually get. A big, frothy, milkshake. CHOCOLATE, please! What luxury."

"But there's like a steak bomb on the menu?"

"What the fuck is a steak bomb, motherfucker?"

"HEY, that's unnecessary. Back to square one there, Butch."

"It's just a big sandwich. Grinder. Like a sub," I added helpfully.

"Of course there's a chicken patty sub, steak subs, burgers...anything you'll want. Believe me, I've never heard of a kid getting disappointed."

I had to change the subject so Leslie might not hold it against me that I mentioned food. "Do they have phones at the truck stop and restaurant at Trail's End? Whattaya call it again?"

"The Oxbow."

"The Oxbow." We repeated the name of the truck stop as if it was the last oasis in some sub-Saharan landscape. I pictured the Oxbow Truck Stop and Restaurant as if it were made of emeralds and had rushing aqueducts pouring out cold mountain water feeding enormous Roman-style fountains.

The imaginary fountains in front of the...shit, I just remembered that what I was imagining was the cover of a book. The Emerald City, one of the Oz books, had hijacked my daydream, yanking its cover art from my imagination like a... shit – *I'm back to thinking about cheeseburgers.*

We were promised happy reunions with our parents, except me, as Will pointed out for the hundredth time.

"If he's lucky he gets to go to CEDU in California or back to RMA. Provo Canyon won't take him. Oh, you ain't heard that yet? You're too young. They won't take anyone younger'n sixteen. You're only fourteen, ain't ya, Bonnie?"

As usual I bristled at being called by my last name, and for being called out for being youngest. There seemed to be extra conditions on me everywhere I went. For example, I was supposed to write a letter to Rocky Mountain Academy asking them to forgive me for splitting. The letter-writing requirement was held over my head like a guillotine blade: write it or die by blunt force trauma at a lock-up in Utah or Montana. The letter was the first thing to become an extra requirement for "the weakest link" among us. I wish I'd never asked what that phrase meant. Will used it when talking to the group about rescue scenarios.

"They can't deal with him at home. That's why they had sent 'im to RMA. You better write that letter, Bonnie boy. You don't wanna get sent to a lock-up." Will paused to blow into the fire. The open flames lit his face from below. "I don't know why I work with kids."

If I'd been bigger or braver, all it would take was a nudge and some pressure. *I could burn that gay-ass goatee off of Will's face.* Knowing I was incapable of carrying out this primitive impulse only reminded me: *What an insignificant cretin I am.*

On the off chance that I survived malnutrition and bear attack, I might go to a roughneck teen jail where I'd probably get shanked for being small or manipulative, or intellectual, or all the other things that I'd never known I was before Idaho.

Survive the rest of the week, one hour at a time.

Will Bender, like most adults with authority over me in Idaho, had special training in how to get under kids' skins. I couldn't ignore it. Fighting with this bastard would go on for weeks. Maybe I deserved to die in jail. Could this be what my parents meant when they'd said, "You don't know how lucky you are?"

It was true, I didn't. That thought had come up a lot of times, trying to elbow its way in from the little red notebook of my mind that said, "Don't inspect." If I thought of never seeing my parents again – a very real possibility – and dying at gladiator training in juvie, I'd start crying. I had to actively let my mind fly, and keep it light.

Not too dark. I willed myself back to thinking about the Oxbow.

But I couldn't stop thinking that having parents, that part of my life, was over. It wasn't a simple thought to confront: *The life I thought I was going to have before this summer, had ended.* I couldn't even remember the face of the last girl I liked, or a time that I'd been happy, or fed. RMA would call these thoughts "victim thinking."

When had I thought concretely about my own death? Certainly, even after the fights with my parents that were so bad I wanted to die – had even perhaps tried to die – I'd not considered the possibility that the act might make my parents happy. Guilty, I thought they'd feel. Or sad.

My parents might love me, but they definitely don't want me around anymore.

In my most private, darkest hour at home, my parents' feelings had been secondary to my own emotions. I must have decided to never dwell on, to never think of that hour again. The crippled, powerless, self-hatred I felt that dark night, I'd never copped out to in RMA. No sane person would. Not there, in that untherapeutic environment. But that night in the desert, I did think I could die. From apathy and freezing. On that cold night I didn't get out from the wool blanket and do pushups and jumping jacks until my heart thumped. I just lay there shivering with my teeth knocking together.

I couldn't start my bow-drill fire the next night. For this, Will informed the crew that we would be walking extra miles the next day.

"You're our weakest link," Leslie repeated in a nasty hiss.

I reached the end of my patience, and something shifted: a wrinkle in reality lasted two days. A two-day dream of air conditioning, and iced tea with packets of sugar. Imagined bong-hits – more than I'd ever actually taken. Packs of cigarettes in a hospitality basket with fruit, cheese. My reflection in a freezer lined with fluffy white frost, became my mental sanctuary. I rolled across a monotonous plateau that was a giant pillow, into a world-sized waterbed, though I was still hiking. Try as I might, I couldn't find an end to the infinite bed, or wake from the daydream.

When I did finally wake, the days of hiking were also in a dream state: I was starving the staff back at RMA, making them hike at gunpoint. Tying my parents to a chair and making them listen to music I liked for twenty hours. In my evil revenge daydream, which I could control as little as a sleeping dream, I only gave Mom water after a teary apology. In my daydream, when I set them free of their bonds and shut down the music, they loved and hugged me with new acceptance, warmth, and sufficient love – requited love.

I knew they were dreams and weren't really happening, but at times my brain sure made it seem real. Tears formed to wet my eyes from my imaginary reunion, dust in my mouth swelling my tongue as eight, ten, and twelve hours of hiking passed. Once, the convincing stories in my head lent my nose the satisfying smell of the northern Idaho woods awash in a tremendous fire that I had started in the wood corral. Hunger fueled my dark imagination. Daydream and reality, nightmare and reality, blended in a way that made me begin to question my goodness, my sanity.

I wasn't the only one weakening under these conditions. Leslie and Joe were almost sent home for dehydration. Joe babbled incoherently about Shoney's Big Boy, so our group at first thought he was just acting foolish. His dehydration got so bad that he fell over face-first with a dusty thud, the mangled rubber soles of his sneakers turned up to the sun. That's how we knew he wasn't playing what RMA would have called an attention game.

Will squeezed a little tube of nutrient into Joe's mouth and doused water from an extra canteen he pulled from inside his rig. Since Joe was slowing down the pace that Will set for us, I didn't feel as sympathetic toward Joe's condition as I normally would've. I just wanted to keep moving toward camp, wherever that turned out to be. Standing was now much worse on my feet than walking – I don't know why. My feet needed to keep getting closer to where we'd sleep that night.

The most amazing realization I made on Survival was how machinery worked before the combustion engine, before steam, back in the days of Leonardo da Vinci when they used math, and men cut ships out of burnt logs. I have some understanding, because of events in the desert that September.

When starting a fire with the bow-drill method, I needed the damn thing all still and plumb. At first there were always little mistakes. It took me a while to guess right on the hitches and knots at both ends of the bow. Then you adjusted for tautness once you got the spindle in there. There had to be enough to allow the spindle to flip one time, but still spin with predictability. Fortunately that final crucial adjustment could be made with a finger while sawing. Here, in the hole-with-a-pie-slice-missing of your fireboard, you put the end of the spindle with the mantle on top. Usually the spindle would flip out in front of you at two and ten o'clock. Once you got up and down from your knees about twenty or forty times, you might get it spinning right for a second. That bumpy-feeling squeak let you know it was starting to work.

The tricky part, if you got the mantle squeezing the spindle into the fireboard right, was to continue spinning until you began to sweat. You couldn't let the sweat drip into the fireboard's pie-hole where the coal should be born. Underneath all this you had a piece of bark or the sheath of your knife to catch the smoldering pulp created by friction.

You had to make sure your knee or bare foot was holding that damn fireboard steady; any motion would throw everything out of whack. You had to saw it – fast enough for the tension to hold the spindle straight, but at the same time, displacing your sawing activity proportionately. You leveled it all out. Then as you kept spinning, *whirr-whirr-urrr* – the smoke started.

When the smoke was billowing from the board, it was like holding the end of a cigar a foot beneath you. Next you GENTLY took everything away except the smoldering pile of pulp on the bark or sheath, and popped it into a ready-made tinder bundle. From here, I was golden. As I got better, the pulp bit could be small, and the tinder bundle would always work. I carried little nests of dried sage in my sack or my pocket for tinder, to use if it was raining.

It was the whirr and whistle of the bark or shoelace winding the spindle back and forth in the fireboard that you needed. Once the smell of burning sage floated into a nostril, you were halfway there. Whirr and whistle. Whirr and pull and whirr. Whirr. If you'd been steady, persevering, and a bit lucky the first time, you'd have a fire to cook rice and lentils in a used peach can we called a billy can.

When I made my bow-drill fire for the first time, I was beyond happy. I was proud, and I didn't have much to be proud of. Making a nice big circle around that requirement on Will Bender's piece of paper was the highlight of my first week.

I had made flame.

Zack got his first bowdrill fire by himself today. He was jumping around camp, singing and hollering. Strange that a small fire made by rubbing two sticks together can make a person so happy. Good job, Zack!
—Official Journal of group leader, Day 8 of SUWS expedition

THIRTY-ONE

I was in the third day of my swearing requirement. This was made possible by my all-day daydreams. Remaining silent is easy when your brain operates in a weakened haze. However, because I was SO unhappy, the despair peeked through. I noticed the fury and tears in my conscious mind when it came back from its dream dimension.

Outdone, tired, and beyond thirsty, all our canteens were empty.

Voices ahead jarred me out of another dream, this one involving a carpet of macaroni and cheese. Will yelled, "Camp Ho." With a holler, Todd and Nick were both singing "'SPRI-ING'! There's a SPRING OVER HERE!"

We rushed toward the voices and water source, a cattle trough with running water dripping needlessly over its rusted sides. The extra water fell into a muddy pit that was a mosaic of cow hoof prints. Muddy water sat in the little pockets. No grazing grasses or plants were to be seen. Just Planet Mars with sage. We crowded around, submerging our canteens in the cattle trough. I jammed an arm between the others, filled mine halfway, and retracted it to my dry gob. I was in heaven as I gulped down the strange tasting water. Like most of us, I had always taken water's existence for granted.

The moment of serenity with my canteen was interrupted as Nick and Joe began barfing. Two minutes after discovering the spring, their bodies rejected the large amounts of water their bodies so needed. What's funny is both of them were laughing while they were retching and burping up the water. The whole group, except Will, who looked on with a disapproving shake of his head, laughed with them. The putridity dribbled from their noses and chins.

From his place away from the crowded trough and growing puddle, Will mentioned that people had better drink plenty – Oh, and drink it slowly.

Now you tell us.

†

Our instructors are skilled, good role models,
responsive listeners, and caring individuals. Mother

Nature is the authority figure and brings effective and timely consequences should the youth's actions or inactions not be appropriate.

—"Dear Parents" letter from Director of SUWS, Member, N.W. Chapter, Society for Adolescent Medicine, Washington Alternative Learning Association

I rendered one of my canteens of water useless the next day. Because I had seen Will suck on a little stone that he said was salty, which caused him to salivate more during the hike, I put a whole bouillon cube into my remaining canteen water. I stupidly thought that the more bouillon salt I added to my water, the more I would salivate when I drank it. Like Will, I'd be more refreshed.

Will saw me try to take a sip of the gooey substance during a break. After coming to investigate, he started screaming. He cursed me for purposeful sabotage in front of the group. Closing the distance, he stuck his finger in my face. "What in God's name did you do? Why would you do this?" He pecked his index finger into my forehead ferociously to the beat of his syllables. "You are a little moron, aren't you? Dumb kids, surrounded by DUMB KIDS!"

It had been a bad idea on my part, nothing more. Even though it hadn't affected anyone else, it was another failure, something more I did wrong. I tried to lead the group hiking the remainder of the day, to compensate, thinking maybe this way Will won't punish the whole group.

Finally, we stopped and made a base camp. Everyone was glad to have a place for longer than one night and one scrimpy meal. We would have two days to camp here, interspersed with a day trip to go see some petroglyphs.

To hike without our bedrolls was easy. I'd been losing weight, and felt light and agile as a spider. I couldn't do much right, but I sure could hike! I don't think Will and Leslie realized how the temperature fluctuations and the hiking wore us down. At the beginning of the expedition the group members had competed to stay at the head of our forced procession, but that nonsense had ended as we realized there was nothing to see.

The visual highlight of the whole trip came the next day.

"OK, people! Rise and shine and shit if you can!"

I hadn't shat in four days.

"I've got a surprise for us! No bedrolls today, just fill your canteens, give me your food bags, and get ready for a day hike. We leave in thirty minutes….Because they have to be buried or hung high enough to keep the coyotes from getting to them. Nobody is going to steal any of your frickin' food, guys! Hand 'em over!"

About two miles later we entered a pasture with protruding round rocks about the size of school buses. Six of them had white marks all over them. Next to the last hunk of rock was a sharp bluff with lots of pictographs scraped on its face. I noticed some dating back to '82. I'm not sure how old the other stuff was that we were supposed to be looking at? Perhaps ten or twenty thousand years?

"See the little dude with the bow, there? And the horse?"

"That kind of looks like a fish. Yeah, that's a fish for sure."

"Does this tribe still exist?" I asked.

"These were the Owyhee, but not really. And some of these were here before them, even. According to what I've been told. And Mr. Jade has a book on local anthropology that has this nice photo spread of these rocks."

Leslie chimed in. "It's too bad there's assholes that actually steal some of this. Mr. Jade told us, remember? Look here, somebody just drove a truck out here and took the entire chunk of this one. What's worse is they fractured it on purpose, so they could take it with them. Shameful pricks!"

Sure enough, we could see the rock had been broken off from a scratched patchwork of hands, animals, and eye shapes with wings that reminded me of UFO saucers.

When we came back from seeing the ancient chalk drawings, the group got to work making natural cordage from sage bark. Braiding bark in the shade as the late afternoon sun faded to evening, I reflected that the day trip to see the petroglyphs was one of the hottest days yet. That we now had water helped, but it had been hot as hell on the day hike. Back by my rig, looking at my remaining rations – after Will returned with them – was disheartening. I was almost out of food, and went to sleep without eating anything.

When six hungry people could share in the killing and roasting of a minuscule mouse, it must be said that we were desperate. The mouse's demise on the next day's hike did succeed in providing our group with plenty of laughs, if not adequate mouthfuls. As soon as the mouse, the size of a large cockroach, astonished us by brazenly skittering into the middle of our hiking formation, Will yelled, "Get it, kill it. Whoever kills it gets the requirement done!"

It amused me to watch the other boys thrash about like scrabbling, starving English Bobbies. I knew I'd just get shoved out of the way if I went for the kill. Incredibly fast, dodging blows from above that rattled the sandy earth, the little rodent scurried in and out of tiny caves in the rocky terrain and under sticks and other debris, only to be flushed out anew. The malnourished group lashed out like drunken blind men with unproductive whacks of the sticks that we carried, all trying to peg the little bugger into unconsciousness.

Butch, the kid who'd arrived in handcuffs, wasn't armed with his "digging stick." Holding his deteriorating shoe over his head, he was waiting for the right moment. It was absurd how smoothly Butch brought his footwear down from above, with one targeted thud. As Butch ground his shoe into the rock, we heard the mouse yelp. The group crouched next to Butch. When he lifted his shoe, you would have thought we had brought down our first wooly mammoth. Butch lifted his face toward the open sky and let out a terrific, primal yell that ended in a low growl. He seemed to be attempting to turn into a werewolf, or was regressing one step backwards, into an ape.

Immediately, a little fire was built and the six of us celebrated the hunt and the shared, pitiful treasure. I had a leg. The forepaw, about the size of two inchworms joined at the head, joined the thigh in a tiny "L" shape. I ate the bone after the meat, and for the next few hours we often broke out in laughter as we walked back to base camp, reenacting Butch's triumphant Tarzan yell.

†

A certain pet owner has just purchased a young dog that has much potential to become a quality hunting dog. The owner searches out and locates a dog trainer with a top reputation. He contracts to have the dog trained over a period of time. After many weeks the trainer calls and says your dog has completed his formal training. The trainer gives you the necessary orientation, the commands, etc., and says as you leave, "Be clear in your commands, be consistent and follow through. Above all, demonstrate your love and caring for the dog and you will be pleased with the dog's performance for years to come."

Now the question. If the owner is inconsistent, uses different commands (mixed signals), or pretty much ignores the dog, what kind of a hunting dog will he have in a month or a year? He will probably have wasted the money and just have a common mutt. The owner must do his part.

—"Dear Parents" letter from Director of SUWS, Member, N.W. Chapter, Society for Adolescent Medicine, Washington Alternative Learning Association

THIRTY-TWO

Will's goatee had grown in, Leslie had fur developing on her ankles, and it was even colder at night. The days were tolerable in coolness, a change from the desert inferno. Except when it rained, I thought my spirits were high. I was only one more night away from completing my swearing requirement. I presented my natural cordage to Will just before sunset. I used the cordage, made from sage bark as required, to complete my Paiute dead-fall traps.

He had made traps earlier in the week and showed us later how to bait and set them. Setting a trap wasn't easy, but making natural cordage was even more tedious. It took a lot of focus and steadiness that I had a hard time marshaling in my brain fog. The cordage I had made was strong, I was confident of that. But Will tugged on my cordage much harder than he or Leslie had ever done to any of the other kids, or to my cordage before. When Will tugged, my first trigger line broke. He hadn't just triggered the trap, he wrenched my cordage in such a way that it was sure to break. He was onto the second trap ten feet away while I followed behind, begging him to stop. He snapped three of my traps up, sending the carefully notched sticks and hand braided bark in all directions. He took what was left and shoved the broken lengths of sticks and cordage into my face.

"Make 'em stronger. These traps won't catch! These were put up too quickly."

"I can't believe this."

Flustered, I raspberried a sigh while turning to the devastation he had wrought. Asshole, ass fucking hole fuck, I sputtered. I had worked diligently on those traps.

Will came up behind me and shoved me in the direction of my rig.

"What did you say?"

I stared at him. "What do you mean? N-n-nothing," I stammered, wondering if I was about to receive the physical thrashing in front of the rest of the kids that, if I didn't deserve it, I had predicted. The blood rushing up to my face was doing a hairpin around my earlobes and racing back down to my jaws. A lightheaded feeling overtook me and I couldn't think of anything but the word I'd been searching for: Precognition, that was the word.

"Nothing. I said I can't believe this, I think. OK?"

Striking an innocent pose, staring into Will's light beard, as the rest of the crew looked over at us, I worried that I had caused us another needless hike. Will grabbed my T-shirt from the front and pumped his finger in my face again. *He's about to punch me in the face.*

"Zack, you won't or you can't? If you won't, you won't finish your requirements. If you say 'you can't' then I'm putting 'I can't' on your swear list along with 'Jesus,' because I'm really tired of hearing either from you. You understand? I don't want to hear you say either EVER AGAIN!"

The fear of Will beating me down, or letting the rest of the group kick me to death, almost caused me to cry. I couldn't take much more picking on, fear, hunger, uncertainty, embarrassment, or public humiliation.

I remained silent through the nightly requirement routine. I set my traps, did the required stupid entry in the workbook, dug a pit, started a fire, and kept to myself. Talking to no one, I nibbled on ashcakes – a combination of stirred flour, water, and fire. As I slept that night I dreamed even more wildly. More food, as much as imagination would allow me. Every sense accompanied every image.

Food in freezers in grocery aisles, pillows of cheesy lasagna, dispensers of juice like at the Hill School flowed colorful, sweet liquids onto empty floors. At some point my supposed parents appeared in my dream. My mother was young, herself a young child.

I didn't open my eyes and didn't want to leave my blanket when I awoke the first time. No sunrise, no light, bitterly cold. I was shivering. Lifting my blanket a crack to be imperceptible, but mostly just to remain warm, I let a stream of liquid and steam fly from my groin. It landed with splashing near my head, but I wasn't there. With the reserve of fluid released from my bladder, I was warmer and fell back into nurturing blackness.

And dreaming again, peacefully dreaming, back to the food, back to thick carpet, bunny rabbit costumes, smiles of memories of aunty and uncles, smells from Mom's kitchen. Dad's making eggs, and they're growing into chickens before dropping down into soufflés in the frying pan. Now sizzling bacon and pancakes. "But it's dinnertime! Dad!"

I awoke with a start, and felt a pain in my spine.

Butch had kicked me in the back.

"You pissed in my shoe, fucker!"

A stream of glazed, half frozen liquid led to where I lay. Butch stood over me enraged, holding one shoe, just as he had stood over the mouse. He pointed at the shoe's mate, lying in a frozen, slushy layer of my urine.

"Jesus, I'm so sorry Butch…"

And that's how that happened.

"Butch, please, don't tell them. I'll give you my powdered milk if you don't tell Will? Oatmeal from my next rations, too. Please, please, man!"

It was obvious by Butch's expression that he had noticed.

I'd broken the swearing requirement. There wasn't going to be time to pass it now before Trail's End. It was a mistake! I WAS sorry and embarrassed. I'd never been a bed pee-pee-er. Jesus – the swear word.

"Awww…You just broke your swearing requirement, Blood. I'm sorry but I hope he fucking kills you."

My complexion, already rosy red with embarrassment, was no defense when Will was roused sufficiently to rush over to learn the cause of the morning fuss. Butch greeted him loudly, tattling like the little rat he had murdered.

From my blanket on the ground, I protested: "I just woke up. I had just been jarred awake, I was asleep! Butch kicked me! Please! Will, WAIT?"

Will Bender was already running back to the field counselor's site. He frisked his rig, returning a second later holding his field counselor fanny pack. He grabbed the neck of my shirt roughly with one hand again, pulling me out of the blanket. He yanked at me until I was standing, and pulled me toward the nearest high crest. I had no shoes on. He reached into his fanny pack after we had climbed up and away from the group. He pulled out a bulky walkie-talkie with a big rubber antenna that beeped once before he called to Mr. Jade.

"Field Group 42 to Base. Field Group 42 to Base, come in, Base. Over."

"This is Jade, go ahead Will, I hear you. Over." The radio crackled back.

"Yeah, Bonnie is unable to keep up. Can't meet his swearing requirement. He's burnt! I recommend pulling him. Maybe he'll be useful to the other group? Come and get him. Over and out."

"Fuck you, Will, you goddamn cocksucker. I hate you. I hope you get a rattlesnake up your ass! Hit me, you fucking torturing bastard! I SWEAR I AM GOING FUCKING CRAZY! BASTARD!"

I cursed. I had nothing to lose. My dignity was long gone. I'd thought I'd never have use of that again, anyway. No dignity. So I let it rip for another minute.

"Are you done yet?"

I had never been as angry as I was that moment. Will existed only to make my life unbearable – even more than Darlayne Hammer had succeeded in those long weeks at RMA. At this moment, from which there was no physical escape, I considered stabbing Will in the back as we returned over the crest, but my knife was at camp. If I had had more strength, I could have become a murderer.

On the way back to the base camp with the bastard, Will Bender, I tried to compose myself. I didn't want to keep crying. I was shaking with rage, and shame for having to again face the group for peeing. I wanted to ask a practical question, but refrained. If I opened my mouth to speak again, it was going to be all curse words, and I'd probably start crying.

And there was an important consideration that was left unclear: *If I was held back, would I still get next week's food ration?*

I wouldn't eat my rice and lentil rations until Mr. Jade arrived with an answer to that question. Mr. Jade would arrive with my fate in his hands, to take me somewhere. It would be my third day without eating almost anything. I made flame with my bow drill to prepare another ashcake. It would be something to eat, and something to do to avoid having to interact with the expedition kids.

THIRTY-THREE

The next day I didn't move from my sleeping rig. I was faint, and still seething. Also, I was concerned that I might get violently jumped by the rest of the kids in the group. I'd been scapegoated from the first week when I was blamed for having caused extra hiking. And since this wasn't RMA, things were different because there was no violence Agreement. The others might be punished because I was kicked out of the group – that might be a SUWS program technique.

If a group mauling began, I couldn't see Will stopping it very quickly. He hated me. The group hated me. I hated me. I was away from the group in my mind, already. Todd Jerde was still trying to talk nicely to me through my blanket. But I knew I'd never see him again after daylight. *This must be what despair feels like.*

Mr. Jade appeared with the freezing morning. We could hear the Land Rover approach, and then the sound faded to silence. I shook the ash and desert dust off of myself and stood up slowly. Would there be a quick beatdown waiting as I put my boots on? No, all of us were more focused on food. That's what Mr. Jade's arrival meant. Today was to be the final re-supply, not just my removal to another group and more expedition time.

Mr. Jade and his overstuffed frame pack arrived while I was getting my rig together. Whispering about the possible whereabouts of the Land Rover, I could hear Butch say to Nick that he knew how to hot wire a car. But they didn't try.

A novelty of technology trumpeted my future. A fax machine had spit out a facsimile of a handwritten note from my father. He had dribbled ink from his Montblanc pen in his illegible, scratched hand-writing, reminiscent of Hebrew, on a lined legal pad. Then some lights read my dad's words, and a similar machine in SUWS headquarters reproduced them exactly on flimsy white paper.

Mr. Jade heralded my fate with a stiff blue envelope in his hand. This impersonal seeming paperwork transmitted from 2,500 miles away painfully confirmed my fears. Not only would I would not see my parents at the last day and the Trail's End ceremony, I'd be staying in the desert. I wasn't going home at all after this. Whenever that is.

I read my dad's note, scrawled in black on the lightweight paper.

Zack, I am beyond disappointed with you. Your mother and I want you to know that the time has come for you to understand the consequences of your actions. Running away from RMA, where they are trying to help you, will not be tolerated. You WILL NOT be welcome at home unless you graduate the program at RMA. No excuses, no exceptions – no more "splitting." They will repatriate you if you show proper remorse. We expect you to write a letter asking that they invite you back to stay on campus. That is the ONLY place for you. Don't test them, or us, again. You will be very sorry if you do.

We do love you, sorry we cannot be at Trail's End, but we will be proud when you finally succeed in completing this chapter. Listen to [Mr. Jade] and be good.

Again, we DO love you, honey. Love Mom and Dad.

Back to RMA? What had I even split for? I must write a letter to RMA groveling so they'd "allow me" to return to their program? To grovel for more of what I knew was wrong: the yelling, my continued brainwashing?

There was no pretense any more that RMA was a boarding school. Everybody in the desert knew it to be one of the worst places a kid could be sent. A kid who had never been arrested!

Mr. Jade pulled me over the little hill that Will radioed him from. Although I knew how to drive a car, I wasn't going to try to bring the legendary survivalist down, and run off with his keys. Besides, I still couldn't see where he had parked the vehicle. The rest of the group packed away their new stores while Mr. Jade and I talked in private. My situation was dire, he admitted.

"I understand the predicament you're in, buddy. I've seen a lot of kids here. And what you probably don't now understand, is that I do see your point of view. Having to go back to RMA has got to be tough, Zachary. Zack? OK, Zack – but you'd better take it just one day at a time, little by little. Right. You know, I started a school for kids just like you a few years back. It's in Wyoming. Splendid Grove used to work with, um, well, younger older souls. You know what I mean, son? Let's just get you to another group, and to Solo, and out of the desert. Life is more than these couple of weeks. I can tell by looking at you that you're a strong kid. You're also smart enough to know when to surrender. Right?"

Mr. Jade was more sympathetic than anyone, so far, out West. He waved off my questions about his program, Splendid Grove.

"It's defunct now. Foreclosure and legal issues."

Did the place get busted?

He continued. "I don't believe that RMA is the right place for you, anyway, but don't ever tell anyone I said that, got me?" He winked benignly. "I don't think, to be honest, it would be good for anyone your age, from what I know of their heavy-duty emotional curriculum.

"'s too sophisticated," he added after a pause.

"Tell me about the lock-ups in Wyoming, please, Mr. Jade. Are they worse than RMA? I felt like I was going crazy up there, to be reciprocally honest, sir."

Mr. Jade looked at me in a way that said: Man to Man. He let a moment linger and casually spit out a breakfast crumb. "Well, I know that some real legitimate juvenile offenders, murderers, have been in some of what you call 'lock-ups.' A lot of them under court order. It's a different world now, I guess, with the money, politics, and insurance companies. I know that's not how you got here, Zack, and remember, you can't let things get so far out of hand that your whole life is ruined. You gotta get back on track so you can get back to a school. Hope for college. Forget what I said. RMA is a safe place, if nothing else, and it's expensive. There are places out there where horrible things happen. I'm sure you'll pull through OK at RMA. It's a good place. Better than lots out there, OK? Seriously."

I scratched my neck, nodding in silent skeptical understanding.

"Your parents do care about you, you know, or you wouldn't have gotten here and met me. If they didn't care, you'd already probably be worse off, believe me."

I believed him wholly in the sincerity department. Mr. Jade was the first person to treat me with any kindness in a long time, and the watermelon slices he gave me were sweet. While I slurped the melon, eating the entire rind, I strongly felt this conversation with Mr. Jade was circular; I had no choice in any matter that pertained to me. It was the same Catch-22 that plagued the thoughts of the students up in northern Idaho. My parents' choices now would play a pivotal role in the rest of my natural duration. Mr. Jade showed me that my parents were willing to continue to make decisions. I had zero control. And it could get worse, even, than this.

"If you think about it, it could get out of hand...hasn't it already?

Imagine living like this, every single day! Life on the street is like that. A lot of kids go missing. They get murdered too, son! Think about that."

Mr. Jade asked, "Would you mind if we did a little exercise? Think back to a time that you can remember clearly. A good time. Got one? OK, what are you doing? Eating, heh, OK. Lunch hour? Good. Remember your school? Think about lunch hour there. Try to think about the next year. Sixth grade? OK. Was that your last school?"

"No, there's at least two more."

"That's fine, son. Take your time."

This was easy and I could almost taste the lunch at the Hill School again.

"OK. Did you get to the last place? What about RMA? Think about eating in their dining area. OK. Good. And close your eyes for a few seconds. Just breathe, son. OK. Now. Let's go backwards. Open your eyes, and take me back, every year, the same memories – starting at RMA, a few moments each...OK, good. Good. And until you get back to sixth grade. OK, now let me see you try to remember the year before that?"

I remembered all the hubbub and swirling shrieks of little kids. *The noises of trays banging against tables, kids wearing hats and Indian head bands with feathers, and pretend feathers sticking up, and cake I never ate. I never liked cake, or mustard* – I flashed back to RMA for a heartbeat.

"Now can you remember eating lunch in fourth? Fourth grade. How about third? Good. Well, I see an indication of good recall. But..."

He snapped me out of some pleasant peanut butter and jelly sandwich in public school to tell me that my eyes looked left, which in most people is to the future, when I remembered lunch in my past. Or something like that.

"You have an unusual way of storing stimuli, Mr. Bonnie. I bet you have a great memory. Let me tell you something. Remember how I was telling you how much bigger life is than these few weeks, months, and years of your life? Not just longer, life is bigger – you will know more. You'll probably have to take my word for it. You'll *think* differently."

Mr. Jade opened a pack of peanuts from his breast pocket, tore the plastic with his teeth and poured half of the contents into my hand.

271

"Thanks."

"When you're eighteen you're going to do what you want, nobody will stop you. Do you think I could tell you how I learned how big and empty the world is? Why I know it's – life – is so hard on you? And how I had to relearn how to remember?"

I sat and listened. He pulled a Snickers bar from his pocket and handed it to me. I knew what to do with it.

A boating accident killed his wife and daughter. An uncle had taken them out in his sailboat and it caught fire. I'd never met anyone who had sustained such loss. His whole family, gone in a fire. While Mr. Jade told me the details about the accident, I felt a little queer eating the candy bar.

I'd been queasy about death my whole life. Especially since the death of my grandfather, and my best friend's father, in the same year. Injury and blood I could deal with, but the certainty of ceasing to exist was too puzzling for me to focus on. I'd tried to solve that little conundrum, as unsuccessfully as I had attempted to solve the history of god. That stuff boggled my mind.

I wasn't sure why Mr. Jade, who visibly winced during his recollections, shared all of this with me. As he began to cry, I hugged him. I would have hugged a weeping man who had lost his family whether I had been to RMA, where everybody always hugged, or not. My holding him while he sobbed seemed to make a huge impression on him. The private and tragic story he told, and the exercises he did with me, the time he took, talking to me in private, all made me feel an indescribable connection to him. I wanted to know what he wanted me to know in a different way, not the way every other adult I'd yet known thought I needed to know something.

Here's what imprinted: *We'd die. Every one of us. We were alone. We were all alone. When we weren't alone, the possibility of suddenly being alone would always isolate us from one another. Every single one of us would always be alone, and any feeling contrary to that fact would be short lived. This feeling could only be mitigated by positive relationships with my parents, and doing my homework at school. That meant going back to RMA, where I'd learn the rest.*

It had never occurred to me to just surrender and accept my doomed fate. I'd grown up, my parents had kicked me out of the nest, and I'd just been too dumb to see it. By being on Survival, wasn't it obvious that they knew I would live, or I would die? And if I don't die, then RMA, if I'm lucky, will be where I'm sequestered until I graduate. Thinking beyond that, from a practical point of view, was impossible for me to grasp.

I'm not sure my parents "want" me to die; I'm sure they'll be thrilled to see me succeed at Survival, but if I had died, or will die, incontestably their lives would run smoother.

Something clicked into place. I suddenly stopped resenting my predicament out there. It was Survival, after all. As they said at RMA: Just Do It. The much quoted Nike advertisement that Tess Turnwell had used in the Truth propheet played in my head with a new understanding: *I have to Do It! Just. Do. It.* The "It" changed, situation to situation, day to day, and even hour to hour out here.

Mr. Jade made me realize that I might just have to do whatever it takes until I was eighteen. If I didn't have a choice, despite the word games from my parents and CEDU especially, I'd have a choice. I decided to ignore that discrepancy.

Just Do It trumps semantic arguments and philosophical thoughts of predetermination.

I saw it, in my first intellectual thought since Survival began.

Go back to RMA. Write the letter, don't fight. Just be complacent and do it because life will roll over me.

Life was steamrolling right over me, flattening me out.

It happened because I wasn't eighteen, not because I needed to change. I couldn't stop the steamroller any more than I could have been born to different parents — perhaps parents that didn't care if I had a rat tail and stayed out all night. Parents who didn't punish me for growing up in a hurry. This wasn't something that started in the Owyhee or Mojave or Great Basin Desert, wherever I was! My lack of choice was clear.

How I reacted to the lack of choice was the only thing I could control.

[T]he interrogator may, by virtue of his role as the sole supplier of satisfaction and punishment, assume the stature and importance of a parental figure in the prisoner's feeling and thinking. Although there may be intense hatred for the interrogator, it is not unusual for warm feelings also to develop. This ambivalence is the basis for guilt reactions, and if the interrogator nourishes these feelings, the guilt may be strong enough to influence the prisoner's behavior....Guilt makes compliance more likely...."

—CIA Interrogation Manual, KUBARK Counterintelligence Interrogation, July 1963, Approved for Release 2014/02/25, at page 83, quoting Biderman, Albert D., and Herbert Zimmer, The Manipulation of Human Behavior, John Wiley and Sons Inc., New York and London, 1961.

THIRTY-FOUR

What did it matter what had gone wrong at this point? Why did I want to sneak out, get high, fuck girls, meet older people? Was that a problem?

To me, it still seemed my parents were "what went wrong." Maybe I would never be able to convince my parents that independence was good, that I was fine the way I was. Maybe I couldn't articulate to them that splitting from RMA and Minnehaha were in different categories. Leaving from summer camp was a form of expressing freedom and independence; splitting from RMA a desperate act of self-preservation.

Sitting next to Mr. Jade, with half of my flannel pocket filled with peanuts, clicking through these nuggets of self-preservation, I felt sedate. I was content, maybe for the first time ever! Immersed in my mysteriously unfolding personal saga, I was present and calm. Normally, I would be angry at being taken into yet another unknown situation, but this time, I felt peace. All because I had no control.

The freedom I enjoyed before being sent to RMA was over. That life had been vanquished. You could say that that Zack was dead.

Say a prayer for the person I was three months ago, because whatever I become in the future is dependent on NOT going to a fucking lock-up! And I've got to get out of the fucking desert! I don't want to die!

"Just Do It." The mantra lived in me.

Mr. Jade let me help him up. He wiped tears off his shaven face, and reached again into a pocket. Retrieving a summer squash and handing it to me with another wink, Mr. Jade led us down to join the others. Will Bender glared at me as I nibbled on the squash near the group. His stare bored into me his design to be hurtful. He had been intimidating me the entire expedition. Will had chosen me, the youngest, smallest, and weakest link, as the enemy. He had wanted to fight me, to hurt me physically and mentally, in front of the group. How else could he display his dominance? His eyes conveyed disgust and malice. His testing me was never to make me a better survivalist, to strengthen my resolve, or toughen me up. Will Bender did it because he was a weak-willed brute. I was brave, he was a wuss.

Squash should not be eaten raw. I sliced the second half into thin coins and wrapped them in my bandanna after taking a few communion-sized slices for immediate consumption. Returning to the fire, I packed my bedroll, safely storing the squash and a handful of flour, this my only remaining food besides my one emergency meal of rice and lentils.

"Zack, if you want to say anything else to your group here, or say any goodbyes, now is the time."

Mr. Jade tied closed the garbage bag we'd be packing out. The group was cordial to me, not callous, as I'd anticipated. Maybe it was Mr. Jade's presence, or perhaps the realization that they themselves had more days of involuntary adventure ahead. Todd even gave me a hug after jotting an address in my journal.

Mr. Jade and I walked a few hundred yards away from the group until we could see his Land Rover. He knew better than to keep it near juvenile delinquents alert to any opportunity for escape. It didn't take much for something to look shiny out there in the Mojave. I'm not even sure what a Mojave is, but it's one of the terms that Leslie, Will, and Mr. Jade tossed around. He stored his rattlesnake skin fedora on the back seat and we drove on a cattle trail that eventually brought us to The Cut Above.

THIRTY-FIVE

A big bearded fellow named Torque ran my next expedition. I prepared myself for what was bound to be more confrontation and possible violence. It did still ache that I would return to RMA, but unconsciously, I had helped myself. I had inadvertently given myself more time to prepare for my impending incarceration.

Hiking was easy now. Even if there was a lot of elevation, I was the strongest hiker. I had lost significant weight. I didn't need anything except my knife, water, the food I was given, and my wool blanket. When we were told to expect rain overnight, we rigged our ponchos as lean-to's or pup-tents. On nights when it rained unexpectedly, I did pushups under the blanket, shook the water out, slept, got up and did jumping jacks, and repeated the calisthenics program throughout the night.

Being dropped into this new group that proudly called themselves "The Cut Above" turned out to be the best thing that could have happened. These were my final days of Survival. With my mantra "Just Do It" playing over every mile I hiked, my attitude adjusted. Will had been wrong about things: I was not more vocal than other kids. I had been away from home longer than anyone I met. I had gone longer without seeing parents, I had been without three square meals for longer than any other kid in the desert, and now I was also expected to hike further, with less sustenance, than any kid in either group.

An aching, gnawing pain that started in the small of my back and traveled to the top of my skull woke me. The pain from the area between my shoulders to my crown was worse than that. The pain behind my eyes didn't ache. It was sharp. My feet both had pins and needles. It was the third day that I had woken with that pain going throughout my body.

I suddenly went to the bathroom. Suddenly – I had about four seconds' notice.

Great. What is this? Exhaustion? Injury? Malnutrition?

I learned later I had giardiasis. It's caused by a parasite, maybe from the water in that cattle trough. This condition would last about three weeks, and although I wasn't in pain, I did crap myself with liquid a few times. Neither RMA nor Sheriff Snipes ever offered medical support, even though I leaked butt-water all over the back seat of the Sheriff's cruiser.

> Giardia infection (giardiasis) is an intestinal infection caused by a microscopic parasite that's found world-wide, especially in areas with poor sanitation and unsafe water. Giardia infection is marked by abdominal cramps, bloating, nausea and bouts of watery diarrhea.
>
> Giardia infection is a waterborne infection and can be caused by parasites found in backcountry streams and lakes.....
>
> Giardia infections usually clear up within a few weeks. But you may have intestinal problems long after the parasites are gone. Several drugs are generally effective against giardia parasites, but not everyone responds to them. Prevention is your best defense.
>
> —The Mayo Clinic website

✝

The way I felt about clothes and food changed permanently after this experience. Clothes are made to be worn rough, and food remained a point of scarcity in my mind forever.

Solo was in a few more days, a time when we didn't have to hike. I just prayed nothing bad would happen before I could sit around doing nothing but heating my food for several days. We would meet clerical requirements like finishing SUWS' stupid workbook and writing mandatory letters to parents, and in my case, RMA. I would write that wretched letter and hope for the long-awaited day when the Sheriff would meet me at Trail's End. Sheriff Snipes, my surrogate parent with a gun and a squad car, who would take me back to CEDU's therapukic boarding program, my shitpit called RMA.

For now, we hiked in the closing September light for several hours. My walking dreams concluded as we reached a campsite. I noticed my brain haze was especially cloudy as I met nightly requirements. I never cursed anymore, because I seldom spoke.

We heard signs of Mr. Jade's Land Rover at sunset. It was one of the last days of The Cut Above's expedition days before Solo, so we knew he would have fresh food rations for us. We could hear him off in the distance bogging down, then speeding toward us. Mr. Jade rendezvoused with us just as the sun split around the horizon. Besides the famous Idaho potatoes he handed out, he also had a dog.

A dead dog, disagreeable to the palate of most people in this world, was frozen solid and tied up in a clear plastic bag. It did not matter that I could see its snout and open mouth. I knew it to be food. The previous morning a hunter had shot it. The farmer didn't recognize it as a dog until too late and had no use for it, dead or alive. The farmer notified his friend, Mr. Jade, who arranged to take the little dog's corpse from the farmer's freezer.

Do Mr. Jade and Torque exchange a bag of frozen domesticated canine often?

My new group passed the weighty bag around for inspection. It was sealed up well, the plastic bag airtight. On our walk, my new group passed around the thawing mass of meat with disgust and amusement, sharing in carrying its weight.

Will Bender had only been a few inches bigger than Butch, and only a few years older. The other group haunted me. Why had Will and Butch been bullies? Why would god make those violent, evil people? Now removed from him, I wondered if I'd ever again have to see his face.

I knew I'd have to see Darlayne Hammer's again at RMA.

Torque was an excellent field counselor. A towering bald man with a full beard, he liked kids, and was like a desert Santa. He was compassionate and kindly to everyone in his group. Though scary looking, his eyes exuded patience, tolerance, and kindness. He taught us right, and made me feel welcome from the first day. Torque treated us with respect, like we were adults. He didn't yell once, and on my first day he shook my hand like he was privileged that I had joined his group. He made Survival seem voluntary, assisting us with our traps or fires, instead of making it a requirement, or a chore. Torque taught all of us that being in nature could bring joy. The bear-sized man also knew many advanced survival techniques we campers did not.

"OK, boys, when we get to camp later on, I fully intend to put you to work. I know that you think I'm a pushover, and tonight, I AM BRINGING THE PAIN! We'll have to hustle since we're running out of daylight. Everybody ready for a work shift? I promise you, you will be happy if we work together!"

"If it's good enough for A Cut Above," one of the kids confidently yelled out.

Though there was some kind of project ahead of us, we responded with enthusiasm. There was no mean dynamic in this group at all, and I was the strong and more experienced survivalist now, showing the group some proper hook making, and primitive fire-making techniques that weren't in the requirements.

We arrived at our site as the dying sun spread over a sky the color of smoked salmon. The dog, a pretty small beast, part spaniel or hound, had a speckled chest and snout, short paws, and stank as only death in a plastic bag does. The requirement to dress the meat was tasked to a boy named Ahmed.

Torque demanded that each of us set two traps. Paiute dead-fall traps were practically second nature to me, so I assisted Ahmed, who was short on time for numerous chores. A good cut of the meat might be mine, if we got his set up ASAP. Torque showed me how to set a sling trap that night, which he also said could be called a skewer trap. That's what happened to the prey when it worked. Now I knew what did and didn't work in catching small prey, and could spot a baited trap that wouldn't catch. I had always been so afraid of Will in the previous group, that to learn to set the traps took me longer because I felt him breathing down my neck like an angry dragon.

Tonight, a feast. We followed Torque's order to go by the old creek bed and haul back several large flat rocks. "Nice going, men, that's enough stone. Now we need to make mortar. Zack, you look like a muck-man, get over here and sweep up as much of this smooth dirt as possible. That's it, just use your hands. We're going to make a pile of smooth dust and then a big ball, just like you'd make a milk ball, or ashcake. Pour some more water. Just like that. Pour some more in the middle. Keep stirring. Keep stirring. Presto. Good. OK, boys everybody grab a double handful and smear it on. Like this. See what I'm doing? Smear it on, and we'll have ourselves an adobe oven!"

The pile of dust acted as a bonding agent. We had primitive cement. With some group cooperation and Torque's instruction, we built a sturdy looking oven with a stone shelf. There were smiles all around that night as we brought enough dry sage and aspen firewood for a group fire, and added some freshly unearthed onions that I knew where to gather. We wrapped the dog meat in tin roofing we had found. With the onions, and cayenne that Torque gave us, we shoved whatever we had in the dog. That night, among cheerful faces illuminated by the crackling oven, we waited for the little spaniel to cook. I watched as the stumps of legs burned and spit juice.

Meat treat was served. When it came off the fire we set in on it with no remorse, no compunction or guilt in eating dog. We wiped slime on our faces, watching Torque – the only one with a beard. He'd have to wash before bedding down. We laughed out of fake disgust watching him eat, pretending to be a caveman. I fell asleep quickly after the nutritious meal, and when I woke in the morning, I was energized, fueled enough for one of the last hikes before Solo.

I didn't get mad or chastise other campers who needed a break, and Torque didn't seem to mind that we hiked less. Since I'd been tutored in flaking pyrogenic rock to be used as knives, arrowheads, and spear tips, the obsidian, quartz, and red lava rocks were my friends. Plants could be used for diuretics and toilet paper, and I had a good idea what uses each one had and how to identify them. Most important, I paid attention to the plants that were edible, so I would be able to identify them for life.

Even the sonic booms that cracked and caused such wonder in the first days of both groups had ceased to amuse us, unless it was one of the funny-looking aircraft they were testing. Sometimes they made a streaking noise, but sometimes they floated by silently, looking like a cross between a lake-sized boomerang and a slow-flying bullet. They kept flying after sunset, too. At night, on the few occasions I was up, the sky was alive with activity.

That night, the campfires were out. I'd made a teeny sit-fire and was cooking some little desert onion bulbs I had gathered. I lay them over the little flame in a pit between my legs. I knew the tiny flame in a pit would not incinerate anything. I took my wool blanket over by some scrub and wiggled. My deteriorating jeans dropped to the ground. There I was exposed, urinating, when I saw it. Up in the sky. Stars out. Clear. What the fuck?

Only two of us had noticed earlier, when one of those funny-looking aircraft had shot by without noise. Now, alone, I saw shooting stars, three and four at once. Shooting up, outward from in front of me. Green, glowing, flashing through the sky.

Have the planets waged war on Earth?

Celestial occurrences combined with satellite activity and stuff I couldn't identify. But it was too dizzying to stare up like that for long. I slept well that last week.

Mr. Jade visited one last time before Solo. He came laden with our usual meager rations and another separate treat. A freshly killed raccoon was still soft, dry and warm to the touch. Nobody ever asked from where this fat, furry fellow had come.

"Mr. Jade caught him with his bare hands probably, on the way here? Or maybe with the Land Rover?" Ahmed suggested.

The raccoon was bigger and fatter than the dog. In preparing the oven I took charge of squishing the mud between stacked rocks. My oven wasn't an engineering marvel, but it was sufficient to keep the heat on the meat. The fur of the 'coon was given to the kid who had developed a blue blister on his foot and slowed us down that day. The raccoon's pelt would make a soft sock for him.

We had another wonderful meaty meal around the fire together. The raccoon was as greasy and delicious as I'd imagined it would be. Torque told us about expeditions he had done in South America and Alaska. Even though we had just eaten what felt to be the entirety of a twenty-pound raccoon, twice the size of the dog, I couldn't wait to get alone with my food cache.

Solo caused some apprehension in The Cut Above. None of us had ever actually been left alone in the woods for multiple days. Solo should give me time to relax, and break into my hidden food stores freely.

Yeeeeaaaaa Fuck

I just passed my swearing requirement. I have had so much fun today. I am feeling groovy. Ox-Bow here I come. I am hungry. Actually I am so full I can barely eat. I ate 2 times as much as I ate yesterday and have barely gotten into my rations. I have a huge bucket of applesauce.

— Author survival notebook, 22 Sep 1988

THIRTY-SIX

24 Sep 1988

When I was dropped at my Solo site, I hid my food stash. I had been able to keep a meal's worth of rice and lentils because of the meat we had cooked. I made sure there was always something I could eat, just in case. No matter how hungry I got, something always told me to save a little. My life might depend on it.

Torque gave me a piece of paper and two pens, he showed me the limits of my site, and gave me a firm handshake. He would check on each of us, at least once daily, during the four day period.

When he was gone, I unrolled my rig with the hoarded food. I had plenty to eat, and the time and tools to prepare it. Along with my rations, I had a few pieces of potato, half a yellow squash, and the extra rice and lentils I had been saving for when I'd have the chance to cook them up in my peach can. After this many weeks, my peach can was black, black, with accents of black burnt on the patchy bottom. Used for all my cooking needs and never cleaned out, the sediment inside had to be extinguished while my food "cooked" in it.

I shall feast! And there's a water source right here!

My Solo site had everything I needed. Besides the rapidly flowing brook that bordered my limited area, I had a big flat stone to lounge on, and a shady aspen to sit under. I had sticks, rocks, plants, and my rig. There was nothing lacking, though a down pillow would have been sweet.

My strength came back to me, and along with having enough food, my brain reacquired some of its edge. It relaxed me that the starving, hiking part of Survival was officially over. Three days lying on the sunny slab of rock of my Solo site, or lounging in the shade where I had set up my sleeping rig, made me human. I did the cleaning, the cooking, the assigned homework and daily reading that Torque or Mr. Jade brought.

I did it all without a field counselor looking over my shoulder to see if I did it right. I wasn't a kid during Solo. I felt like a man.

How did you feel about your family the first day of the course? Now?

I disliked the idea of my mother and father's decision to send me here. This may have solved some family problems but it also created some. I think basically what I'm trying to say is I loved my parents but didn't know how to express it correctly. Now I am just very confused about telling them.

Can you think of any ways to improve this course so it will help more? What are they?

I think that this course would be improved if the participants understood how it could benefit them. More motivation would definitely help too.

—Author's Survival final evaluation form

†

"Motivation" was Survival code for comfort. It meant working for yourself. It meant food. Will Bender had often asked, "Are you motivated enough to build a coal bed, or a shelter?"

I needed this time to rest – to be alone. To be left alone, to think about nothing but my physical needs, gave me back a sense of control. For three days, I did have complete control of my life, within the 200-foot perimeter of my private campground. If I didn't have to go back to RMA, I could be at peace. I instinctively knew this.

Scrambling to put jeans on and hide my dwindling food stash, I perceived Torque coming to check on me the last day of Solo. He probably didn't know, or even care, that I'd been hoarding food, but I couldn't afford anything to cloud the sunny experience I was having with The Cut Above.

Early on the day of Trail's End, Will Bender surprised me at my Solo site. His intrusion at sunup into my privacy and sleep made me wonder why he was there. Over coffee he brought me – it tasted like shit, but was still better than the cowboy coffee back at RMA – Will declared that I was the youngest kid to ever do the SUWS program, so far. I had set an all time distance record during my 25 days of hiking, too. Will had come with a potato and some other edible items, which I took, careful to make my face look appreciative.

"You need to understand, Zack, that you have a whole lifetime ahead of you. You shouldn't want to clash with those that have authority over you. It's a suicidal move, you get me?" I sensed his apology was genuine. He was gentler in his manner than I had ever seen him. I already knew he was an asshole, a walking Napoleonic complex.

In a few years, I should come back and kick his ass.

I was going back to RMA after all this shit anyway, and I didn't really need to think about anything, or anyone else.

Just do it. Life steamrolls. Don't resist. Tolerate Will. Whatever it takes.

I changed the subject. "Your beard's gone. You're all clean. Thanks for the soap. As soon as you go, I'm going to hit the stream. I know I'm still filthy."

"Don't forget that the Oxbow has hot showers. You just wait... Anyway, I came to tell you that you should be proud of what you've accomplished out here, Zack. I didn't think you were going to make it, but Torque told me you've been a prince. Mr. Jade and I are really hoping you'll have a good experience back at RMA. It's going to be OK, son."

After Will left, I opened the letter he had handed me. It was from my parents. My mom was excited about an RMA parents' weekend workshop they had been to a few weeks earlier.

> While you were starting your Wilderness experience, Daddy and I were attending the Parent Seminar. The first day we began our Values Profeet (spelling?). The experience was very moving and emotional. It gave me a chance to reflect on important values and to look back on parts of my life.
>
> On Saturday, Daddy and I (feeling sad because we wouldn't be visiting you) went to the school. ... That tour, along with the Values Profeet, and the Seminar, reaffirmed our belief in the school. ...
>
> Right now, you have no choices. To run away is hurtful to you and to us. It is not being "tough" but being weak. A strong person deals with problems and tries to solve them. You are a strong person.

[…] Now there's a new start. You'll be working hard in Raps and in staying in agreement. If you have setbacks, you'll be able to deal with them and stay on course.

You're a very fine, sensitive person. I LOVE YOU!!

[…] I support you in your work at RMA. I'll think of you every day with all the love in my heart. If you start writing us, I can write you back.

—Letter to author from mother, dated 5 Sep 1988, delivered 27 Sep 1988

I did the math. The workshop had begun on September 1st, the day Sheriff Snipes told me that my parents would meet me in Boise so we could go home together. Instead, they went to a resort for an RMA indoctrination and sent me on Survival. Now they were more invested in the program than ever.

I wrote the requisite letter to Mom and Dad. Then I wrote to RMA, asking for permission to return to the shitpit. And then I wrote to God, asking for absolution and direction to a normal life.

THIRTY-SEVEN

Mom, Dad,

I cant say I expect you to understand this letter. I am in a position right now where I am not at all sure whether I love you or abhor you. All this moving around which I understand is part my fault has gotten me confused about the person I am and who you and everybody else want me to be.

You don't seem to understand that I am not that person.

Well anyway I am on Solo right now. I've become quite good at making spark rock fires.

Please send me the "Hardy Boys Books." There are these ones for older kids. I read one, it was really good. I was surprised.

How does my sister like her new T-shirt?

Could you send me some food when I get back to RMA? I looked in the mirror in Mr. Jade's car last week and I look like this! [stick figure] My face is so much thinner you wouldn't believe it.

If he is allowed to write me at school I would love to hear my brother's advice.

Oh I almost forgot. Please send me 2001 and 2010 A Space Odyssey books. I saw 2010 the movie. I thought it was the best.

I think you - Mom & Dad - and I should have a long private phonecall. I would like to be totally upfront with you. But I can't do that in front of an older student for 15 min.s. Would you please see if this can be worked out. I would enjoy telling you what I have learned, and what is true.

I want to hear everything you have to say. I won't be at peace until I do the same.

Now, please call the shrink and tell him to call me at RMA. Please try to work this out, it is important to me.

To tell you the truth I think it was kind of stupid to go to the seminar because I know for a fact they fed you a line of shit. But I'm glad to hear you enjoyed it.

How's grandmas and pa? I hope there fine.

Tell Aunt M I miss them and especially J, I've been thinking about him.

When you write tell me how J, K, C, D, and J are.

Oh! How's Aunt Gail? Tell her I miss her.

There coming to get this letter soon so I have to set my traps.

Love,

Your confused son,

Zack

Bonnie

—Letter from author to parents, last day of Solo, 28 September 1988

✝

September, 1988
In the Idaho
desert

Mom, Dad,

I can't say I expect you to understand this letter. I am in a position right now where I am not at all sure whether I love you or Abhor Abhor you. All this moving around which I _____ and _____ part my _____ has gotten me quite confused about the person I am and who you and everybody else want me to be.

You don't seem to understand that I am not that person.

Well anyway I am on Bob right now. I've become quite good and making _____ spark rock fires.

Please send me the

Hardy Boys Books. There are these ones for older kids, I read one it was really good, I was surprised.

How does _____ like her new T-shirt? Could you send me some _____ when I get get back to RMA? I looked in the mirror in _____ scar last week and I look like this! 😊 My face is so much thinner you wouldn't believe it.

If _____ is allowed to write me at school I would like to hear my Brothers advice.

Oh I almost forgot. Please send me _____ A Space Odyssey books. I saw 2010 the movie I thought it was the best.

2

I think you and I should have a long private _____ phone call I would like to be totally up front w/u. But I can't do this in front of an older student for 15 mins, would you please _____ see if this can be worked out. I would enjoy telling you what I know, have learned, and what is true. I want to hear everything you have to say, I won't be at peace until I do the same.

Now, please call Doc. _____ and tell him to call me at RMA Please try to work this out, It is important to me.

To tell _____ the truth I think it was kind of stupid to go to the Seminar Because I know for a fact they fed you a line of shit, But I'm glad to hear you enjoyed it. How's grandma and pa? I _____ hope there Fine. Tell _____ I miss them and especially _____ I've been thinking alot about him.

_____ when you write tell me how _____ and _____ are. Oh! how's Gail? tell her I miss her. There coming to get the letter soon so I have to set my traps Love, your confused son _____

We approached Trail's End. One kid hopped, with the raccoon pelt and a knife sheath lashed to a small board, all tied preposterously to his foot. We were supposed to be running, but since he had to hobble, we all went slower. We were still out of breath, sweaty, smelly, and sufficiently hungry for the assembled parents and guardians. Behind them streamed the passing cars we'd been hearing for the last thirty minutes.

The truck stop was nearby. We slurped water out of Dixie cups dispensed from a yellow cooler in Mr. Jade's Land Rover, while kids reunited with their parents and stared longingly at the Oxbow. It had none of the majesty of my daydreams. The industrial cooler sweated beads of condensation that dripped to the ground. Ice. The novelty, the luxury.

Then came the yogurt. The large group of kids, field counselors, and parents congregated by the entrance of The Oxbow Truck Stop and Restaurant. Before we gorged on the delights within, Torque told us that natural occurring yeast in yogurt was essential to producing the enzyme that would break down the meal. He and Mr. Jade produced cups of plain yogurt and disposable spoons. I had never received easier instructions. We had been dreaming of this day for three weeks.

Four weeks, in my case. From September first to 28th.

Generally, you will receive back from the training a son/daughter with newly discovered potential and openness. In baseball lingo, hopefully the wilderness program advanced them to third base. Now it is up to you to get him/her to home plate. Good luck and best wishes.

SUWS, Inc. - Wilderness Program

P.S. Remember that, if parents are not united, you become an easy mark for manipulation.

—SUWS Letter to parents, enclosing copy of Back in Control, a "practical parenting" book.

The Oxbow no longer took the form of the Taj Mahal in my imaginings, but I knew it was going to be sufficient as soon as a wave of smells greeted me within. The last meat I had eaten was raccoon; as soon as the waitress came to the table I ordered the Philly steak and cheese of my dreams. That sandwich was, to me, what a one pound nugget of gold would have been to a Forty-Niner. Within minutes I was brought the biggest, meatiest, greasiest, steak bomb of my life. Steak juice dribbled down my chin. *Hail to the waitresses!*

After the massive feast at the Oxbow, when I could eat no more, Sheriff Snipes brought me to a row of shower stalls and returned my bag that had been confiscated by SUWS at Bray Lake. I immediately opened the bag to get at the stale cigarettes. An unpleasant aroma wafted out.

"I'll buy you a pack of cigarettes. You wanna just throw all that away? I brought you fresh clothes. Don't forget to wash your feet because I can smell them from here. Here, take the towel."

After a hot shower that I wished would last forever, I tried the clothes on. Way too big. Even with my tummy gorged, I had lost a lot of the corporeal me due to burning zillions of calories and sweating my soul out. Clothed, I oozed out of the shower stall, fatigue growing.

The expedition group broke up unceremoniously. Parents took their kids from The Cut Above back to the land of bicycles, music, girls who wear dresses, and freedom; I got sandwiched in the front seat of a police car between the armed sheriff and Albert Guerre, the infamous, freakishly tall bounty hunter, who everyone at RMA said was a retired Army Green Beret. Coincidences in life are funny; Albert Guerre was the same escort who had brought the handcuffed Butch to the Spokane airport, four weeks prior, for my first Survival group. I'd heard of Al Guerre numerous times up near Bonners Ferry.

And now the three of us were heading back there.

Sheriff Snipes had brought more than clothes. He'd brought backup. He and Albert Guerre had car-pooled down to the Oxbow in order to deliver me back to the Rocky Mountain Academy campus. I realized Albert's significance as I let myself be loaded into the police cruiser. Al was hired by my parents and sent to the Trail's End, in the middle of the desert, for little old me, to make sure I didn't resist being taken back to RMA. Nothing could have been further from my mind than to jump out of a moving vehicle or run from a cop. It was humorous that my parents thought I might still have the strength. Mom and Dad had no idea what they had just put me through on Survival, or the insanity their hired escorts would soon thrust me into.

In the car I faded into sleep. Albert and Sheriff Snipes wanted to talk. Didn't they know I'd awoken at 5 AM that day and wasn't interested in playing twenty questions?

Ten hours later, mountains loomed, as familiar as prison walls, and tamaracks waved darkly in the northerly wind. We were closing in on the final, dreaded destination.

I'm going to be at RMA for good this time. Now the re-education program at RMA could begin in earnest.

The RMA was founded especially for adolescents with educational, motivational and behavioral problems. A highly structured residential school, it offers a secondary academic curriculum and the comprehensive counseling support these young people need.

In this environment, students recognize and are able to reach their intellectual, emotional, social and physical potentials.

—RMA brochure

The history of these adolescent residential programs is, in essence, a story of how abusive, dehumanizing practices that reformers of mental hospitals and prisons have attempted to stamp out for centuries have been repackaged and are currently being sold by a booming industry as essential and beneficial for kids. It is also a story of how thousands of well-meaning, caring, and intelligent parents have been taken in by a business that uses exaggerated claims of risk to teens to sell its services. It's a story of splintered families, of parents convinced by program operators that extreme, even traumatically stressful treatments are their children's only hope.

—Maia Szalavitz, *Help at any Cost: How the Troubled Teen Industry Cons Parents and Hurts Kids*, Riverhead Books, New York, 2006.

These strict institutional settings work at cross-purposes with the developmental stages adolescents go through. According to psychiatrists, teenagers need to gain responsibility, begin to test romantic relationships and learn to think critically. But in tough programs, teenagers' choices of activities are overwhelmingly made for them: They are not allowed to date, and they are punished if they dissent from a program's therapeutic prescriptions. All this despite evidence that a totally controlled environment delays maturation.

[M]ost people are unaware that these programs have never been proved safe or effective. It's part of what a recent Institute of Medicine report labeled a "quality chasm" between the behavioral treatments known to work and those that are actually available. So parents rely on hearsay — and the word of so-called experts.

Unfortunately, in the world of teen behavioral programs, there are no specific educational or professional requirements. Anyone can claim to be an expert.

—Maia Szalavitz, "The Trouble with Tough Love," *The Washington Post*, 29 January 2006

ADVANCE REVIEW COPY AFTERWORD

I conceived the **Dead, Insane, or in Jail** series to lead up to and tell the story of the last six months of the two-and-a-half year so-called "emotional growth program" at a CEDU school.

After the initial period portrayed in this, the first book, the program ratchets up pressure on our protagonist, young Zack, and disrupts every connection to ordinary reality and the sense of self that he brought with him to the school. The entire book series, though, is a means to a greater end.

Educating myself and others about the principles of institutionalized persuasion is more than a hobby. The American phenomenon misnamed as the "troubled teen industry" demands further study, within neuroscience, and in all the other fields – bioethics, social psychology, trauma and epigenetic medical research, and public health among them – that will surely be related in the future. (Any studies related to group psychology in teens, and adults who were in high control groups as teens, will be very revealing.) There is hope for fair and unbiased research. For me, to work on collecting and interpreting that data would be an honor.

It is sad that the groups that are meant to save or protect children are so frequently instrumental in harming them along the way. Unfortunately, and especially in a country where you need a license to catch a fish, but not to have a child, more oversight is needed in every sector where the future healthy lives of children hang in the balance. Because of this, I ally myself with persons and groups that advocate for a declaration of human rights for young people.

Some within the US government are working to join the rest of the world in ratifying the United Nations Convention on the Rights of the Child. Quickly adopted by 194 nations, it has formed part of international law since shortly after it was adopted by the UN General Assembly in 1989. Of all UN member nations, only the United States has not yet ratified it. See website: https://en.wikipedia.org/wiki/Convention_on_the_Rights_of_the_Child

Today, public, private, governmental, religious, and "treatment oriented" institutions are negatively affecting millions of lives. Young people deserve a protective standard to shield them from the corruption, predation, and greed of the systems and individuals meant to protect them! Teens have the affirmative right to develop into the persons they become without undue influence, and without threats to their individual autonomy and free expression.

Please join me as I build a personal strategy to these ends. I am already inspired by organizations and individuals continuing the work of Margaret Singer and Robert J. Lifton, including the following groups working to protect the rights of minors: Alliance for the Safe, Therapeutic & Appropriate Use of Residential Treatment (ASTART for Teens), Survivors of Institutional Abuse (SIA), International Cultic Studies Association (ICSA), and American Professional Society on the Abuse of Children (APSAC).

As the recipient of this Advance Review Copy, will you consider sharing my contact info with other people and groups, and/or alerting me to them?

I shall continue to do this work until the book series – or my life – is complete. This is what it takes to tell the tale.

Zack Bonnie
Charlottesville, VA
deadinsaneorinjail@gmail.com

PREVIEW

Book Two from the **Dead, Insane, or in Jail** series will be published next.

To be notified when it becomes available, please visit the deadinsaneorinjail.com website and subscribe to the newsletter.

Following is a preview of material from Book Two.

†

Our bodies had been infected by thinking, almost from the beginning. My thinking was strong and I wanted to learn the tools to fight it.

I wasn't going to control Me. I imagined my little kid – my Me – now dressed in the costume of the Masked Crusader, driving a luxury car. A Jaguar maybe. It made sense that our thinking could be blamed for all the things we did to our little kids – our "doogers," our Me's.

I enthusiastically threw myself into being aware. I knew well every time my thinking tried to tell me negative thoughts. They only quieted when I was taking care of my feelings, and for the brief moment after. I could scrub and scrub my thoughts but they were still there.

†

I had so much love to share, so much honesty to be aware of. I could make people aware by being honest and aware with myself. I had vision. I had my little kid's set of eyes too. I was so proud of the rest of the kids in my PG, and I did kind of worship the staff now. They showed us all of this, improved our vision, revealed Rock Bottom to us, taught us how to fight our thinking.

It was all coming together for me. I was succeeding in the program. I was working it. I'd had a good honest cry! It was making sense, and I knew that as long as I trusted the tools, and the emotional work that I did, I would achieve something great.

✝

"OK. We're going to say goodbye to those loved ones now. Say good bye. You'll get to see them again, I promise. But now, goodbye, Daddy! Mommy's got to leave, now, Yu-Yu. It's OK, Zack."

Mumbling and crying stirred around the room as the music came back up. I remembered goodbyes to cousins when I was a young boy. Goodbyes to grandparents at the end of summer. I tried to ignore the goodbyes to friends, and girls from home. They shouldn't be surfacing. I gently chastised myself.

Next to me, Melanie said goodbye to an aborted baby, and Ernesto cried about a grandfather. Moans for dead parents were impossible to block out.

✝

That's it for now! Book 2 (working title: **Dead, Insane, or in Jail: Overwritten***) is coming. For more news, links, and special offers, visit the website at deadinsaneorinjail.com.*

Made in the USA
Charleston, SC
24 July 2015